TRUTH [illegible] TRIUMPHS

ESSENTIAL TOOLS IN THE FIGHT AGAINST PROPAGANDA, DISINFORMATION AND HYPOCRISY

John F. Holliday

For permission requests, contact:
john@johnholliday.net

Available now in paperback, hardcover and eBook formats.
https://www.johnholliday.net

ISBN 979-8-9994800-0-2

First edition
Printed in the United States of America

To my beloved Gurudev Sri Sri Ravi Shankar, whose teachings continue to illuminate the path from ancient wisdom to present action, showing that timeless truth speaks to every age.

And to my darling wife Alice, the perfect companion for this journey - whose very name evokes nobility and truthfulness - and whose unwavering support, piercing insights, and embodiment of the principles within these pages remind me daily that her name is no coincidence - for in her, Truth and Love are one and the same.

Satyameva Jayate
Truth Alone Triumphs

PREFACE

If you've ever felt frustrated trying to reason with someone who seems immune to facts, logic, or compassion—this book is for you. If you've watched loved ones fall down rabbit holes of conspiracy theories, hate, and extremism—this book offers tools that can help. And if you're simply seeking clarity in an era of "alternative facts" and deliberate deception—you'll find it here.

WHY SHOULD YOU READ THIS BOOK?

We live in a time when basic truths about human dignity are under attack. Extremist ideologies spread through social media like wildfire. Family dinners turn into battlegrounds over fundamental values. Friends disappear into echo chambers of misinformation. Traditional fact-checking and logical arguments seem powerless against emotional manipulation and propaganda.

This book offers something different: a 2,000-year-old philosophical toolkit that cuts through modern deception with surgical precision. It's not about winning arguments—it's about revealing truth in ways that can't be denied.

I wrote this book because I believe we're in a crisis of clear thinking. Not a crisis of information—we have plenty of that. Not a crisis of good intentions—most people want to do right. But a crisis of being able to distinguish truth from lies, wisdom from manipulation, righteousness from self-interest dressed up in moral language.

BEFORE YOU START

This book is structured as a series of short, memorable statements intended to capture a deep truth. Think of them as compressed logic — like philosophical zip files that unpack into powerful arguments. "All humans have equal capacity for righteous action" is an example. In just eight words, it demolishes entire ideologies of racial superiority.

The commentary that follows each statement shows you exactly how to apply it to real-world situations. They're designed to be memorable enough to recall in the moment you need them, yet profound enough to shift entire worldviews.

HOW CAN YOU USE THESE TOOLS?

Let me be direct about what you're probably facing. Your uncle shares racist memes on Facebook. Your cousin insists that diversity is "destroying America." Your neighbor claims gun control violates divine law. Your coworker says transgender people are "mentally ill." Your childhood friend now believes elaborate conspiracy theories about global elites.

Traditional responses don't work because:

- Fact-checking fails when people reject the sources
- Emotional appeals fail when empathy has been weaponized against "weakness"
- Logical arguments fail when logic itself is seen as "elitist"
- Religious arguments fail when scripture gets cherry-picked

This book offers a different approach—one that works because it uses the extremists' own stated values against their positions. It's philosophical jujitsu, using the force of their arguments to reveal their contradictions.

WHAT MAKES THIS APPROACH DIFFERENT?

I'm not a professional philosopher or political pundit. I'm a lifelong student of Vedic philosophy who became frustrated watching ancient wisdom that teaches universal human dignity get twisted to justify discrimination and hate. As a student of my teacher Gurudev Sri Sri Ravi Shankar, I've spent decades learning how timeless principles can address contemporary challenges.

The method I'm sharing—called Mīmāṃsā (pronounced "mee-MAHN-sah")—isn't some exotic mystical practice. It's simply a rigorous way of thinking developed over 2,000 years ago by Indian philosophers who needed to interpret sacred texts and resolve contradictions. Think of it as an ancient debugging system for flawed arguments.

> *Note on Sanskrit Terms: Throughout this book, you'll find Sanskrit terms immediately translated. The power of these ideas transcends any particular language, and I want them accessible to everyone, regardless of background.*

Mīmāṃsā works through three simple tests that anyone can apply:

1. The Reality Test (Direct Observation): What can we actually see with our own eyes? When someone claims certain groups are inferior, we can point to countless examples of excellence from those very groups.

2. The Logic Test (Inference): If A causes B, what does B tell us about A? When we see diverse societies thriving while segregated ones stagnate, what does that tell us about diversity?

3. The Authority Test (Legitimate Sources): Which authorities are reliable and why? When extremists claim tradition supports them, we can show how they're cherry-picking while ignoring deeper principles.

HOW TO COUNTER EXTREMIST ARGUMENTS

Here's what makes this approach effective for disarming extremist ideologies: it doesn't attack from outside their worldview—it reveals contradictions from within. For example:

When they say: "It's traditional/It's always been this way!"

You respond: "Tradition contaminated by unrighteousness loses its authority. Slavery was traditional too—did that make it right?"

When they say: "Those people are naturally inferior."

You respond: "Excellence from any group disproves natural inferiority. When we see members of supposedly 'inferior' groups achieving greatness, the theory fails."

When they say: "We need to preserve our culture from diversity."

You respond: "Monocultures lead to collapse in nature and society. Diversity is nature's fundamental principle—uniformity is the deviation."

Each response is backed by both ancient wisdom and modern evidence, making them difficult to dismiss as either "newfangled liberalism" or "outdated philosophy."

AN INVITATION TO CLEAR THINKING

These aren't just my opinions—they're philosophical arguments constructed according to strict logical rules that have been tested over millennia. You don't have to accept them on faith. Test them yourself. Apply them to the situations you face. See if they reveal truth more clearly than the confused rhetoric surrounding us.

This isn't about converting anyone to Eastern philosophy or asking you to adopt my spiritual beliefs. It's about using powerful analytical tools that happen to come from ancient India to address very modern problems. Whether you're Christian, Jewish, Muslim, atheist, or anything else, these tools work because they're based on logic and observation, not religious doctrine.

My teacher often says that truth needs no defense—it only needs to be revealed. These tools can help. They won't magically convert extremists overnight. But they will give you clarity in confusion, firm ground in quicksand, and sometimes—just sometimes—they'll plant seeds of doubt in seemingly impenetrable ideologies.

May these ancient tools help you navigate modern challenges. May rigorous thinking triumph over rhetoric. And may truth alone triumph!

ABOUT THE AUTHOR

John F. Holliday is a software architect, writer, and lifelong student of Vedic philosophy who is committed to demonstrating the relevance of ancient philosophical traditions to contemporary moral challenges. With decades of intensive study in Vedic philosophy, particularly the rigorous *Pūrva Mīmāṃsā* school, John brings a unique perspective to modern debates about justice, equality, and human rights.

John's journey into Eastern philosophy began in his early twenties, eventually leading him to study under renowned spiritual teacher Gurudev Sri Sri Ravi Shankar. This profound engagement with Vedic thought transformed not only his intellectual understanding but his entire approach to ethics and social engagement. He has spent years studying the complex epistemological frameworks of classical Vedic philosophy, particularly the sophisticated analytical tools of *Mīmāṃsā*, which he now applies with precision to contemporary issues.

John holds a J.D. from the University of Michigan and an A.B. in applied mathematics from Harvard College. As a post-graduate fellow in law and computational linguistics at the Institute for Legal Documentation in Florence, Italy, John explored the emerging nexus between law and computing by designing a graphical notation for the language-neutral expression of legal norms based on deontic logic and the Hohfeldian system of legal analysis which he then actualized by building an expert system prototype to recognize legal relationships from natural language expressions.

In his professional role as a seasoned information architect and software engineer, John founded and manages the *SharePoint Developer Network* LinkedIn group with over 13,000 members. John and his wife Alice co-founded *Works of Wonder International*, an NGO committed to empowering individuals and communities to overcome trauma and chronic exposure to stressful conditions.

For speaking engagements, workshops, or correspondence:
Email: john@johnholliday.net

To connect online:
LinkedIn: https://www.linkedin.com/in/holliday
Website: https://www.johnholliday.net

CONTENTS

ON CIVIL RIGHTS

Birth and race do not determine **virtue or worth.***

The claim that racial hierarchy is natural law contradicts direct perception. We perceive directly that virtue and capability manifest equally across all racial groups.

This core principle tears down the false idea that some races are naturally more capable than others. It uses the principle of direct observation—when we see someone being virtuous or good, we see it directly, not through the lens of their race. This challenges fake science like "race realism" that tries to rank people by race. Ironically, these racist ideas emerged during the same period when people were also developing ideas about universal human rights.

* *Timeless Principle: The eternal truth that moral capacity depends on individual consciousness, not physical characteristics, refutes all forms of racism across all eras.*

Across centuries, philosophers have recognized this truth. The Roman emperor Marcus Aurelius said "we were born to work together"[1] regardless of where we come from. Buddhist teachings say our actions—not our ancestry—create our karma. Confucian ideas about basic human goodness cross all family and racial lines.

Modern brain science backs this up. There's no connection between racial categories and people's ability to think morally. Epigenetics (how environment affects our genes) shows that our surroundings—not our race—shape how we behave. Philosophers like Husserl[2] and Merleau-Ponty[3] pointed out something important: when we meet someone, we experience their humanity first, before any racial categories come into play. When we see someone doing good, we recognize it immediately without thinking about their race.

This works in real life too. When organizations use "blind" evaluations (where they don't know applicants' races), they find talent everywhere—not just in certain racial groups. The U.S. military's racial integration succeeded[4] because when people work toward the same goal with equal opportunity, racial barriers disappear. Schools that focus on each student's individual ability rather than racial stereotypes get better, fairer results. Some might point to statistics showing differences between racial groups. But this commits two logical errors. First, the "ecological fallacy"—assuming that group averages tell us about individuals. It's like saying because men are taller on average, every man must be taller than every woman. Second, the "naturalistic fallacy"—even if differences existed, they wouldn't make discrimination okay.

This principle connects to other important ideas, like "all humans have equal capacity for righteous action" and "diversity reflects nature's fundamental principle." Together, they create a framework that makes racial discrimination illogical in any serious ethical system. This means building organizations that let virtue shine through regardless of someone's background. We need to recognize that unfair systems—not natural limitations—cause unequal outcomes. This includes fixing biased AI systems and practicing seeing people without the filter of racial categories. The goal is creating conditions where everyone's goodness can emerge.

FOR FURTHER READING

Marcus Aurelius - Stoic assertion that 'we were born to work together' regardless of origin

Marcus Aurelius (167-180 CE). Meditations, Book II. Various modern translations available.

Edmund Husserl - phenomenological tradition supporting direct perception of moral agency

Husserl, Edmund (1913). Ideas: General Introduction to Pure Phenomenology. Translated by W.R. Boyce Gibson. New York: Macmillan, 1931.

Maurice Merleau-Ponty - phenomenological insights on perception preceding categorization

Merleau-Ponty, Maurice (1945). Phenomenology of Perception. Translated by Colin Smith. London: Routledge, 1962.

U.S. military racial integration - historical example of successful institutional change

Executive Order 9981 (1948). Desegregation of the Armed Forces. Harry S. Truman Presidential Library.

Systemic racism exists even when not visible.

Claims that systemic racism doesn't exist because it's not always visible ignore the reality of unseen forces. Just as we don't deny gravity because we can't see it, or radiation because we can't feel it, we cannot deny institutional discrimination simply because its mechanisms—like accumulated biases and inherited structures—are often invisible.

This statement tackles a difficult question: how can we recognize systemic racism when we can't always see it happening? It draws on the idea that just because we can't see something doesn't mean it isn't real—like how our actions can have hidden consequences. Discriminatory practices create invisible barriers in institutions that lead to unfair outcomes, even when there's no obvious discrimination happening.

For generations, thinkers have recognized these invisible forces. W.E.B. DuBois wrote about how Black Americans had to constantly see themselves through two lenses—their own and how white society saw them.[1] Antonio Gramsci explained how power often works through culture and "normal" practices rather than obvious force.[2] The Frankfurt School showed how bias gets built into everyday institutions in ways we don't notice.[3] Today, researchers have proven that unconscious racial biases affect decisions in hiring, lending, healthcare, and criminal justice—even when people think they're being fair.

This statement challenges the idea of being "colorblind"—the belief that since open discrimination is illegal, racism must be over. But studies show that seemingly neutral policies can still hurt certain racial groups more than others. Think about standardized tests that favor wealthy students, neighborhoods still segregated because of old discriminatory housing policies, or jobs filled through personal networks that exclude people who weren't already "in the club." Eduardo Bonilla-Silva calls this "racism without racists"—unfair systems that keep running even when no one's actively trying to discriminate.[4]

In practice, this means organizations need to look at their results, not just their rules. If a company keeps hiring mostly white employees despite having "fair" policies, they need to find and fix the invisible barriers, not deny they exist. This is why affirmative action and diversity programs matter—they counteract advantages that some groups have without even realizing it.

This connects to other important ideas, like "invisible barriers need visible remedies" and "prejudice requires ignoring evidence." Together, they show that we first have to admit systemic racism exists before we can fix it. For today's leaders, this means learning how unconscious bias shows up in supposedly neutral systems. It's not enough to avoid active discrimination—we need to actively measure outcomes and fix problems when we find them.

FOR FURTHER READING

W.E.B. DuBois - concept of 'double consciousness' affecting African Americans

DuBois, W.E.B. (1903). The Souls of Black Folk. Chicago: A.C. McClurg & Co.

Antonio Gramsci - theory of hegemonic power structures maintaining dominance through cultural means

Gramsci, Antonio (1971). Selections from the Prison Notebooks. Edited and translated by Quintin Hoare and Geoffrey Nowell Smith. New York: International Publishers.

The Frankfurt School - analysis of the 'culture industry' and embedded institutional bias

Horkheimer, Max and Theodor W. Adorno (1947). Dialectic of Enlightenment. Stanford: Stanford University Press, 2002.

Eduardo Bonilla-Silva - concept of 'racism without racists' describing systemic inequalities through race-neutral processes

Bonilla-Silva, Eduardo (2003). Racism Without Racists: Color-Blind Racism and the Persistence of Racial Inequality in the United States. Lanham, MD: Rowman & Littlefield.

All humans have **equal capacity for righteous action**.*

The principle of eligibility for moral action, when universalized, establishes that all humans possess equal capacity for righteous action. This directly contradicts claims of inherent superiority of any group.

|| ॐ ||

This core principle lays the groundwork for why all people deserve equal rights. It says that every human being has the same ability to be good or bad, regardless of their background. This goes beyond just saying people should be treated equally under the law—it means that at the deepest level, we all have the same capacity to make moral choices. The philosopher Kant believed this too: he said all people have dignity simply because they can think and reason.

* *Timeless Principle: The eternal truth that moral capacity depends on individual consciousness, not physical characteristics, refutes all forms of racism across all eras.*

Throughout history, thinkers from different cultures have reached this same conclusion independently. The Roman emperor Marcus Aurelius (who lived around 150 CE) believed all humans were part of one global community.[1] Buddhist teachers like Nagarjuna taught that everyone has the potential for enlightenment.[2] The Chinese philosopher Mencius (around 300 BCE) said all people are born with the same basic goodness.[3] Islamic scholars like Al-Ghazali (around 1100 CE)[4] and Christian thinkers like Thomas Aquinas (around 1250 CE)[5] also taught that everyone has equal spiritual and moral potential, regardless of their social status.

Modern science backs this up. Researchers have found that people from all cultures share the same basic moral emotions and ways of thinking about right and wrong. Marc Hauser's studies show we're all born with similar ethical instincts.[6] Frans de Waal's research on primates shows that moral behavior comes from our shared evolution, not from belonging to special groups.[7]

In practice, this means we should build systems that assume everyone has equal moral potential—not systems where people have to prove they're worthy. This challenges ideas that rich or educated people are somehow more virtuous. It also questions racial prejudices and class-based assumptions about who's "good" or "bad." In criminal justice, it means focusing on helping people change rather than just punishing them. In education, it means everyone deserves access to learning because of their basic human dignity, not because they've already proven themselves. Some might argue that people clearly behave differently—some seem more moral than others. But this confuses what people do with what they're capable of. It's like saying someone who never learned to read can't possibly be intelligent. Environment and opportunity explain these differences, not some people being inherently better than others. This principle connects to other important ideas: that your birth doesn't determine your worth, and that consciousness goes beyond physical categories. Together, these ideas show that our ability to make moral choices is what makes us human—making discrimination based on anything else simply illogical. For today's leaders and policymakers, this means creating conditions that help everyone develop their moral potential, rather than assuming some people just don't have it. When we see moral failures, we should look at broken systems, not broken people.

FOR FURTHER READING

Marcus Aurelius - The Roman emperor who believed all humans were part of one global community

Marcus Aurelius (167-180 CE). Meditations. Various modern translations available.

Nagarjuna - Buddhist teacher who taught that everyone has the potential for enlightenment

Nagarjuna (c. 150-250 CE). Mūlamadhyamakakārikā (Fundamental Verses on the Middle Way). Various translations available.

Mencius - Chinese philosopher who said all people are born with the same basic goodness

Mencius (c. 372-289 BCE). The Mencius. Translated by D.C. Lau. London: Penguin Classics, 1970.

Al-Ghazali - Islamic scholar who taught everyone has equal spiritual and moral potential

Al-Ghazali (1058-1111). The Revival of the Religious Sciences (Ihya Ulum al-Din). Various translations available.

Thomas Aquinas - Christian thinker who taught equal moral potential regardless of social status

Aquinas, Thomas (1265-1274). Summa Theologica. Various modern editions available.

Marc Hauser - studies showing we're all born with similar ethical instincts

Hauser, Marc (2006). Moral Minds: How Nature Designed Our Universal Sense of Right and Wrong. New York: Ecco/HarperCollins.

Frans de Waal - research on primates showing moral behavior comes from shared evolution

de Waal, Frans (1996). Good Natured: The Origins of Right and Wrong in Humans and Other Animals. Cambridge, MA: Harvard University Press.

Immanuel Kant - philosopher who argued all people have dignity through their capacity for reason

Kant, Immanuel (1785). Groundwork of the Metaphysics of Morals. Various modern translations available.

Racial categories are **social constructs**, not natural facts.

The claim that racial categories are scientifically valid because we have words for them commits the fallacy of conflating linguistic convention with ontological reality. Words create conceptual divisions, not natural ones.

This statement exposes a crucial truth: racial categories aren't scientific facts—they're ideas that societies made up. Just because we have words for different races doesn't mean those divisions are real in nature. It's like how having the word "unicorn" doesn't make unicorns exist. Language creates conceptual divisions in our minds, but that doesn't make them natural facts.

From ancient times, the proof that race is made up becomes clear when you look at how different societies define it. In America, someone might be considered "Black," but in Brazil, they'd fit into one of many different categories. South Africa's apartheid system created a category called "Coloured" that doesn't exist in America. The U.S. "one-drop rule"—saying anyone with any African ancestry is Black—shows how artificial these boundaries are. Throughout history, groups like the Irish, Italians, and Jewish people were reclassified from "non-white" to "white" when it suited those in power.[1]

Modern genetics illustrates this point. The Human Genome Project found that there's more genetic difference between two people of the same "race" than between people of different "races."[2] Population genetics shows human variation is continuous, like a spectrum, not divided into separate boxes. Anthropologist Alan Goodman's research found that racial categories explain less than 0.1% of human genetic differences—making them scientifically meaningless for biology.[3]

This has huge implications. If racial categories are just made up, then the idea that some races are better than others is obviously nonsense—it's just a social system kept in place by power, not nature. Critical race theorists have shown that racial categories were actually invented to justify slavery and colonization, not the other way around.[4]

In practice, this challenges racial profiling by police, which assumes you can predict behavior based on made-up categories. In medicine, it means moving away from treating patients based on race and instead focusing on actual genetic and environmental factors that affect health.

This connects to other ideas about social constructs, like how gender roles are also made up by society, and how different cultures recognize different numbers of genders. Together, these show how many things we think are "natural" are actually just social agreements. This means seeing how made-up categories shape our institutions and building systems that respond to individuals, not stereotypes based on artificial groupings.

FOR FURTHER READING

Sapir-Whorf hypothesis - theory about language shaping perception

Whorf, Benjamin Lee (1956). Language, Thought, and Reality: Selected Writings. Cambridge, MA: MIT Press.

The Human Genome Project - revealed greater genetic variation within racial groups than between them

International Human Genome Sequencing Consortium (2001). "Initial sequencing and analysis of the human genome." Nature 409(6822): 860-921.

Alan Goodman - research showing racial categories explain less than 0.1% of human genetic variation

Goodman, Alan H. (2000). "Why Genes Don't Count (for Racial Differences in Health)." American Journal of Public Health 90(11): 1699-1702.

Critical race theory documentation of how racial categories emerged to justify slavery and colonization

Omi, Michael and Howard Winant (1994). Racial Formation in the United States: From the 1960s to the 1990s. New York: Routledge.

Equal or comparable achievement demonstrates equal rights to opportunity.

When members of all groups demonstrate equal or comparable achievement given equal opportunity, this establishes their equal right to participation in all spheres of action. Denying opportunity based on group membership violates this observed principle.

This statement uses simple logic: when people from all racial groups achieve equally when given the same chances, it shows they deserve equal opportunities. It's like a scientific experiment—equal results under equal conditions show equal ability. This means denying opportunities based on someone's race violates a basic principle we can observe in real life.

In every civilization, we've seen this proven over and over. During the Harlem Renaissance (1918-1937), African American artists, writers, and musicians created extraordinary work when barriers were temporarily lowered.[1] When Jackie Robinson joined Major League Baseball in 1947, he proved Black athletes were equal to white ones—they just hadn't been given the chance before.[2] After 1965, when immigration laws changed, Asian students excelled in American universities, disproving old ideas about Western intellectual superiority. The pattern is always the same: remove the barriers, and achievement gaps disappear.

Modern brain science backs this up. Studies show no differences in thinking ability between racial groups when you account for things like poverty and education quality. The "achievement gap" in schools matches up exactly with differences in resources, not racial differences. Countries like Finland that made their education systems truly equal saw achievement gaps between ethnic groups vanish.[3]

This has huge practical implications. If we see ongoing achievement gaps, it means opportunities aren't really equal—not that some groups are less capable. This flips the script: instead of making individuals prove they're worthy, institutions need to prove they're providing real equal access. In hiring, if a company has equal representation, that's evidence their process is fair. If they consistently hire mostly one group, that signals hidden barriers that need investigation. Some might argue that "cultural differences" explain achievement gaps. But this is circular reasoning—using the effects of inequality to justify more inequality. It's like saying people who were never taught to read have a "culture" of not reading. The power of this principle is that it's based on observable facts: results speak louder than theories. This connects to other ideas like "excellence from any group disproves natural inferiority" and "equal results establish equal rights." Together, they create a framework based on evidence that makes discrimination self-defeating.

It means measuring outcomes is the real test of equal opportunity. If disparities persist, that reveals systematic problems needing systematic solutions—not excuses about individual or cultural shortcomings.

FOR FURTHER READING

The Harlem Renaissance - period demonstrating African American achievement when barriers lowered

Lewis, David Levering (1981). When Harlem Was in Vogue. New York: Knopf.

Jackie Robinson's integration of baseball - proving athletic equality when opportunity opened

Robinson, Jackie (1972). I Never Had It Made: An Autobiography. New York: G.P. Putnam's Sons.

Finland's comprehensive school reforms - showing achievement gaps vanish with educational equality

Sahlberg, Pasi (2011). Finnish Lessons: What Can the World Learn from Educational Change in Finland? New York: Teachers College Press.

Discriminatory traditions have **no moral authority**.*

The argument "it's always been this way" regarding discriminatory practices fails because tradition contaminated by unrighteousness loses its authority. Tradition is accepted only when aligned with virtue.

This statement confronts one of the most common defenses of discrimination: "it's always been this way." But tradition gets its authority from being morally right, not from being old. A harmful practice doesn't become acceptable just because it's been around for a long time. This idea revolutionizes how we judge inherited customs—we should keep traditions that help people flourish and abandon those that cause harm.

* *Timeless Principle: Tradition derives authority from righteousness, not antiquity—a principle that invalidates all appeals to discriminatory customs.*

Throughout history, philosophers have recognized this principle. Aristotle distinguished between good and bad customs in his Politics.[1] John Stuart Mill argued that traditions causing unjustified suffering have no validity, no matter how old they are.[2]

This principle devastates many historical justifications for discrimination. Take Confederate monuments—the "heritage not hate" argument fails because the heritage being celebrated explicitly honored slavery, which violates basic moral principles no matter how long it lasted. The Chinese Exclusion Act of 1882 had no moral authority despite lasting over 60 years, because it contradicted human dignity.[3] Anti-miscegenation laws (banning interracial marriage) weren't justified just because they existed for centuries.

The principle works by distinguishing between righteous and unrighteous traditions based on their effects. Traditions that help humans flourish keep their authority; those that cause harm lose legitimacy no matter how old they are. This applies today to voter suppression tactics—you can't justify denying people voting rights just because similar tactics were used historically.

In modern life, this challenges discriminatory practices defended as "company culture" or exclusive social customs justified as "tradition." Just because "we've always done it this way" doesn't make it right. In criminal justice, it questions why we maintain sentencing practices that reflect historical racial bias rather than current ideas of justice. Some might worry this means destroying all culture. But that misses the point—we're not advocating cultural destruction but ethical evolution. Keep the beautiful, meaningful, and helpful parts of tradition while fixing what causes harm. It's like renovating a historic building—you preserve the architectural beauty while updating the dangerous wiring. This connects to other principles like "eternal principles of justice supersede unjust laws" and "discriminatory traditions must yield to justice." Together, they show that real progress means abandoning unjust practices, not preserving them.

For today's leaders, this requires courage to break with discriminatory precedents. True respect for tradition means keeping its best elements while correcting its failures. Age doesn't make discrimination acceptable—righteousness does.

FOR FURTHER READING

Aristotle's distinction between good and bad customs

Aristotle (350 BCE). Politics. Translated by Ernest Barker. Oxford: Oxford University Press, 1995.

John Stuart Mill's harm principle that invalidates traditions causing unjustified suffering

Mill, John Stuart (1859). On Liberty. London: John W. Parker and Son.

Chinese Exclusion Act - example of discriminatory law lacking moral authority

Chinese Exclusion Act (1882). 22 Stat. 58, enacted May 6, 1882.

Excellence from any group **disproves natural inferiority**.

Claims of natural inferiority of any group fail the test of inference. When we observe members of supposedly "inferior" groups achieving excellence, we must infer equal inherent capacity, falsifying the original claim.

This statement uses simple logic to destroy claims that any group is naturally inferior. It works like this: if even one person from a supposedly "inferior" group achieves excellence, it demonstrates that the whole group has the same potential. It's like a scientific theory—you only need one counterexample to prove the theory wrong. When we see members of any group succeed, it shows equal ability exists in everyone.

Over millennia, individual achievements have shattered group stereotypes. Frederick Douglass's powerful speeches in 1845 disproved racist claims about African intellectual inferiority.[2] Marie Curie winning Nobel Prizes in 1903 and 1911 demolished theories that women couldn't do advanced science.[3] Jackie Robinson's baseball excellence in 1947 destroyed ideas that Black athletes were inferior in sports requiring strategy and thinking.[4]

Modern brain science backs this up through studies of neuroplasticity (the brain's ability to change and grow). When people from any background achieve excellence given the right conditions, it demonstrates everyone has the underlying capacity—these aren't just rare exceptions. This shifts the focus from questioning whether people have ability to asking what barriers prevent that ability from showing.

In practice, this revolutionizes how organizations think about diversity. Instead of asking whether underrepresented groups "can" succeed in certain fields, we should ask what's blocking their proven potential. When we see excellence, we need to examine our systems, not question people's abilities. Some might argue these are just "exceptional individuals" who don't represent their groups. But this is flawed logic—it's like saying "all swans are white" and then claiming black swans don't count when you find them.[1] If the capacity exists in some members of a group, logic suggests it's present throughout the group. Environmental factors—not genetics—explain why it shows up differently.

This connects to other principles like "equal or comparable achievement demonstrates equal rights" and "achievement from the oppressed shows universal potential." Together, they create a framework of evidence that makes discrimination illogical. This means treating any individual's excellence as proof of their entire group's capacity. It requires changing institutions to enable potential rather than test for it. We need to stop thinking about what underrepresented groups lack and start recognizing what they have—then remove the barriers keeping that potential from flourishing.

FOR FURTHER READING

Karl Popper's philosophy of science - falsification through counterexamples

Popper, Karl (1959). The Logic of Scientific Discovery. London: Hutchinson.

Frederick Douglass's eloquence disproving claims about African intellectual inferiority

Douglass, Frederick (1845). Narrative of the Life of Frederick Douglass, an American Slave. Boston: Anti-Slavery Office.

Marie Curie's Nobel Prizes falsifying theories about women's scientific incapacity

Nobel Prize Awards: Marie Curie - Physics (1903) and Chemistry (1911). Nobel Foundation Archives.

Jackie Robinson's athletic excellence demolishing theories about Black athletic inferiority

Robinson, Jackie (1972). I Never Had It Made: An Autobiography. New York: G.P. Putnam's Sons.

Judge individuals by **their actions**, not their group.*

The principle that action and its fruits attach to individuals, not groups, refutes collective guilt or merit based on race. Each person's actions determine their virtue, not their birth group.

This statement establishes a fundamental principle: judge people by what they do, not what group they belong to. It's based on the idea that moral responsibility belongs to individuals, not races or ethnicities. Just as you can't inherit guilt or virtue from your racial group, you shouldn't be judged based on it either. Each person's actions—not their ancestry—determine their character.

* *Timeless Principle: Moral responsibility transcends cultures and time periods.*

Wisdom traditions teach that this principle has deep philosophical roots. Aristotle wrote in his Nicomachean Ethics that virtue depends on individual voluntary actions, not group membership.[1] Throughout history, violating this principle has led to terrible injustices. The Japanese American internment during World War II (1942-1945) imprisoned people based solely on ancestry, not individual actions or loyalty.[2] On the flip side, affirmative action works best when it addresses individual circumstances and barriers rather than making assumptions based on group membership alone.

Today, this principle challenges all forms of racial profiling—from police stopping people based on appearance to hiring algorithms that use race as a shortcut for predicting performance. The criminal justice system should evaluate what individuals actually did and their specific circumstances, not apply stereotypes about their racial group.

The philosophical point goes deeper than just being fair. If every person has their own moral agency (their ability to make choices), then judging them by their group commits a basic logical error. It's like judging all books by their covers instead of reading them. Kant argued that treating people based on group membership uses them as statistics rather than recognizing them as unique individuals with their own dignity.[3] Some might argue that recognizing patterns helps predict behavior. But there's a crucial difference between noticing statistical patterns and using them to judge individuals. Even if certain patterns exist across groups, moral judgment requires looking at what each person actually does, not what statistics might suggest.

This connects to other principles like "birth and race don't determine virtue" and "judge work results, not gender." Together, they create a framework focused on individual evaluation. This means building systems that see individual circumstances, achievements, and character rather than using racial categories as shortcuts. It challenges both obvious discrimination and well-meaning policies that reduce people to their group membership instead of recognizing their unique ability to make moral choices.

FOR FURTHER READING

Aristotle's Nicomachean Ethics - virtue depends on voluntary action by rational agents

Aristotle (350 BCE). Nicomachean Ethics. Translated by Terence Irwin. Indianapolis: Hackett Publishing, 1999.

Japanese American internment - historical violation of individual judgment principle

Executive Order 9066 (1942). Authorizing the Secretary of War to Prescribe Military Areas. Franklin D. Roosevelt Presidential Library.

Kant's categorical imperative - treating people as ends in themselves

Kant, Immanuel (1785). Groundwork of the Metaphysics of Morals. Translated by Mary Gregor. Cambridge: Cambridge University Press, 1997.

Claims of racial superiority are **propaganda, not truth**.

Claims of racial or cultural superiority function as persuasive speech rather than valid statements of fact. Like ritual eulogies, they serve emotional rather than epistemic purposes.

This statement reveals that claims of racial superiority aren't scientific facts—they're propaganda designed to manipulate emotions. It's like the difference between a commercial trying to sell you something and a documentary trying to inform you. Supremacist ideologies always function as emotional manipulation disguised as logical argument. They use the language of science and reason, but their real purpose is persuasion, not truth.

Ancient philosophers like Aristotle recognized the difference between speech aimed at finding truth and speech aimed at persuading people.[1] Racial superiority claims always fall into the second category, even when they pretend to be the first.

History shows this pattern repeatedly. Nazi racial theories stole the language of science to push their ideology. Alfred Rosenberg's "Myth of the Twentieth Century" (1930) looked like a scholarly book but was really just propaganda for German superiority.[2] In America from the 1890s to 1930s, "scientific racism" manipulated statistics and cherry-picked evidence to "prove" Anglo-Saxon superiority—starting with the conclusion they wanted and working backwards.[3]

Today, we see the same tactics in "race realism" movements. They dress up white supremacist ideas in academic language, citing IQ studies while ignoring all the problems with those studies and the role of poverty and education. The giveaway is how they only present evidence that supports their view while dismissing everything else. This shows they're motivated by emotion, not a genuine search for truth.

This pattern extends beyond race. Claims about "Western civilization" being superior work the same way—they list Western achievements while ignoring contributions from other cultures and how much human progress comes from cultures learning from each other. These claims are about building group identity and feeling superior, not about accurate history. Some might say they're using "objective" measures to compare cultures. But choosing which measures to use is itself biased. Real comparative analysis would look at both good and bad across all civilizations without trying to rank them. The desire to create hierarchies reveals political goals, not scholarly ones.

This connects to other principles like "racial categories are social constructs" and "society needs multiple voices as in music." Together, they show that supremacist claims fail both scientifically and ethically. This means developing "propaganda literacy"—learning to recognize when something that looks academic is actually emotional manipulation. Instead of debating these claims as if they were serious scholarship, we need to expose them as the propaganda they are and respond politically rather than academically.

FOR FURTHER READING

Aristotle's distinction between epistemic discourse (truth-seeking) and deliberative rhetoric (persuasion)

Aristotle (350 BCE). Rhetoric. Translated by W. Rhys Roberts. New York: Modern Library, 1954.

Alfred Rosenberg's 'Myth of the Twentieth Century' - example of propaganda disguised as scholarship

Rosenberg, Alfred (1930). Der Mythus des 20. Jahrhunderts. Munich: Hoheneichen-Verlag.

American 'scientific racism' period using statistical manipulation

Gould, Stephen Jay (1981). The Mismeasure of Man. New York: W.W. Norton & Company.

Prejudice requires **ignoring evidence** of human equality.

Lived experience reveals equal human capacities across racial lines, whereas discriminatory ideologies require imagining differences that lived experience simply does not support.

This statement reveals that prejudice works by deliberately ignoring what's right in front of us. When we interact with people from different races, we can see directly that they have comparable capacities for intelligence, creativity, and moral conduct. But prejudice requires pretending not to see this evidence. It's like closing your eyes to avoid seeing something that contradicts what you want to believe— making prejudice a form of willful blindness rather than honest mistake.

Psychologist Leon Festinger's cognitive dissonance theory explains how this works: when what we see contradicts our beliefs, prejudiced people protect their beliefs by dismissing the evidence rather than changing their minds.[1] This shows prejudice is willful ignorance, not innocent error.

History is full of examples. Southern slaveholders saw enslaved people's intelligence and creativity every day but maintained beliefs about Black inferiority by calling these obvious abilities "exceptions" or "mimicry." Nazi officials witnessed Jewish contributions to German science and culture while clinging to conspiracy theories about "Jewish parasitism" to avoid admitting what was obvious.

Modern research confirms this. Jennifer Eberhardt's studies show how racial stereotypes literally change what people see—police officers see weapons that don't exist when suspects are Black.[2] This reveals prejudice as distorted perception, not just bad attitudes.

Philosophically, this raises deep questions about how we form beliefs. If prejudice requires actively suppressing evidence, then fighting it needs more than just presenting facts—we need to understand why people reject obvious truths. Prejudice works like motivated reasoning: starting with the conclusion you want and ignoring anything that contradicts it.

Practical solutions focus on making it harder to ignore evidence. When orchestras started doing blind auditions (musicians play behind screens), gender bias disappeared because evaluators couldn't see who was playing.[3] Similar approaches—standardized testing, anonymous applications, structured interviews—force people to evaluate actual performance instead of their assumptions.

This connects to other principles like "racial prejudice stems from misperception becoming delusion" and "physical differences don't extend to consciousness." Together, they show prejudice as a systematic error in perception that needs deliberate correction. This means creating systems that make ignoring evidence difficult. It's not enough to educate people about bias—we need structures that force objective evaluation of performance while minimizing chances for prejudiced interpretation. We must recognize that prejudice isn't just lack of information but active rejection of available evidence.

FOR FURTHER READING

Leon Festinger's cognitive dissonance theory - explaining how people reject evidence contradicting beliefs

Festinger, Leon (1957). A Theory of Cognitive Dissonance. Stanford: Stanford University Press.

Jennifer Eberhardt's research on how racial assumptions override direct observation

Eberhardt, Jennifer L. (2019). Biased: Uncovering the Hidden Prejudice That Shapes What We See, Think, and Do. New York: Viking.

Blind auditions in orchestras eliminating gender bias

Goldin, Claudia and Cecilia Rouse (2000). "Orchestrating Impartiality: The Impact of 'Blind' Auditions on Female Musicians." American Economic Review 90(4): 715-741.

Failed segregation shows racial divisions are **artificial**.

Segregation and discrimination fail to produce their claimed benefits (social harmony, purity, etc.), proving these divisions are artificial rather than natural. Failed results invalidate the theoretical basis.

This statement uses simple logic to prove racial divisions are artificial: if segregation actually worked as promised, it would create harmony and prosperity. But history shows the opposite—segregation always fails, creating violence, poverty, and dysfunction. When a system's actual results contradict its promised benefits, it demonstrates that the theory behind it is wrong. The failure of segregation reveals that racial separation isn't natural but forced.

Through the ages, segregation has never delivered what it promised. American segregation from 1877 to 1964 claimed it would create social harmony, economic efficiency, and preserve culture for everyone. Instead, it produced constant violence, wasted economic potential by limiting where people could work, and cultural stagnation by reducing the exchange of ideas. The "separate but equal" doctrine failed completely—it created neither real separation nor equality, just a hierarchy that needed constant force to maintain.[1]

South African apartheid from 1948 to 1994 provides even clearer proof. Despite elaborate theories about "natural" racial boundaries and how separation would help everyone develop, the system created widespread violence, economic decline, international isolation, and social problems for all racial groups. It didn't collapse just from outside pressure—it fell apart from its own contradictions, needing more and more repression to maintain boundaries that weren't natural in the first place.[2]

We see this pattern today in American cities. Segregated areas consistently perform worse than integrated ones in economic mobility, education, and community well-being.[3] This happens everywhere, regardless of region or local culture, suggesting that separation itself causes these problems.

The deeper insight is philosophical: if racial differences were truly natural, they wouldn't need laws, violence, and social pressure to maintain them. Nature doesn't need enforcement—water flows downhill without police making it happen. The very fact that segregation requires force reveals it's artificial. Some might argue that people "voluntarily" segregate today. But this ignores how past coercion created current patterns and how existing structures make integration difficult. Real voluntary association would look very different from patterns created by historical force.

This connects to other principles like "racial categories are social constructs" and "society needs multiple voices." Together, they show that artificial divisions hurt rather than help communities. This means judging policies by actual results, not promised benefits. When social problems persist, it often signals we're maintaining artificial divisions rather than addressing natural differences. The solution isn't better segregation but removing the artificial barriers that segregation created.

FOR FURTHER READING

American segregation period promising but failing to deliver social harmony

Woodward, C. Vann (1955). The Strange Career of Jim Crow. New York: Oxford University Press.

South African apartheid system and its internal contradictions

Thompson, Leonard (2001). A History of South Africa. New Haven: Yale University Press.

Contemporary residential segregation patterns and their negative outcomes

Massey, Douglas S. and Nancy A. Denton (1993). American Apartheid: Segregation and the Making of the Underclass. Cambridge, MA: Harvard University Press.

Excluding any group **diminishes society's virtue**.

When any group is denied eligibility for social participation, the entire society suffers loss of virtue. Exclusion diminishes collective virtue, not just individual opportunity.

This statement reframes discrimination in a powerful way: when we exclude any group from society, we don't just hurt them—we hurt ourselves. It's like a body rejecting one of its own organs; the whole system suffers. Society works as an interconnected system where damaging any part weakens everything. As Martin Luther King Jr. said, "injustice anywhere is a threat to justice everywhere."

History illustrates this principle repeatedly. The pre-Civil War South excluded enslaved people from education and innovation, which left the entire region technologically backward for generations. When Nazi Germany expelled Jewish scientists and thinkers, they crippled their own scientific progress. Those same German-Jewish physicists helped develop technologies for the Allies, contributing to Germany's defeat.

Modern research confirms this pattern. Scott Page's studies show that diverse groups consistently solve complex problems better than uniform ones.[2] Richard Florida's research reveals that cities with more diversity have faster economic growth and more innovation.[3] When we exclude any group's perspectives, talents, and contributions, we reduce our collective ability to solve problems.

The philosophy behind this is what John Stuart Mill called the "marketplace of ideas"—truth emerges when different viewpoints compete and interact.[4] When societies exclude groups, they lose unique insights and experiences that only those groups can provide. This creates what philosophers call knowledge loss that makes everyone poorer.

In practice, this means judging organizations by how inclusive they are, not just their stated goals. Companies that exclude women, minorities, or other groups consistently perform worse than inclusive ones in innovation, adaptability, and long-term success. This shows that diversity isn't just morally right—it's strategically smart. Some might argue that certain groups have specific advantages in some areas. But this misses the point: even if true, excluding others prevents the mixing of ideas that drives real progress. It's like trying to paint with only one color—you might make something, but you'll never create a masterpiece.

This connects to other principles like "multicultural environments increase collective strength" and "equal treatment serves the common good." Together, they show that inclusion is essential for society to thrive. This means seeing diversity as a necessity, not a luxury. Excluding any group isn't just unfair to them—it's self-sabotage. Organizations need all available talent and perspectives to succeed in complex environments.

FOR FURTHER READING

Martin Luther King Jr.'s assertion about injustice affecting justice everywhere

King, Martin Luther Jr. (1963). "Letter from Birmingham Jail." American Friends Service Committee.

Scott Page's work demonstrating diverse groups outperform homogeneous ones

Page, Scott E. (2007). The Difference: How the Power of Diversity Creates Better Groups, Firms, Schools, and Societies. Princeton: Princeton University Press.

Richard Florida's research on diversity driving economic growth and innovation

Florida, Richard (2002). The Rise of the Creative Class. New York: Basic Books.

John Stuart Mill's concept of the 'marketplace of ideas'

Mill, John Stuart (1859). On Liberty. London: John W. Parker and Son.

Racial prejudice stems from **misperception becoming delusion**.

Racial prejudice stems from false perception—seeing difference where none exists meaningfully. This misperception hardens into certain delusion through repetition and social reinforcement.

This statement explains how racial prejudice works like an optical illusion that becomes permanent. It starts with seeing differences that don't really matter—like thinking skin color determines character. This false perception gets reinforced by selective attention (noticing only what confirms our bias) and social agreement until it becomes an unshakeable delusion. It's like how a small misunderstanding can grow into a completely false belief when people keep repeating and believing it.

Across cultures, we can trace how these false perceptions became "scientific facts." In the 1800s, scientists like Samuel Morton measured skulls to "prove" racial hierarchies. But his racial bias led him to make measurement errors that supported what he already believed. He saw what he expected to see and ignored anything that contradicted his assumptions.[1]

Modern brain science shows exactly how this works. Jennifer Eberhardt's research shows that racial categories actually change what people see—our brains process the same information differently based on racial cues.[2] Claude Steele's work on stereotype threat shows how expectations become self-fulfilling prophecies. When people expect certain groups to perform poorly, that expectation itself can create poor performance.[3]

Philosophically, this connects to Buddhist ideas about how mental habits create persistent illusions. Once we see something falsely, that creates a mental pattern that filters everything else we see, making the illusion seem more and more real. Sociologist Georg Simmel showed how social categories get treated as natural facts rather than made-up concepts.[4]

In practice, this means we need training that catches these misperceptions before they harden into unchangeable beliefs. Harvard's Project Implicit shows how unconscious biases work below our awareness, suggesting we need to change systems, not just minds.[5] This also explains why logical arguments often fail against established prejudice—you can't reason someone out of a delusion the same way you'd correct a simple mistake. Some might claim that racial differences are "real." But this misses a crucial point: human variation exists on a spectrum, like height or hair color. Racial categories artificially divide this continuous variation into separate boxes, creating false perceptions of distinct groups where none naturally exist.

This connects to other principles like "prejudice requires ignoring evidence" and "racial categories are social constructs." Together, they show prejudice as a thinking disorder that needs systematic correction. This means understanding prejudice as a perception problem, not just a bad attitude. We need interventions that address unconscious processes, not just conscious beliefs. It's like treating an vision problem—you need corrective lenses, not just telling someone to "see better."

FOR FURTHER READING

Samuel Morton's cranial studies exemplifying measurement errors from racial bias

Morton, Samuel George (1839). Crania Americana. Philadelphia: J. Dobson.

Jennifer Eberhardt's studies on how racial categories prime perception

Eberhardt, Jennifer L. (2019). Biased: Uncovering the Hidden Prejudice That Shapes What We See, Think, and Do. New York: Viking.

Claude Steele's stereotype threat research on self-fulfilling prophecies

Steele, Claude M. (2010). Whistling Vivaldi: How Stereotypes Affect Us and What We Can Do. New York: W.W. Norton & Company.

Georg Simmel's sociology on how social categories become reified

Simmel, Georg (1908). Sociology: Investigations on the Forms of Sociation. Berlin: Duncker & Humblot.

Harvard's Project Implicit revealing unconscious associations

Greenwald, Anthony G., Debbie E. McGhee, and Jordan L.K. Schwartz (1998). "Measuring Individual Differences in Implicit Cognition: The Implicit Association Test." Journal of Personality and Social Psychology 74(6): 1464-1480.

Human worth **cannot be ranked** or compared.*

Human dignity admits no valid comparison that would establish hierarchy. Like revealed truth itself in this philosophical system, human worth is self-evident and incomparable.

This statement declares something radical: human worth can't be measured or ranked like test scores or athletic performance. Just as you can't rank love or beauty objectively, human dignity exists beyond comparison. Drawing from philosopher Kant, it says people have absolute worth as "ends in themselves," not relative worth based on their usefulness. This makes any attempt to rank races, cultures, or individuals philosophically impossible.

* *Timeless Principle: Human dignity is self-evident truth requiring no external validation—a principle that undermines all attempts at racial ranking.*

Historically, this principle destroys all attempts to rank civilizations or races that were popular in the 1800s. Auguste Comte[2] tried to rank "primitive" cultures below "advanced" ones, but this fails because he arbitrarily chose certain measures (like technology) while ignoring others (like ecological wisdom or social harmony). Social Darwinists[3] who applied evolution to rank human societies made a basic error—confusing cultural differences with moral superiority.

Today, this challenges ranking systems everywhere. Standardized tests that rank students or countries assume you can measure human value with numbers, reducing complex abilities to artificial scores. Even well-meaning tools like the Human Development Index become problematic when they suggest some civilizations are "better" than others overall.

The philosophical point goes deep: to compare things, you need shared criteria. But human worth goes beyond any particular quality. Intelligence, kindness, productivity, creativity—these show up differently in different people and cultures. Even if we could measure them perfectly, deciding which matters more involves value judgments that can't be objective. It's like trying to rank whether music is "better" than painting.

Practically, this means rejecting systems that confuse performance with worth. Universities can evaluate applicants for admission without suggesting accepted students are worth more as humans. Immigration policies can make practical decisions without implying some cultures deserve preference. Some might say we need rankings for practical purposes. True—but there's a crucial difference between functional assessment ("who can do this job?") and worth ranking ("who's a better person?"). Society needs performance evaluation, but that doesn't mean high performers have greater human dignity.

This connects to principles like "birth and race don't determine virtue" and "physical strength doesn't determine worth." Together, they establish human worth as beyond measurement. This means creating evaluation systems that serve practical needs without implying human hierarchy. We can assess function without ranking worth, recognizing that practical measurements serve temporary goals, not ultimate values.

FOR FURTHER READING

Kant's categorical imperative establishing rational beings as 'ends in themselves'

Kant, Immanuel (1785). Groundwork of the Metaphysics of Morals. Translated by Mary Gregor. Cambridge: Cambridge University Press, 1997.

Auguste Comte's positivist hierarchy attempting to rank cultures

Comte, Auguste (1830-1842). The Course of Positive Philosophy. Paris: Bachelier.

Social Darwinist theories misapplying evolution to human societies

Hofstadter, Richard (1944). Social Darwinism in American Thought. Philadelphia: University of Pennsylvania Press.

Universal ethics override discriminatory rules.

When discriminatory prohibitions contradict the positive injunction to treat all with righteousness, these prohibitions are simply invalid. Positive ethical imperatives override negative discriminatory rules.

This statement establishes a crucial hierarchy: universal ethical principles always outrank discriminatory rules. It's like how the Constitution overrides local laws—when a specific rule violates fundamental human rights, the rule loses its authority, not the rights. This principle says that when we face a conflict between treating all people with dignity and following discriminatory regulations, human dignity wins. Rules that contradict universal ethics have no legitimate authority, regardless of who made them or how long they've existed.

Throughout history, this principle has guided movements for justice. Henry David Thoreau's "Civil Disobedience" (1849)[1] argued that unjust laws have no moral authority when they violate universal human dignity. Martin Luther King Jr.'s "Letter from Birmingham Jail" (1963)[2] built on this, distinguishing between just laws that align with moral principles and unjust laws that contradict them. The Underground Railroad[4] put this into practice—people broke fugitive slave laws because the universal principle against human bondage outweighed any specific law supporting slavery.

Today we see this in sanctuary cities that prioritize humanitarian needs over immigration enforcement, healthcare workers who treat patients regardless of legal status, and teachers who educate all children despite documentation requirements. In each case, people recognize that universal ethical duties override discriminatory regulations.

The philosophy works like constitutional interpretation—fundamental principles judge specific rules, not the other way around. When laws violate universal principles, the laws lose legitimacy. Legal philosopher Ronald Dworkin[3] explained this by distinguishing between rules (specific directives) and principles (general standards), with principles taking priority during conflicts.

Practically, this challenges the "just following orders" defense. Professional ethics recognize this hierarchy—doctors' oath to "do no harm" overrides discriminatory hospital policies. Teachers' duty to serve all students supersedes exclusionary administrative rules. When institutional rules conflict with human dignity, we must choose dignity. Some might argue that laws are valid simply because they were properly enacted, regardless of moral content. But this misses the key distinction between legal validity and moral authority. Even if a discriminatory rule is legally valid, it lacks moral legitimacy when it contradicts universal principles. This connects to ideas like "eternal principles of justice supersede unjust laws" and "universal duties override gender-based prohibitions." Together, they create a framework for ethical decision-making.

For today's leaders, this demands courage to choose human dignity over institutional compliance when they conflict. It means recognizing that moral authority stands above bureaucratic authority, and being willing to act on that recognition even when it's difficult.

FOR FURTHER READING

Henry David Thoreau's argument that unjust laws lack moral authority

Thoreau, Henry David (1849). "Civil Disobedience." Aesthetic Papers. Boston: Elizabeth P. Peabody.

Martin Luther King Jr.'s distinction between just and unjust laws

King, Martin Luther Jr. (1963). "Letter from Birmingham Jail." American Friends Service Committee.

Ronald Dworkin's jurisprudence distinguishing between rules and principles

Dworkin, Ronald (1977). Taking Rights Seriously. Cambridge, MA: Harvard University Press.

The Underground Railroad as practical application of universal principles over law

Still, William (1872). The Underground Railroad: A Record of Facts, Authentic Narratives, Letters, &c. Philadelphia: Porter & Coates.

Equal treatment serves **the common good**.

The injunction for equal treatment serves universal welfare, a highest value. Discrimination violates this cosmic ordering principle, proving its unrighteous nature.

|| ॐ ||

This statement reframes civil rights in a powerful way: equal treatment isn't just about fairness to individuals—it actually makes society better for everyone. Drawing from ancient ideas about the "common good" and modern theories of justice, it shows that equality helps communities thrive while discrimination hurts everyone, including those it claims to benefit. It's like removing roadblocks on a highway—everyone moves faster when artificial barriers disappear.

History demonstrates this principle repeatedly. The Jim Crow South stayed economically backward partly because racial restrictions prevented people from doing the jobs they were best suited for. W.E.B. DuBois[4] showed how racial discrimination actually hurt white Southern workers by keeping wages artificially low and preventing workers from organizing together effectively. South Africa under apartheid became economically isolated and inefficient because discriminatory policies wasted human talent.

Modern research confirms this pattern. Diverse, inclusive societies consistently outperform exclusive ones in innovation, economic growth, social trust, and quality of institutions. Countries with greater gender equality rank higher on every measure of human development. Nations that include different ethnic groups show more political stability and economic success. Economists call these "efficiency gains"—when you remove discriminatory barriers, resources (including human talent) flow to where they're most useful.

Philosophically, this connects to utilitarian ethics—policies should maximize overall well-being, not protect certain groups' privileges. But this teaching goes deeper, suggesting that equality serves a kind of cosmic order. Discrimination doesn't just hurt people; it violates natural principles of harmony and balance that keep societies healthy.

In practice, this means judging policies by how they affect everyone, not just certain groups. Affirmative action serves the common good by developing previously wasted human potential. Educational equity makes society stronger overall. Even when these policies seem to disadvantage currently privileged groups, they ultimately benefit everyone by creating more productive, stable, and innovative communities. Some think equality is zero-sum—that helping disadvantaged groups must hurt advantaged ones. But this misses the key insight: discrimination creates artificial scarcity and prevents society from functioning optimally. It's like having a sports team where only certain players are allowed to play certain positions regardless of skill—the whole team loses. This connects to principles like "excluding any group diminishes society's virtue" and "multicultural environments increase collective strength." Together, they show equality isn't just morally right—it's functionally necessary.

This means evaluating policies by whether they help society flourish overall, not just protect current advantages. Real common good requires inclusion, not privilege protection. When everyone can contribute their best, everyone benefits.

FOR FURTHER READING

Aristotle's concept of the common good (koinon agathon)

Aristotle (350 BCE). Politics. Translated by Ernest Barker. Oxford: Oxford University Press, 1995.

Cicero's concept of res publica (public good)

Cicero, Marcus Tullius (54-51 BCE). De Re Publica. Translated by Clinton W. Keyes. Cambridge, MA: Harvard University Press, 1928.

John Rawls's theory that just institutions benefit society as a whole

Rawls, John (1971). A Theory of Justice. Cambridge, MA: Harvard University Press.

W.E.B. DuBois's economic analyses of how discrimination harmed Southern workers

DuBois, W.E.B. (1935). Black Reconstruction in America, 1860-1880. New York: Harcourt, Brace and Company.

Eternal principles of justice supersede unjust laws.

When human-made laws conflict with eternal principles of justice, the eternal principles prevail. This invalidates "it's the law" defenses of discrimination.

This statement declares that eternal principles of justice always outrank human-made laws. When legislation violates fundamental moral principles, the principles win. This idea has ancient roots—Aristotle distinguished between man-made and natural justice, Cicero said unjust laws aren't really laws at all, and Thomas Aquinas placed God's eternal law above human law. This framework directly challenges the idea that laws are valid just because they were properly passed, regardless of their moral content.

History demonstrates that people have used this principle to justify resisting unjust laws. In ancient Greece, Sophocles's play Antigone (441 BCE) showed this conflict when divine law required burial rites that the king had forbidden[4]. The Underground Railroad operated on this principle—helpers knew that assisting escaped slaves was morally required despite federal laws saying otherwise. During the Nazi era, people who rescued Jews invoked universal human dignity against genocidal laws. Civil rights activists challenged segregation by appealing to constitutional principles that transcended discriminatory state laws.

Today we see this in sanctuary cities that protect undocumented immigrants despite federal enforcement orders, healthcare workers who treat patients regardless of legal status, and teachers who educate all children despite documentation rules. In each case, people recognize that eternal justice principles override specific laws that violate human dignity.

The philosophy works through what legal scholars call "constitutional interpretation"—fundamental principles judge specific rules, not vice versa. Ronald Dworkin explained this by distinguishing between rules (specific commands) and principles (general standards), with principles winning when they conflict[5]. This supports courts striking down discriminatory laws by appealing to constitutional principles that embody eternal justice.

Practically, this challenges arguments that equate following the law with being moral. While societies need general legal compliance to function, specific unjust laws lack moral authority and may require resistance. Professional ethics recognize this—doctors must care for all patients even if laws say otherwise, journalists must tell truth despite secrecy laws. Some worry that questioning laws threatens social stability. But unjust laws actually create instability by violating principles needed for legitimate government. Laws that contradict eternal justice generate resistance, not compliance, ultimately undermining social order rather than supporting it. This connects to principles like "universal ethics override discriminatory rules" and "personal virtue choices supersede state authority." Together, they create a framework for ethical resistance to unjust authority. This means measuring legal directives against universal justice principles, recognizing that moral authority stands above bureaucratic compliance when they conflict. Sometimes the highest form of respect for law is refusing to follow unjust laws.

FOR FURTHER READING

Aristotle's distinction between conventional and natural justice

Aristotle (350 BCE). Nicomachean Ethics, Book V. Translated by Terence Irwin. Indianapolis: Hackett Publishing, 1999.

Cicero's assertion that unjust laws aren't truly laws

Cicero, Marcus Tullius (52 BCE). De Legibus (On the Laws). Translated by Clinton W. Keyes. Cambridge, MA: Harvard University Press, 1928.

Thomas Aquinas's hierarchy placing eternal law above human law

Aquinas, Thomas (1265-1274). Summa Theologica, I-II, Question 91. Various modern editions available.

Sophocles's Antigone dramatizing conflict between divine and human law

Sophocles (441 BCE). Antigone. Translated by Robert Fagles. New York: Penguin Classics, 1984.

Ronald Dworkin's legal theory distinguishing rules and principles

Dworkin, Ronald (1977). Taking Rights Seriously. Cambridge, MA: Harvard University Press.

Achievement from the oppressed demonstrates **universal potential.***

The acceptance that even those of lowest social position can achieve spiritual and moral excellence demonstrates universal human capacity. If the "least" can achieve greatly, hierarchy is false.

This powerful teaching uses logic to destroy systems of oppression from within. It works like this: if people from the "lowest" social positions can achieve greatness, then the whole idea of social hierarchy is proven false. It's the ultimate philosophical checkmate—using a system's own evidence against it. When supposedly "inferior" people achieve excellence, it forces us to admit that all humans have equal potential.

* *Timeless Principle: Excellence emerging from unexpected sources disproves all systems of inherent hierarchy.*

Since antiquity, excellence from oppressed groups has forced societies to face their contradictions. Frederick Douglass's brilliant speeches and writing made Americans confront the absurdity of enslaving "inferior" people while witnessing their intellectual genius[1]. When Phillis Wheatley published her poetry in 1773, it created mental conflict—some questioned slavery while others desperately tried to explain away her talent[2]. More recently, Barack Obama's presidency embodied this principle—undeniable excellence from a group subjected to centuries of oppression[3].

The logic is simple but devastating. If you claim a group is inferior, but then someone from that group achieves excellence, only three things are possible: either the achievement didn't happen (but we can see it did), the person doesn't really belong to that group (which denies reality), or your hierarchy is wrong. If there is no credible evidence supporting the first two, the hierarchy must be false.

Today, this principle helps us understand success stories correctly. When women excel in science, immigrants build successful businesses, or working-class students master complex subjects, these aren't rare exceptions—they reveal universal human capacity. The real issue is systemic barriers, not natural limitations. This shifts our focus from questioning people's ability to examining what's blocking it. Some try to dismiss these achievements as "exceptional individuals" who don't represent their groups. But this is flawed logic—like saying "all swans are white" and then claiming black swans don't count. If the capacity exists anywhere in a group, logic suggests it exists throughout the group. Environmental factors explain why it shows up differently.

This connects to principles like "excellence from any group disproves natural inferiority" and "birth and race don't determine virtue." Together, they create a logical framework that makes racial hierarchy impossible to defend. This means seeing individual excellence as proof of universal capacity, not rare exceptions. We need to change institutions to enable potential rather than test for it. Instead of asking "why can't they succeed?" we should ask "what's preventing their success?" When we see achievement from oppressed communities, it reveals human potential waiting for opportunity to flourish.

FOR FURTHER READING

Frederick Douglass's oratory and writing demonstrating intellectual brilliance

Douglass, Frederick (1845). Narrative of the Life of Frederick Douglass, an American Slave. Boston: Anti-Slavery Office.

Phillis Wheatley's poetry creating cognitive dissonance about slavery

Wheatley, Phillis (1773). Poems on Various Subjects, Religious and Moral. London: A. Bell.

Barack Obama's presidency as contemporary example of excellence from oppressed group

Obama, Barack (2009-2017). 44th President of the United States. Presidential Archives.

ON GENDER EQUALITY

Physical differences don't extend to **consciousness or capability**.*

Physical sexual differentiation doesn't extend to consciousness or capacity for knowledge and virtue. The principle that the self transcends physical attributes refutes claims of mental or spiritual gender hierarchy.

This foundational teaching separates physical bodies from consciousness and capability. Just because men and women have different physical characteristics doesn't mean they have different mental or spiritual capacities. The principle says that consciousness operates independently of physical sex—making any claims about women being less intelligent or spiritually capable a basic logical error. Our true human capacity goes beyond our physical form.

* *Timeless Principle: Consciousness knows no gender—an eternal truth that invalidates all claims of mental or spiritual gender hierarchy.*

Throughout history, many philosophical traditions have recognized this separation. Plato distinguished between soul and body.[1] Hindu Vedantic thought separates the eternal self (atman) from temporary physical form.[2] Even Descartes recognized mind as separate from physical matter.[3] Each of these traditions implicitly rejected the idea that mental capacity comes from physical characteristics, laying philosophical groundwork for gender equality.

Modern brain science confirms this. Research shows that cognitive differences between males and females are tiny, mostly caused by environment and upbringing, and vary so much between individuals that gender-based generalizations don't work. Studies of brain plasticity (the brain's ability to change) show how social conditioning shapes brain development. Research on gender-diverse individuals demonstrates that consciousness works independently of biological sex.

The philosophical principle here is that consciousness is the true self, while physical characteristics are just temporary attributes—like clothes we wear. When society says women can't do certain mental tasks because of their bodies, it confuses the essential (consciousness) with the accidental (physical form).

In practice, this means educational policies should assume equal intellectual capacity regardless of gender. Workplaces should evaluate performance, not demographics. Social norms should encourage everyone to develop their full potential without gender-based restrictions or expectations. Some might point to statistics showing gender differences in certain cognitive tasks. But these ignore how different social conditioning creates these patterns, and how variation within each gender far exceeds average differences between genders. Biology provides potential—it doesn't determine what we actually achieve. This connects to principles like "all humans have equal capacity for righteous action" and "in highest consciousness, gender becomes irrelevant." Together, they establish consciousness as beyond gender.

This means treating mental capacity as individual, not gender-determined. We must recognize that consciousness has no gender boundaries—a person's body doesn't limit their mind.

FOR FURTHER READING

Platonic philosophy separating soul from body

Plato (380 BCE). Phaedo. Translated by G.M.A. Grube. Indianapolis: Hackett Publishing, 1977.

Vedantic thought distinguishing eternal self (atman) from physical form

Shankara (8th century CE). Vivekachudamani (Crest Jewel of Discrimination). Translated by Swami Madhavananda. Kolkata: Advaita Ashrama, 1921.

Cartesian dualism recognizing mind as separate from material extension

Descartes, René (1637). Discourse on Method. Translated by Donald A. Cress. Indianapolis: Hackett Publishing, 1998.

Contemporary philosophy of mind on consciousness transcending physical properties

Chalmers, David J. (1996). The Conscious Mind: In Search of a Fundamental Theory. Oxford: Oxford University Press.

Gender **cannot restrict eligibility** for action.*

The principle of eligibility for action cannot be restricted by gender. This principle (adhikara in Sanskrit), traditionally depended on one's capacity and preparation, not on the characteristics with which one is born. When we include irrelevant factors like gender in eligibility criteria, we corrupt the selection process and prevent the best outcomes for everyone.

This statement declares that gender can never be a valid reason to exclude someone from any activity or role. Using religious evolution as an example—if women can now participate in the most sacred rituals that were once forbidden to them, then certainly they can't be excluded from secular activities. The principle is simple: if you're capable of doing something, your gender shouldn't stop you. All areas of human achievement must be open to everyone regardless of gender.

* *Timeless Principle: This captures the universal principle that gender is simply irrelevant to determining what someone should be allowed to do - only their actual ability to perform the action matters.*

For millennia, we've seen gender barriers fall one by one. Women entered religious leadership despite fierce resistance, proving gender didn't affect spiritual authority. As women became doctors, lawyers, politicians, and entered other professions, it became clear that gender restrictions came from social prejudice, not natural limitations.

Today, we still see inappropriate gender restrictions. Military combat roles, corporate leadership, STEM fields, and certain trades show gender imbalances that reflect systemic barriers, not natural differences in ability. Each restriction violates the principle that capability—not identity—should determine who can do what.

Practically, this means examining all requirements to ensure they relate to actual job needs, not demographics. Organizations that achieve real gender equality focus on demonstrated competence while actively removing barriers that unfairly affect certain groups. Some might argue that certain roles have physical requirements that favor one gender. But we need to distinguish between genuine job necessities and artificial barriers. Most roles require mental rather than physical capabilities. Even physically demanding positions often accommodate different body types and strengths through adaptive technologies and techniques. This connects to principles like "intelligence, not gender, determines educational access" and "equal or comparable achievement demonstrates equal rights to opportunity." Together, they establish universal access as a moral principle.

This means examining whether any gender-based restrictions serve real purposes or just preserve historical discrimination. True eligibility depends on what you can do, not what gender you are.

Equal capacity demands equal opportunities.

Observable equal capacities between genders necessitate equal rights to action. Denying women opportunities despite demonstrated ability violates the principle of inference from capacity to rights.

This statement follows simple logic: when we can see that men and women have equal abilities, they deserve equal opportunities. It's like observing that two students get the same test scores—you can't then say one deserves college admission while the other doesn't. The principle says that once we observe equal capabilities (which we have), continuing to deny equal opportunities is both illogical and unjust. Evidence of equal ability creates an obligation for equal access.

History repeatedly illustrates this principle. When women entered medicine, they performed as well as or better than men, disproving claims they weren't suited for science. Women's success in law, academic research, and business leadership provided hard evidence that gender restrictions came from prejudice, not real capability differences. Today, women make up the majority of medical students in many countries.

Modern research confirms equal capabilities across all fields. Studies show girls and boys achieve similarly in all subjects when given equal encouragement and opportunity. Workplace evaluations reveal that when women underperform, it's typically due to different treatment, not different ability. Individual variation within each gender far exceeds any average differences between genders.

The philosophical logic is straightforward: when we see equal effects (same performance), we must infer equal causes (same capability). It's basic reasoning—if two people produce the same quality work, they must have similar abilities. Continuing to restrict opportunities after seeing proof of equal capability violates logic and perpetuates injustice based on disproven ideas.

Practically, this means evaluation systems should focus on actual performance, not gender assumptions. Recruitment should actively seek qualified candidates regardless of gender. Advancement should reward achievement, not conformity to traditional gender expectations. Some might claim that average differences between genders justify treating individuals differently. But this commits a logical error—applying group statistics to individuals. It's like saying because men are taller on average, every man must be taller than every woman. Even if statistical differences existed (which research largely disproves), we must evaluate individuals, not stereotypes. This connects to principles like "equal or comparable achievement demonstrates equal rights to opportunity" and "equal results establish equal rights to participation." Together, they create an evidence-based foundation for gender equality.

This means letting demonstrated capability, not gender identity, determine who gets opportunities. When we see equal performance, we're obligated to provide equal treatment. The evidence is clear—now we must act on it.

Women's virtue encompasses **all spheres**, not just domestic.

Restricting women's virtue to domestic spheres contradicts their observed capacities in all fields. Like men, women's virtue encompasses all righteous action, not arbitrary limitations.

|| ॐ ||

This statement challenges the idea that women's goodness or moral contribution should be limited to home and family. It says that trying to confine women's virtue to domestic roles ignores their proven abilities in all areas of life. Just as men can express virtue through any righteous action—in business, politics, science, or family—so can women. True virtue doesn't follow gender boundaries; it flows wherever there's opportunity to do good.

History is full of women who proved this principle by demonstrating virtue across many domains despite pressure to stay in domestic roles. Florence Nightingale didn't just care for the sick—she revolutionized medical care and hospital systems.[1] Eleanor Roosevelt went beyond being a supportive wife to advance human rights globally.[2] Marie Curie transformed our understanding of physics and chemistry.[3] Each showed that women's moral capacity extends far beyond traditional boundaries, and that restricting it actually diminishes virtue rather than preserving it.

Today, we still see attempts to limit women's moral authority to "appropriate" spheres. Religious institutions might welcome women's charity work but deny them leadership roles. Political systems expect women to focus on "family issues" rather than economics or foreign policy. Corporate cultures channel women toward "nurturing" roles while keeping them away from strategic decisions. All of these perpetuate artificial limitations.

Philosophically, virtue (dharma) consists of universal principles, not context-specific rules. When society tries to restrict women's virtue to certain areas, it violates the universal nature of moral action and prevents the best expression of righteousness in all spheres of life.

In practice, this means recognizing women's moral authority everywhere—in business ethics, political leadership, scientific research, military service, spiritual guidance, and technological innovation. Organizations that embrace this principle typically see better moral clarity and decision-making. Some claim women have "natural" inclinations toward certain spheres. But these often reflect what girls are taught to value, not inherent limitations. Even when preferences exist, they should expand rather than restrict options for expressing virtue. This connects to principles like "gender cannot restrict eligibility for action" and "self-determination is a universal human right." Together, they establish that women's virtue is comprehensive, not limited.

This means recognizing women's moral authority as universal, not restricted to certain domains. Virtue flourishes through expanding opportunities for expression, not limiting them. When we confine anyone's goodness to narrow channels, we rob society of their full contribution.

FOR FURTHER READING

Florence Nightingale revolutionizing medical care and hospital sanitation

Nightingale, Florence (1859). Notes on Nursing: What It Is, and What It Is Not. London: Harrison.

Eleanor Roosevelt advancing human rights globally

Roosevelt, Eleanor (1958). On My Own. New York: Harper & Brothers.

Marie Curie transforming scientific understanding

Curie, Marie (1923). Pierre Curie. New York: The Macmillan Company.

Gender roles are **social constructions**, not natural law.

The fundamental nature of consciousness is identical across genders, yet society imagines limitations that don't exist. Gender roles are social constructs, not natural laws.

This statement reveals that gender roles—the behaviors and expectations society assigns to men and women—are made up by cultures, not dictated by nature. While consciousness works the same way in everyone regardless of gender, societies create elaborate rules about how men and women should act based on physical differences that have nothing to do with mental or moral capacity. These artificial rules limit human potential rather than express it.

History shows this through the wild variation in gender roles across cultures and time. What one society calls "masculine," another considers "feminine." Roles that seem essential in one era disappear in the next. Ancient Sparta expected women to train physically and manage property—activities medieval Europe later banned for women. Today's Nordic countries show egalitarian possibilities that seemed impossible just generations ago.

Modern anthropology finds no universal gender roles beyond those directly tied to biological reproduction. Different societies assign caregiving, leadership, economic activity, spiritual authority, and artistic expression to different genders based on cultural logic, not natural law. Even within one society, gender expectations vary dramatically by class, region, and time period.

Philosophically, this involves distinguishing between essential nature and cultural additions. Gender roles are cultural impositions on human consciousness, not natural expressions of real differences. When societies mistake their own cultural constructions for natural law, they create artificial limitations that block human potential.

Practically, this means questioning whether workplace cultures, family structures, educational approaches, and social expectations reflect real needs or just historical habits. Organizations that examine and revise gender-based assumptions typically find better performance and satisfaction. Some might argue that biology influences behavior. But we must distinguish between statistical tendencies and individual destiny. Even where biology creates general patterns, these should expand rather than limit choices. Plus, cultural conditioning often takes tiny biological differences and amplifies them into major social restrictions. This connects to principles like "racial categories are social constructs" and "restrictive gender roles obstruct self-realization." Together, they show how identity categories are constructed, not natural.

This means examining whether organizational practices reflect real operational needs or just perpetuate arbitrary gender expectations. Authentic human expression goes beyond conventional role limitations—people flourish when they can be themselves, not when forced into predetermined molds.

FOR FURTHER READING

Anthropological research on cultural construction of gender roles

Butler, Judith (1990). Gender Trouble: Feminism and the Subversion of Identity. New York: Routledge.

Women achieve all life goals **without needing men**.

Women achieve all four life goals (righteousness, prosperity, pleasure, liberation) without being male, demonstrating that gender irrelevant to human fulfillment. Capability, not anatomy, determines achievement.

This statement asserts women's complete independence in pursuing all aspects of human fulfillment. It references the four traditional life goals—righteousness, prosperity, pleasure, and spiritual liberation—and states that women can achieve all of them without needing men. The principle is clear: consciousness has full capacity regardless of gender. Women don't need male guidance, protection, or partnership to reach any life goal. Their ability to succeed independently in every area demonstrates that achievement depends on capability, not gender.

History offers countless examples of women achieving complete success independently. Queen Hatshepsut ruled Egypt successfully for over 20 years.[1] Marie Curie made groundbreaking scientific discoveries. [2] Mother Teresa achieved spiritual realization.[3] Countless businesswomen have built economic empires. Each shows that women can excel in every area of human achievement without depending on or needing guidance from men.

Modern research confirms this across all life domains. In education, women often outperform men academically. Women-led businesses frequently show better financial performance than male-led ones. Single women increasingly achieve economic independence and career success. Female spiritual teachers and philosophers make major contributions to wisdom traditions worldwide.

Philosophically, consciousness contains complete potential for all achievements. When society claims women need male partnership or guidance to be complete, it contradicts the self-sufficient nature of human consciousness. This creates artificial dependency that actually diminishes rather than enhances human capacity.

In practice, this means recognizing women's complete capability in business leadership, spiritual development, intellectual achievement, and personal fulfillment—all without requiring male partnership or approval. Organizations that truly acknowledge women's independent capacity typically see better innovation and decision-making. Some might point to traditional partnership models as ideal. But we must distinguish between voluntary cooperation (which can benefit anyone) and enforced dependency. While partnerships can enhance life for all people, claiming that women inherently need men to be complete violates their fundamental autonomy and capability. This connects to principles like "self-determination is a universal human right" and "true freedom means choosing one's own path." Together, they establish women's complete autonomy in all aspects of life.

This means seeing women as fully capable individuals, not incomplete beings needing male completion. Authentic human development transcends gender dependencies. Women's independent achievements across all life goals prove that fulfillment comes from within, not from any external completion by another gender.

FOR FURTHER READING

Queen Hatshepsut ruling Egypt successfully for decades

Tyldesley, Joyce (1996). Hatchepsut: The Female Pharaoh. London: Viking.

Marie Curie achieving scientific breakthroughs

Curie, Eve (1937). Madame Curie: A Biography. Garden City, NY: Doubleday.

Mother Teresa embodying spiritual realization

Spink, Kathryn (1997). Mother Teresa: A Complete Authorized Biography. San Francisco: HarperSanFrancisco.

Intelligence, not gender, determines educational access.

When intelligence is the criterion for learning, gender-based restrictions in any field - religious or secular - become questionable. Intelligence knows no gender.

|| ॐ ||

This statement uses sacred learning in some religious traditions as the ultimate example: if even the most holy studies require only intelligence—not a specific gender—then certainly regular education can't exclude based on gender. The principle is straightforward: intellectual capacity has nothing to do with being male or female. If gender doesn't matter for the highest forms of learning, it definitely can't matter for secular education or job training. Intelligence crosses all gender boundaries.

In all cultures, excluding women from education reflected prejudice, not reality. When barriers fell, the truth emerged. Medieval abbesses like Hildegard of Bingen produced brilliant theological and scientific works despite limited access.[1] The few women who got into universities consistently excelled. Once modern education opened to women, they showed equal or better academic performance across all subjects—proving that previous exclusions wasted human potential rather than protecting anything.

Today's educational data confirms intellectual equality. Girls outperform boys in reading and writing worldwide. In math and science, they achieve equally when cultural biases are removed. Women now make up the majority of university graduates in many countries, with higher completion rates and grades than men.

The philosophy here is that qualification for learning depends on your mind's capacity, not your body's characteristics. When schools impose gender restrictions, they violate the basic relationship between mind and learning that makes education what it is.

Practically, this means ensuring equal access from preschool through professional training. It means eliminating gender-biased teaching methods and curricula. It means creating learning environments where all students can develop intellectually, regardless of gender. Some might defend historically gender-segregated education. But we must distinguish between segregation that preserved male privilege and arrangements that truly served educational needs. Real educational grouping would focus on learning styles, not gender categories. This connects to principles like "physical differences don't extend to consciousness" and "gender cannot restrict eligibility." Together, they establish intelligence as beyond gender.

For today's leaders, this demands educational policies based on intellectual capacity, not demographics. Authentic learning serves human development, not gender conformity. When we limit education by gender, we rob society of half its intellectual potential.

FOR FURTHER READING

Hildegard of Bingen producing sophisticated theological and scientific works

Newman, Barbara (1987). Sister of Wisdom: St. Hildegard's Theology of the Feminine. Berkeley: University of California Press.

Self-determination is a universal human right.*

Autonomy is a universal human virtue, not a male privilege. Women's dependence on male relatives violates this fundamental principle of human dignity and self-determination.

This statement declares that self-determination—the right to make your own choices—belongs to all humans, not just men. It says autonomy is a fundamental human virtue that can't be restricted by gender. Systems that make women depend on male relatives for permission violate natural order, not preserve it. They deny basic human dignity. True virtue requires individual autonomy for everyone, regardless of gender.

* *Timeless Principle: Self-determination is intrinsic to human nature—a truth that transcends cultural variations in gender roles.*

Philosophical traditions recognize that legal systems that required male guardianship for women violated this principle. From ancient Roman patria potestas to modern guardianship laws, these systems treated adult women like permanent children who couldn't govern themselves. But when these laws were eliminated—when coverture laws ended, when property restrictions fell, when financial dependencies were removed—women immediately showed they could make competent decisions. The barriers were artificial all along.

Today, we still see violations of women's self-determination. Some countries require male guardian permission for women to travel, work, or get medical care. More subtle forms exist too: workplace cultures that funnel women's decisions through male colleagues, or families that expect women to sacrifice personal goals for male relatives' preferences.

Philosophically, consciousness has inherent capacity for moral decision-making. When outside authorities override individual judgment based on gender, they violate the essential connection between consciousness and ethical action that makes us human. It's like saying someone has a mind but can't use it—a fundamental contradiction.

In practice, this means legal systems must recognize women's independent standing. Economic policies must ensure women's financial autonomy. Healthcare systems must respect women's medical decisions. Social norms must support women's life choices without requiring male approval. Some might defend traditional family structures where men make decisions. But we must distinguish between voluntary cooperation and forced dependency. Healthy relationships involve mutual consultation and support—that's completely different from systems that deny women legal or practical autonomy. This connects to principles like "women achieve all life goals without needing men" and "control over one's body is the foundation of autonomy." Together, they establish complete self-determination as a human right.

This means recognizing women's complete autonomy in personal, professional, and civic decisions. Authentic human dignity requires individual self-determination—it doesn't threaten it. When we deny anyone's right to make their own choices, we deny their humanity.

FOR FURTHER READING

Kantian philosophy on autonomy as fundamental to human dignity

Kant, Immanuel (1785). Groundwork of the Metaphysics of Morals. Translated by Mary Gregor. Cambridge: Cambridge University Press, 1998.

Work results demonstrate **gender is irrelevant** to achievement.

The gender of the agent has no bearing on the accomplishment of any task. Results depend on skill and effort, making gender restrictions pragmatically absurd as well as ethically wrong.

This statement makes a practical argument: when you judge by results, gender doesn't matter. Work outcomes depend on competence, not whether the worker is male or female. This makes gender-based restrictions both morally wrong and practically stupid. When success is measured by achievement quality, the achiever's gender becomes irrelevant. Gender discrimination thus fails both ethically and in terms of efficiency—it's bad for business and bad for society.

History demonstrates this repeatedly. When gender barriers fell, work quality stayed the same or improved. Katherine Johnson's calculations sent astronauts to the moon.[1] Female CEOs often deliver better stock performance than male ones. In every case, removing gender restrictions improved results—proving those restrictions protected privilege, not quality.

Modern research confirms this across industries. Companies with women in leadership show higher profits, better risk management, and more innovation. These outcomes prove that including women helps rather than hurts organizational excellence.

The philosophy focuses on results as the ultimate test of action. When gender restrictions fail to improve outcomes—and often make them worse—this shows that the restrictions are invalid, no matter what traditional excuses people give. Real merit focuses on achievement, not demographics.

Practically, this means evaluation systems should focus only on results and competencies. Recruitment should emphasize proven capability, not assumptions about "cultural fit." Advancement should reward achievement regardless of the achiever's gender. Some might worry about team chemistry or workplace culture. But they need to show how these actually relate to performance, not just comfort with familiar demographics. Real teamwork gets better with diversity, not worse.

This connects to principles like "equal capabilities demand equal opportunities" and "judge individuals by their actions, not their group." Together, they establish evaluation based on results. It means focusing on work quality, not worker demographics. Excellence comes from recognizing merit, not from demographic preferences. When we judge by results, gender becomes irrelevant—and organizations that understand this outperform those that don't.

FOR FURTHER READING

Katherine Johnson's NASA calculations

Shetterly, Margot Lee (2016). Hidden Figures: The American Dream and the Untold Story of the Black Women Mathematicians Who Helped Win the Space Race. New York: William Morrow.

Those who create life possess **fundamental agency**.

Women's creative power in birth establishes their fundamental agency. Those who create life cannot be denied agency in other spheres. This greater power cannot be trumped by the exercise of lesser powers.

This statement uses powerful logic: if women can create life itself—the ultimate creative act—they obviously possess agency for everything else. The principle says that beings capable of creating and nurturing human life have inherent power that can't be denied in other areas. It's like saying someone who can build a skyscraper surely can build a house. If women can create conscious beings, they can certainly create businesses, policies, art, or anything else humans achieve.

Throughout history, societies showed a strange contradiction: they honored women's power to give birth while denying their power to lead, think, or create in other ways. But this revealed how illogical gender restrictions are. How could beings powerful enough to create life be too weak for leadership or intellectual work? The reverence for motherhood actually proves, rather than disproves, women's fundamental creative power.

Today, this principle challenges attempts to reduce women to just reproductive roles while denying their broader abilities. Women who excel as both mothers and professionals show that reproductive capacity enhances rather than limits other forms of creativity and achievement.

Philosophically, this works through the principle that greater powers include lesser ones. Creating conscious life is the ultimate creative act—it requires intelligence, patience, sacrifice, and transformative power beyond any other human activity. No business deal, scientific discovery, or artistic creation demands comparable creative capacity. So it's illogical to deny women agency in areas that require less creative ability than what they already demonstrate.

Practically, this means recognizing that parenting experience provides leadership skills, not detracts from them. Women's life-creation capacity demonstrates their potential for all creative achievements. We need systems that support rather than force choices between motherhood and professional fulfillment. Some might argue that biological reproduction differs from other creative activities. But this misses the point—consciousness capable of nurturing human development has all the qualities needed for any creative achievement, from art to technology.

This connects to principles like "women's virtue encompasses all spheres" and "women achieve all life goals without needing men." Together, they establish comprehensive creative agency. This means seeing women's creative power as evidence of universal capability, not limited function. Life-creation capacity demonstrates fitness for all forms of human achievement. When we deny this, we deny basic logic along with basic justice.

Equal work demands equal pay, regardless of gender.

Pay discrimination violates basic economic principles recognized even in ancient economics—equal work merits equal compensation. Gender-based pay gaps contradict both virtue and practical economics.

This statement states a simple economic truth: if two people do the same work equally well, they should get the same pay. Gender-based pay gaps violate both moral fairness and basic economics by paying people differently for irrelevant reasons. It's like charging different prices for identical products based on who's buying—it makes no economic sense. True economic virtue means rewarding what people contribute, not their demographic characteristics.

Historically, paying women less reflected systematic undervaluing of their work, not actual quality differences. When equal pay laws were implemented, employers discovered that women often delivered better value for the money. Modern examples like Iceland's strict pay equity laws show that equal pay actually improves economic efficiency rather than harming it.[1]

Current research shows that organizations with pay equity perform better. Companies with transparent, merit-based pay systems have happier employees, less turnover, and higher productivity. These patterns show that equal pay helps rather than hurts organizations by keeping and motivating the best talent.

The philosophy is straightforward: effects should match causes. If two people contribute equally, they should be rewarded equally. When gender affects pay despite equal performance, it breaks the logical connection between effort and reward that makes fair exchange possible.

In practice, this means creating transparent salary structures based on job requirements and performance. It means regular pay audits to find and fix disparities. It means compensation systems that focus on contribution value, not negotiation tactics or demographic assumptions. Some might argue that "market rates" or negotiation explain pay gaps. But these factors often reflect systemic bias, not merit. Real market efficiency requires eliminating discriminatory distortions, not perpetuating them.

This connects to principles like "work results prove gender is irrelevant" and "equal or comparable achievement demonstrates equal rights." Together, they establish fair compensation as both moral and practical necessity.

For today's leaders, this demands pay systems that reward performance, not demographics. Equal work deserves equal pay regardless of who does it. This isn't just about fairness—it's about running efficient organizations that reward real value.

FOR FURTHER READING

Iceland's pay equity requirements demonstrating improved economic efficiency

Act on Equal Status and Equal Rights of Women and Men No. 10/2008, as amended by Act No. 56/2017 (Iceland).

Physical strength differences **don't determine human worth**.

Physical strength differences are bodily, not essential. The self that performs all significant human actions transcends physical limitations, making strength-based arguments for inequality invalid.

This statement declares that human worth has nothing to do with physical strength. It distinguishes between our true self—our consciousness—and our physical body. Since all important human actions (thinking, deciding, creating, loving) come from consciousness rather than muscles, using physical strength to justify gender inequality is philosophically wrong. Human value comes from moral and intellectual capacity, not how much weight someone can lift.

Experience shows that arguments about male physical strength became less relevant as societies evolved. The industrial revolution showed how technology could amplify anyone's capability regardless of individual strength. The information age proved that intellectual capacity, not physical power, determines most achievements. Each technological advance further separated human worth from physical attributes.

Today, strength-based arguments ignore reality. Most jobs require mental rather than physical ability. Even physically demanding roles increasingly rely on training, technique, and equipment rather than raw strength. Emergency responders, military personnel, and manual laborers succeed through skill and tools, not just muscle power.

Philosophically, this involves distinguishing between the essential self (consciousness) and the physical body. Since consciousness performs all significant human actions while the body just provides support, creating hierarchies based on physical differences violates the basic nature of human identity.

Practically, this means workplace policies should focus on job-relevant abilities, not physical assumptions. Social norms should value intellectual and moral achievement over physical prowess. Cultural stories should celebrate diverse forms of excellence rather than just physical strength. Some might point to evolution or history to defend strength-based hierarchies. But modern human flourishing depends on capabilities that go beyond physical strength. Cooperation, innovation, and cultural development require qualities that have nothing to do with muscle power.

This connects to principles like "physical differences don't extend to consciousness" and "human worth cannot be ranked." Together, they establish worth as consciousness-based, not body-based. This means evaluating people based on relevant capabilities, not physical traits. Human value transcends bodily attributes. In a world of technology and ideas, physical strength matters less than ever—making strength-based discrimination not just wrong but obsolete.

Restrictive gender roles **obstruct self-realization**.

Imagining a separate, restricted "women's virtue" obstructs women's pursuit of all four life goals. This conceptual error harms both individual women and society by limiting human potential.

|| ॐ ||

This statement shows that restrictive gender roles block rather than help human flourishing. When society creates narrow categories of "proper" behavior for women, it prevents them from reaching their full potential in all areas of life. The principle says that limiting women to restricted virtues violates natural order instead of preserving it. True self-realization means going beyond, not conforming to, limiting gender expectations.

Since ancient times, women who achieved remarkable things consistently broke rather than followed restrictive gender roles. Joan of Arc led armies when women weren't supposed to fight.[1] Elizabeth I ruled England powerfully when women were told they couldn't lead.[2] George Sand became a celebrated writer by adopting male dress and a male name to escape gender restrictions.[3] Their successes showed that restrictive roles block rather than help authentic human expression.

Modern research shows how gender restrictions hurt both individuals and society. Countries with more equal gender norms have happier citizens, stronger economies, and more stable societies. Women in societies with flexible gender roles report greater life satisfaction and achieve better outcomes in all areas of life.

Philosophically, self-realization requires developing all human capacities, not artificially limiting them. When society forces people into partial roles based on gender, it violates the comprehensive nature of human flourishing. This prevents both individual and collective development from reaching full potential.

In practice, this means schools should encourage all students to develop their full range of abilities. Workplaces should support diverse career paths regardless of gender. Social institutions should celebrate rather than constrain individual potential and achievement. Some argue that traditional roles provide structure and meaning. But we must distinguish between freely chosen paths and forced limitations. Real structure enhances human potential rather than restricting it. Meaningful roles come from authentic self-expression, not external rules imposed on us.

This connects to principles like "gender roles are social constructions" and "true freedom means choosing one's own path." Together, they show that self-realization transcends gender. This means creating environments that support rather than limit individual development. Human flourishing requires freedom from restrictive gender expectations, not conformity to them. When we box people into narrow roles, we rob them—and society—of their full potential.

FOR FURTHER READING

Joan of Arc transcending gender roles through military leadership

DeVries, Kelly (1999). Joan of Arc: A Military Leader. Stroud: Sutton Publishing.

Elizabeth I succeeding by rejecting gender limitations

Somerset, Anne (1991). Elizabeth I. London: Weidenfeld & Nicolson.

George Sand achieving literary success by transcending gender restrictions

Harlan, Elizabeth (2004). George Sand. New Haven: Yale University Press.

Universal duties override gender-based prohibitions.

Prohibitions on women's participation lack logical foundation, while positive injunctions for righteous action apply universally. Invalid prohibitions cannot override valid universal duties.

This statement establishes a clear hierarchy: universal moral duties always outrank gender-based restrictions. When positive obligations to do what's right conflict with negative rules saying "women can't do that," the moral obligations win. The principle shows that universal calls to pursue righteousness apply to everyone and override particular rules that exclude based on gender. True virtue means participating in righteous action, not avoiding it because of your gender.

Thinkers across traditions have recognized that women have followed this principle by choosing moral duty over gender restrictions. Florence Nightingale broke Victorian rules about proper ladies to care for wounded soldiers.[1] Rosa Parks defied expectations about how Black women should behave to advance civil rights.[2] Each showed that universal moral obligations beat social restrictions when they conflict with doing what's right.

Today, we see this conflict continue. Women challenging workplace discrimination, fighting for social justice, or pursuing public service careers often face pressure to prioritize traditional gender roles over moral duties. This principle says that universal obligations to pursue justice and serve humanity override expectations to conform to gender roles.

The philosophy distinguishes between positive commands ("do good") and negative prohibitions ("women can't do that"). When they conflict, positive duties to pursue righteousness carry more weight. Universal duties apply to all conscious beings, while gender restrictions are just particular limitations without strong philosophical foundation.

Practically, this means recognizing women's obligation to pursue justice even when it challenges traditional expectations. It means supporting women who prioritize moral duties over gender conformity. It means creating social structures that enable rather than block women's participation in righteous action. Some might claim that gender roles themselves are moral duties. But they'd need to show how these restrictions serve rather than violate universal principles of justice and human flourishing. Real moral duties enhance our capacity for righteousness—they don't diminish it.

This connects to principles like "universal ethics override discriminatory rules" and "gender cannot restrict eligibility for action." Together, they establish that universal duties come first. This means recognizing that moral obligations transcend gender expectations. Authentic virtue requires participation in righteous action regardless of demographic characteristics. When gender rules conflict with moral duty, duty wins.

FOR FURTHER READING

Florence Nightingale violating Victorian gender norms to serve wounded soldiers

Bostridge, Mark (2008). Florence Nightingale: The Making of an Icon. London: Viking.

Rosa Parks defying social expectations to advance civil rights

Parks, Rosa with Jim Haskins (1992). Rosa Parks: My Story. New York: Dial Books.

In highest consciousness, **gender becomes irrelevant.***

At the most consequential levels of human endeavor, gender becomes irrelevant. Since the highest human capacity transcends gender, lower activities cannot validly impose gender restrictions.

This statement uses the highest form of human experience to prove a point about all experience. It says that in moments of deepest understanding or spiritual realization, gender simply doesn't matter—consciousness at its peak transcends male/female categories. The logic is powerful: if gender becomes irrelevant at humanity's highest achievement, it can't be essential for lesser activities. When the greatest mystics and thinkers reach ultimate realization, they operate beyond gender identity.

* *Timeless Principle: Ultimate truth transcends gender—therefore gender cannot be the ultimate determinant in any sphere.*

Throughout history, spiritual and intellectual traditions have recognized that consciousness transcends gender. Great mystics, philosophers, and sages gained recognition for their transformative insights regardless of gender. Hildegard of Bingen's mystical visions,[1] Rumi's spiritual poetry,[2] and contemporary spiritual teachers all show how ultimate realization works independently of whether someone is male or female.

Today, we see this in peak performance across all fields. Scientific breakthroughs, artistic masterpieces, humanitarian achievements, and leadership excellence come from consciousness, not demographics. The most profound human contributions go beyond gender categories rather than reflecting them.

The philosophy works through hierarchical logic. Direct knowledge or enlightenment represents humanity's highest capacity, and it operates beyond gender. Therefore, all lower forms of knowledge and activity can't legitimately impose gender restrictions. What transcends at the top can't be essential at the bottom. It's like saying if the summit of a mountain is above the clouds, you can't claim clouds are essential to the mountain.

Practically, this means recognizing that peak achievement in any field goes beyond gender considerations. We should evaluate contributions based on their value, not the contributor's gender. We need pathways for everyone to pursue their highest realization regardless of gender identity. Some might claim biological differences affect consciousness. But the most sophisticated human achievements consistently transcend rather than reflect gender patterns. At its highest expression, consciousness shows universal rather than gendered characteristics.

This connects to principles like "physical differences don't extend to consciousness" and "you alone know your own identity." Together, they establish consciousness as beyond gender. This means recognizing that real excellence operates beyond gender categories. If consciousness transcends gender at its highest point, then gender restrictions violate human potential at all levels. The deepest truth about humans isn't male or female—it's consciousness itself.

FOR FURTHER READING

Hildegard of Bingen achieving recognition through mystical insights

Newman, Barbara (1987). Sister of Wisdom: St. Hildegard's Theology of the Feminine. Berkeley: University of California Press.

Rumi's spiritual poetry transcending gender categories

Barks, Coleman (1995). The Essential Rumi. San Francisco: HarperSanFrancisco.

Equal or comparable results establish equal rights to participation.

When women achieve equal or comparable results in any field, this definitively establishes their equal rights to participation. Observable outcomes override theoretical prejudices about capacity.

This statement uses simple logic based on evidence: when women achieve equal results in any field, they've proven their equal right to participate. It creates an undeniable chain of reasoning—if results are the same or comparable, capacity must be the same, and if capacity is the same, participation rights must be equal. Observable achievement beats theoretical speculation about gender limitations every time. You can't argue with results.

History shows this pattern repeatedly. When women entered medicine, law, business, and academic research, they consistently performed as well as or better than men. This demonstrated clearly that gender restrictions arose from prejudice, not real capacity differences. Each breakthrough created precedent for more opportunities.

Today's data confirms this across all fields. Female students have higher graduation rates and grades in higher education. Women-led companies often outperform male-led ones financially. Female leaders show superior performance in many management metrics. These outcomes don't just suggest equal rights—they establish them.

The philosophy uses inference from effects to causes. When equal results show up consistently across different contexts, logic demands we recognize equal underlying capacity. Denying equal participation rights after seeing equal outcomes violates both logic and evidence. It's like seeing two runners finish a race at the same time but claiming one is slower.

Practically, this means using performance data rather than assumptions in promotions. It means expanding opportunities where women show excellence. It means removing barriers that prevent the best talent from being used, regardless of gender mix. Some might point to isolated examples of different performance. But they must explain the overwhelming pattern of equal or better outcomes when barriers fall. Statistical outliers can't override systematic evidence of equal capacity and achievement. This connects to principles like "equal capabilities demand equal opportunities" and "excellence from any group disproves natural inferiority." Together, they establish equality based on evidence.

This means letting demonstrated performance, not demographics, determine participation rights. Equal results establish equal capacity and thus equal entitlement to opportunity. When the scoreboard shows a tie, you can't claim one team is inferior.

True freedom means **choosing one's own path**.

True freedom includes choosing traditional or non-traditional paths. Forcing either domesticity or career on women violates the principle of autonomous choice essential to virtue.

This statement defines real freedom as having genuine choice about your life path. Forcing either domesticity or career on women violates the principle of autonomous choice, which is essential to virtue. The principle goes beyond simply opposing tradition; it says true liberation includes the right to choose traditional options if that's what you really want. Freedom means more choices, not different requirements. Whether someone chooses full-time parenting or a high-powered career, what matters is that they chose it themselves.

Historically, the key to fulfillment has been genuine choice rather than the choice itself. Women who truly chose domestic focus found happiness when it reflected their authentic preference, not social pressure. Women who chose non-traditional paths thrived when freed from expectations to conform. The difference wasn't what they chose but whether they really had a choice.

Today, this principle challenges extremes on both sides. Conservative movements that pressure women into domestic roles violate autonomy just as much as progressive movements that look down on domestic choices or pressure career focus. Real equality means creating conditions where all choices—from full-time parenting to CEO positions—reflect what individuals actually want, not what society expects.

Philosophically, virtue requires voluntary action, not coerced behavior. When society mandates particular life paths based on gender, it corrupts the voluntary nature that makes virtue and self-realization possible. It's like forcing someone to donate to charity—the coercion destroys the virtue of the act.

Practically, this means policies that support diverse life choices: flexible work arrangements, comprehensive childcare options, economic security for various family structures, and cultural narratives that celebrate rather than judge different paths to fulfillment. Some worry that unlimited choice creates social chaos. But authentic choice typically produces more social harmony, not less, by reducing conflict between what people want and what they're told to do. When people can follow their genuine preferences, society benefits from their authentic contributions. This connects to principles like "self-determination is a universal human right" and "restrictive gender roles obstruct self-realization." Together, they establish choice as fundamental to human dignity.

This means creating conditions for real choice rather than pushing particular outcomes. True gender equality comes through expanded options, not mandated paths. The goal isn't to make all women choose careers or all women choose family—it's to ensure whatever they choose is truly their choice.

Marriage means **partnership, not ownership**.

Marital unity implies cooperative partnership, not male ownership of women. This sacred union models equal partnership, not hierarchical possession.

This final teaching on gender equality defines marriage as a cooperative partnership between equals, not an ownership relationship. Using the example of joint ritual performance where both partners participate equally, it shows that true marital unity comes from collaboration, not control. The principle reveals that authentic harmony in marriage emerges through mutual respect and shared responsibility, not through dominance and submission. Real partnership means working together, not one person owning the other.

The historical record shows that the evolution of marriage laws shows society slowly recognizing this truth. Old legal systems that transferred women from father's ownership to husband's ownership violated the true nature of marriage bonds. Modern laws recognizing mutual rights and responsibilities better reflect what authentic partnership means. The most successful marriages throughout history have always involved mutual respect rather than dominance.

Current research demonstrates that egalitarian marriages work better across every measure—they last longer, partners are happier, children develop better, and families are more financially stable. Couples who share decision-making, housework, and career support achieve better results than those following traditional hierarchical patterns. These findings show that partnership models help rather than hurt marital success.

The philosophy draws from the concept of ritual cooperation, where joint performance requires equal participation, not subordination. When marriage partners approach their relationship as a collaborative enterprise rather than an ownership arrangement, they create conditions for real unity and mutual flourishing.

Practically, this means laws that recognize equal marital rights. It means cultural stories that celebrate partnership rather than dominance. It means financial arrangements ensuring mutual security and autonomy. It means solving conflicts through collaboration, not authority. Some might defend traditional family structures by citing leadership needs. But we must distinguish between real leadership and dominance. True leadership serves the relationship and all family members rather than privileging one partner. Genuine authority comes from competence and wisdom, not gender identity. This connects to principles like "self-determination is a universal human right" and "women achieve all life goals without needing men." Together, they establish marriage as voluntary partnership between complete individuals.

This means supporting relationship models based on mutual respect rather than gender hierarchy. Authentic marital unity comes through partnership, not ownership—through cooperation, not control. When two whole people choose to build a life together as equals, that's when marriage reaches its highest potential.

ON DIVERSITY, EQUITY & INCLUSION

Diversity is nature's **fundamental principle.***

Diversity constitutes the fundamental virtue of creation itself. Attempts to enforce uniformity violate natural law, which manifests through variety.

This foundational teaching says diversity isn't some modern social invention—it's the basic organizing principle of existence itself. It directly challenges those who call diversity initiatives "unnatural social engineering." The principle comes from both scientific observation and philosophical wisdom: nature always creates variety, not sameness. Think about it—genetic diversity keeps species alive, ecosystem complexity maintains environmental balance. Life's essential strategy is variation, not uniformity.

* *Timeless Principle: The cosmos manifests through infinite variety — uniformity contradicts the creative principle itself.*

Throughout history, philosophers have recognized this truth. The ancient Greek philosopher Heraclitus (who lived around 535-475 BCE) saw that reality works through the unity of opposites—he said "the path up and down are one and the same," meaning opposing forces create harmony[1]. Hindu cosmology describes creation as infinite variety emerging from original oneness. Charles Darwin's evolutionary theory in 1859 proved scientifically that diversity drives adaptation and survival[2]. Today's complexity science shows that varied systems are stronger than uniform ones.

Modern ecology illustrates this philosophical insight. Research shows that biodiverse ecosystems beat monocultures on every measure—health, productivity, sustainability. Think of farms: single-crop fields need constant artificial support and can fail catastrophically from one disease. But diverse farms growing a variety of crops and using crop-rotation methods show natural resilience. The same is true for organizations. Research consistently demonstrates that diverse teams solve complex problems better than uniform ones.

The philosophy goes deeper than just observing nature. If diversity is existence's fundamental principle, then forcing uniformity actually goes against natural order. This completely reframes diversity initiatives—they're not newfangled social experiments but restoration projects, returning our social systems to alignment with how the universe actually works.

Practically, this means seeing diversity as institutional necessity, not moral luxury. Organizations that embrace natural variety consistently perform better, adapt faster, and last longer. Resistance to diversity shows misunderstanding of natural principles, not legitimate concern for keeping institutions strong. Some worry about "too much" diversity creating chaos. But they miss that nature's variety works within coherent systems, not random disorder. A forest has tremendous diversity but still functions as a unified ecosystem. Diversity needs coordination and shared purpose, not abandonment of organizational goals.

This connects to principles like "society needs multiple voices as in music" and "excluding any group diminishes society's virtue." Together, they show diversity as essential to social order, not threatening to it.

This means embracing diversity rather than just managing it. Recognize variation as strength, not challenge. When we align with nature's fundamental principle of diversity, we tap into the same force that has made life resilient and creative for billions of years.

FOR FURTHER READING

Heraclitus's identification of unity of opposites as reality's fundamental structure

Heraclitus (535-475 BCE). Fragments. In Kirk, G.S., Raven, J.E., and Schofield, M. (1983). The Presocratic Philosophers. Cambridge: Cambridge University Press.

Charles Darwin's evolutionary theory demonstrating how diversity drives adaptation

Darwin, Charles (1859). On the Origin of Species by Means of Natural Selection. London: John Murray.

Population genetics showing genetic diversity essential for species survival

Frankham, Richard (2005). "Genetics and extinction." Biological Conservation 126(2): 131-140.

Ecosystem complexity and stability relationship

McCann, Kevin Shear (2000). "The diversity-stability debate." Nature 405(6783): 228-233.

Uniformity leads to **systemic collapse.***

Monocultures lead to collapse in nature and society. The principle of maintaining cosmic order requires preserving diversity for system resilience.

|| ॐ ||

This principle reveals that systems with too much uniformity become fragile and prone to collapse, just like a forest with only one tree species. For everyday people, it matters because it shows that diversity in our teams, communities, and ideas isn't just nice to have—it's essential for creating resilient organizations that can weather crises and adapt to change.

* *Timeless Principle: Direct, first-person knowledge of internal states supersedes external observation - a fundamental epistemological truth.*

Think of a forest where every tree is identical. If a disease strikes, the entire forest dies because there's no natural resistance. This same danger applies to organizations and societies: when everything becomes too similar, the whole system becomes brittle and vulnerable to collapse. The core idea here is that systems need different perspectives and approaches to handle unexpected challenges—what experts call 'requiring variety' to survive.

History shows us clear examples of this pattern. The Irish Potato Famine occurred because farmers relied solely on one potato variety that couldn't resist blight, leading to mass starvation[1]. Similarly, the 2008 financial crisis happened when banks all used the same risky lending practices, creating a domino effect that diverse approaches might have prevented[2].

Modern science confirms this principle through studies of complex systems. Research shows that diverse teams in companies make better decisions during crises, just as ecosystems with more biodiversity recover faster from disasters[3]. The biological concept of 'genetic bottlenecks'—where populations lose adaptability by becoming too similar—applies equally to organizations: without diverse 'idea genes,' institutions can't evolve when faced with new challenges.

Practically, this means valuing diversity is smart risk management, not just social responsibility. Organizations mixing different backgrounds and perspectives develop better solutions, like an orchestra blending instruments to create richer music than any single instrument could alone. When people worry diversity causes chaos, remember that shared goals combined with varied approaches create harmony and strength.

This connects directly to other principles like 'Diversity is nature's fundamental principle' (6.1) and 'Multicultural environments increase collective strength' (6.11). For today's leaders, embracing diversity acts as insurance against failure—uniform teams might look efficient initially, but they plant the seeds of their own collapse by being unable to adapt when the world changes around them.

FOR FURTHER READING

The Irish Potato Famine historical event

Irish Potato Famine. (1845-1852). [Historical Event]

The 2008 global financial crisis

Global Financial Crisis. (2008). [Economic Event]

Stuart Kauffman's research on complex systems

Kauffman, Stuart. (1993). The Origins of Order: Self-Organization and Selection in Evolution. Oxford University Press.

Ecological research on monoculture vulnerability

Tilman, David (1999). "The ecological consequences of changes in biodiversity: a search for general principles." Ecology 80(5): 1455-1474.

Present action must address **historical injustices**.

Addressing historical injustices through present action fulfills virtue. The principle that past actions require present remediation applies to systemic discrimination.

This principle shows that simply stopping discrimination today isn't enough—we must actively repair past wrongs because their effects still hold people back. For everyday people, it matters because it explains why efforts like affirmative action or community investment are necessary to create truly equal opportunities in our neighborhoods and workplaces.

Imagine your neighbor breaks your fence and says 'I'll stop breaking it' but doesn't fix the damage. The fence remains broken. Similarly, historical injustices like discrimination create lasting damage that requires active repair, not just an end to harmful practices. When systems have created disadvantages that accumulate over generations, true justice means restoring what was lost, not just promising equal treatment from now on.

History shows us how this repair work succeeds. After WWII, Germany paid reparations to Holocaust survivors and their families—not as punishment, but to acknowledge harm and help rebuild lives[1]. South Africa's Truth and Reconciliation Commission helped heal apartheid wounds by openly addressing past crimes[2]. The Marshall Plan saw America invest in rebuilding war-torn Europe, turning former enemies into allies through practical restoration[3].

Today, we see this in efforts like affirmative action. When past policies denied home loans to certain neighborhoods (redlining) or excluded groups from good jobs, simply ending discrimination now doesn't fix the wealth or education gaps created. Economists call this 'path dependence'—the past shapes present opportunities. For example, families denied homeownership couldn't build wealth to pass down, putting their children at a lasting disadvantage.

The philosophy here comes from Aristotle's idea of corrective justice: when harm occurs, we must restore balance[4]. Think of it like helping someone up after you knock them down—justice isn't just stopping yourself from pushing others, but making amends for the harm done. This differs from distributive justice (fair sharing going forward) because it specifically addresses lingering imbalances from the past. Practically, this means policies must look beyond current fairness. Equal school funding today can't undo decades of underfunding in some communities—we need extra resources to close gaps. In hiring, pure 'merit-based' systems ignore how historical exclusion left some groups with fewer networks or preparation opportunities. Some worry this creates 'reverse discrimination,' but that misunderstands the goal. This isn't about punishment—it's about repairing systems so everyone truly starts from equal footing. When we fix these gaps, we unlock talent and strengthen entire communities, benefiting society as a whole.

This connects to principles like 'Pure meritocracy ignores systemic advantages' (6.4) and 'Systemic racism exists even when not visible' (1.2). For today's leaders, it means designing policies that actively repair historical damage—recognizing that true equality requires more than just equal rules moving forward.

FOR FURTHER READING

Germany's reparations to Holocaust survivors

Reparations Agreement between Israel and West Germany. (1952). [Historical Agreement]

South Africa's Truth and Reconciliation Commission

Truth and Reconciliation Commission (South Africa). (1995-1998). [Commission Report]

The Marshall Plan for European recovery

European Recovery Program [Marshall Plan]. (1948-1951). [U.S. Legislation]

Aristotle's theory of corrective justice

Aristotle. (c. 350 BCE). Nicomachean Ethics. Book V.

Pure meritocracy **ignores systemic advantages.**

Believing hiring occurs purely on merit ignores systemic advantages and biases. True merit recognition requires acknowledging and correcting structural inequalities.

This statement exposes a major flaw in "colorblind" meritocracy: it shows how supposedly neutral evaluation systems actually keep inequalities in place rather than fixing them. The principle reveals that you can't judge merit in a vacuum—you have to consider the conditions that help people develop, show, and get rewarded for their abilities. When we ignore systematic advantages and disadvantages, we mistake privilege for talent while missing real capability in people who faced more barriers.

Evidence shows that we've seen this pattern in schools and workplaces that claim to be objective while actually reproducing existing hierarchies. Elite universities that gave preference to "legacy" applicants (children of alumni) from the 1930s through 1990s showed how talk of merit masked hereditary privilege. Similarly, companies that hired based on "cultural fit" and employee referrals created an appearance of meritocracy while systematically excluding qualified candidates who lacked the right social connections.

Modern research shows this happens. Studies show that identical résumés get different responses based on whether the applicant's name sounds white or Black. Marianne Bertrand and Sendhil Mullainathan's groundbreaking 2003 study found that "white-sounding" names got 50% more callbacks than "Black-sounding" names, even with identical qualifications[1]. Similar bias shows up in performance reviews, where the same work gets different ratings depending on the reviewer's perception of the worker's gender, race, and class background.

Philosophically, this works through what Pierre Bourdieu called "cultural capital"—the knowledge, skills, and tastes that schools and employers reward but that get distributed unequally based on your social background[2]. Standardized test scores correlate more with family income than natural ability. "Soft skills" often just mean knowing upper-class cultural codes, not having universal capabilities.

In practice, this means developing evaluation systems that account for different opportunities people have had. Medical schools that consider socioeconomic background along with test scores often discover exceptional talent from under-resourced communities. Tech companies using structured interviews and blind coding tests consistently find more diverse talent than traditional networking-based hiring. Some claim that accounting for background means "lowering standards." But this misses the point: current standards often measure privilege rather than potential. Real meritocracy requires equal opportunity to develop and show merit, not just equally applying biased criteria.

This connects to principles like "present action must address historical injustices" and "equal or comparable achievement demonstrates equal rights." Together, they show that recognizing true merit requires fixing systemic problems.

This means creating evaluation systems that measure real capacity rather than privilege. True meritocracy needs structural equity to work properly. When we only look at outcomes without considering starting points, we're not finding the best people—we're finding the most advantaged.

FOR FURTHER READING

Marianne Bertrand and Sendhil Mullainathan's study on racial bias in hiring

Bertrand, Marianne and Sendhil Mullainathan (2003). "Are Emily and Greg More Employable Than Lakisha and Jamal? A Field Experiment on Labor Market Discrimination." National Bureau of Economic Research Working Paper No. 9873.

Pierre Bourdieu's concept of 'cultural capital'

Bourdieu, Pierre (1986). "The Forms of Capital." In J. Richardson (Ed.), Handbook of Theory and Research for the Sociology of Education (pp. 241-258). New York: Greenwood.

Just institutions require **representative participation**.

Just institutions require representative participation. When decision-makers reflect affected populations, justice becomes possible.

This statement says that for institutions to be truly just, the people making decisions need to reflect the diversity of people affected by those decisions. It builds on democratic theory's core idea: legitimate governance requires consent of the governed, which means all affected groups need meaningful participation. Without diverse voices at the decision-making table, institutions develop blind spots that keep systemic inequalities going. It's like trying to design a building while only looking at it from one angle—you'll miss crucial problems.

History illustrates this principle through successful democratic movements worldwide. The U.S. Civil Rights Movement in the 1950s-60s demanded not just the right to vote but actual political representation that could advocate for Black community interests.[1] South Africa's transition from apartheid (1990-1994) needed more than just majority rule—it required institutional structures ensuring all groups had a voice, not just the majority.[2] Today's movements for indigenous sovereignty similarly demand decision-making power over policies affecting indigenous communities.

Modern research backs this up with hard data. Corporate boards with gender and racial diversity show better financial performance and risk management. Diverse judicial panels produce more thorough legal reasoning and get reversed less often. Medical research including diverse populations creates more effective treatments, while all-male or all-white research teams consistently miss crucial factors affecting other groups.

The philosophy works through what experts call "standpoint theory"—different social positions give you access to different knowledge. Groups experiencing discrimination have insights about systemic barriers that privileged groups literally can't see. It's like how only someone who uses a wheelchair really understands which buildings are inaccessible. Without representative participation, institutions lack information they need to make fair decisions.

Practically, this means requiring diversity in hiring and promotion for leadership roles. It means creating advisory councils that actually reflect community demographics. It means designing decision-making processes that amplify marginalized voices, not just include them. Tokenism fails because one person can't represent an entire group—you need critical mass for meaningful participation. Some argue we should focus on "merit over demographics." But this misses two points. First, demographic diversity often indicates merit because underrepresented groups had to overcome extra barriers to reach leadership positions. Second, this principle is about how institutions function, not individual qualifications. A brilliant all-male engineering team might still design products that don't work for women.

This connects to principles like "excluding any group diminishes society's virtue" and "multicultural environments increase collective strength." Together, they show representation as key to institutional effectiveness, not competing with it.

This means seeing diversity as necessary for good governance, not just a moral nice-to-have. Homogeneous leadership simply can't adequately serve diverse populations—it's a functional impossibility, not just an ethical problem.

FOR FURTHER READING

U.S. Civil Rights Movement demanding meaningful political representation

Branch, Taylor (1988-2006). America in the King Years (trilogy). New York: Simon & Schuster.

South Africa's transition from apartheid requiring inclusive representation

Sparks, Allister (1995). Tomorrow is Another Country: The Inside Story of South Africa's Road to Change. Chicago: University of Chicago Press.

Democratic theory on consent of the governed

Locke, John (1689). Two Treatises of Government. London: Awnsham Churchill.

Including everyone maintains **social harmony**.

Including all people in social institutions serves universal welfare and maintains social order. Exclusion creates instability; inclusion creates harmony.

This statement directly challenges the common fear that diversity threatens social cohesion. Instead, it shows that including everyone creates real harmony, while exclusion creates instability. The principle distinguishes between fake peace maintained by keeping people down and authentic harmony achieved through justice. It's like the difference between a quiet classroom because students are engaged versus one that's quiet because everyone's afraid. True social stability comes from addressing tensions, not ignoring them.

History shows that societies achieving lasting harmony embraced diversity rather than resisted it. The Roman Empire's greatest periods (27 BCE-180 CE) happened when they had inclusive policies granting citizenship and opportunities across ethnic lines.[1] The empire declined when it became more exclusive. Medieval Spain's Golden Age (711-1031 CE) flourished through convivencia—Christians, Muslims, and Jews living peacefully together.[2] When Spain later expelled Jews and Muslims, it triggered cultural and economic decline.

Modern research illustrates this principle. Studies show that diverse, inclusive societies have more political stability, economic prosperity, and social trust than uniform or exclusionary ones. The Social Cohesion Index consistently ranks diverse democracies like Canada, Australia, and New Zealand among the world's most harmonious societies. Meanwhile, ethnically uniform but exclusionary societies often face internal conflict and stagnation.

The philosophy works through what social psychologists call "contact theory"—when diverse groups interact meaningfully, prejudice decreases and mutual understanding grows. Exclusion prevents this contact, letting stereotypes and fears grow unchecked. Inclusive environments create chances for people to recognize shared humanity and appreciate each other's contributions.

Practically, this means designing institutions that bring diverse groups together for common purposes, not allowing separate segregated systems. Integrated schools, workplaces, and neighborhoods consistently create more harmonious communities than segregated ones. Diversity training and inclusion initiatives prevent conflict rather than create it. Some point to short-term tensions during integration as proof that diversity causes problems. But this confuses temporary adjustment challenges with long-term outcomes. Research consistently shows that initial integration difficulties turn into better harmony than exclusion ever provides. It's like exercise—it might be uncomfortable at first, but it makes you healthier.

This connects to principles like "society needs multiple voices as in music" and "equal treatment serves the common good." Together, they show inclusion as essential to social order, not threatening to it.

This means seeing diversity initiatives as community building, not social engineering. Exclusion creates the very instability that inclusion solves. Real harmony comes through justice, not through suppressing differences. When everyone has a seat at the table, the whole community becomes stronger and more peaceful.

FOR FURTHER READING

Roman Empire's inclusive policies during peak periods

Garnsey, Peter and Richard Saller (1987). The Roman Empire: Economy, Society and Culture. Berkeley: University of California Press.

Medieval Spain's convivencia period of peaceful coexistence

Menocal, María Rosa (2002). The Ornament of the World: How Muslims, Jews, and Christians Created a Culture of Tolerance in Medieval Spain. Boston: Little, Brown and Company.

Invisible barriers need visible remedies.

Systemic barriers often operate invisibly, requiring visible, intentional efforts to overcome them. Passive equality cannot address active inequality.

॥ ॐ ॥

This statement explains a crucial truth: discrimination often works invisibly, but fixing it requires visible, intentional action. You can't cure an invisible disease with invisible medicine. The principle recognizes that discriminatory systems hide inside seemingly neutral processes—like a computer virus that looks like a normal program. These hidden barriers are hard to spot but need active countermeasures to eliminate. Simply being "colorblind" or passive won't fix systems that actively create inequality.

In diverse societies, we've seen the gap between legal equality on paper and real equality in life. The Civil Rights Act of 1964 banned obvious discrimination, but it couldn't touch the subtler bias built into hiring networks, housing patterns, and school tracking systems.[1] These invisible barriers needed visible fixes like affirmative action, fair housing enforcement, and educational equity programs to actually achieve what the law intended.

Modern research shows how unconscious bias works below our awareness while creating real discriminatory results. Harvard's Project Implicit shows that most people have unconscious associations that contradict what they consciously believe.[2] Studies of hiring show how "culture fit" requirements systematically exclude qualified candidates from underrepresented groups—even when decision-makers don't consciously intend to discriminate.

The philosophy involves what sociologists call "institutional racism"—discrimination that happens through neutral-looking processes rather than individual prejudice. Think about seniority systems that lock in historical exclusions, standardized tests that really just measure family income, or networking-based hiring that keeps opportunities within existing circles. These create invisible barriers that passive equality policies can't fix.

Practically, this means using structured decision-making that interrupts unconscious bias. It means setting measurable diversity goals with real accountability. It means creating mentorship programs that give access to informal networks previously closed to underrepresented groups. "Colorblind" policies often preserve racial disparities rather than eliminate them. Some claim visible remedies are "reverse discrimination." But this misses the point: passive approaches preserve active discrimination. Without intentional intervention, discriminatory systems keep running on autopilot. They don't need ongoing prejudice to maintain themselves—just inertia.

This connects to principles like "systemic racism exists even when not visible" and "biased conditioning requires active correction." Together, they show that real equity needs intentional action, not passive neutrality.

For today's leaders, this demands proactive measurement and intervention, not just good intentions. Invisible barriers need visible solutions. You can't fix what you refuse to see or act on. When discrimination hides in the system, justice must be deliberate and visible.

FOR FURTHER READING

The Civil Rights Act of 1964 and its limitations in addressing subtle bias

Civil Rights Act of 1964, Pub. L. 88-352, 78 Stat. 241 (1964).

Harvard's Project Implicit demonstrating unconscious associations

Greenwald, Anthony G., Debbie E. McGhee, and Jordan L.K. Schwartz (1998). "Measuring Individual Differences in Implicit Cognition: The Implicit Association Test." Journal of Personality and Social Psychology 74(6): 1464-1480.

Biased conditioning requires active correction.

Biased conditioning requires active reconditioning. Just as ritual impurities need ritual remedies, social biases need social interventions.

|| ॐ ||

This statement says that unconscious bias is learned behavior that needs deliberate unlearning—you can't fix it by just being aware it exists. It's like having bad posture: knowing you slouch doesn't automatically make you stand straight. You need specific exercises and practice. The principle draws from psychology's understanding that biased mental patterns form through repetition and only change through intentional counter-training, like retraining muscle memory.

History shows that success in reducing prejudice always requires active work, not passive waiting. When the U.S. military integrated in the 1940s-50s, success came not just from policy changes but from deliberate contact programs, cultural training, and leadership development that actively countered existing biases.[1] South Africa's Truth and Reconciliation Commission (1995-1998) recognized that healing from apartheid needed active dialogue and education, not just time passing.[2]

Modern brain science demonstrates that this approach works. Patricia Devine's research shows that motivated people can learn to recognize and correct their automatic biases through practice.[3] It's like learning to catch yourself before you fall. Corporate diversity training that focuses on building skills rather than inducing guilt shows real improvements in inclusive behavior—when it's properly designed and implemented.

The psychology works through what experts call "counter-conditioning"—replacing unwanted automatic responses with better ones through systematic practice. Bias doesn't vanish through good intentions any more than bad habits disappear through wishing. You need deliberate skill development: recognizing triggers, interrupting automatic responses, and practicing new behaviors.

Practically, this means bias interruption training that teaches specific techniques for catching and correcting unconscious biases in hiring, evaluations, and daily interactions. Good programs focus on changing behavior, not just attitudes. They provide tools for inclusive decision-making, not just awareness that bias exists. Some worry this is "thought control." But there's a crucial difference between changing automatic responses and controlling conscious beliefs. This is skill development, not ideological indoctrination. It's like learning any professional skill—from public speaking to data analysis.

This connects to principles like "invisible barriers need visible remedies" and "racial prejudice stems from misperception becoming delusion." Together, they show that fixing bias requires systematic intervention.

This means treating cultural competency as a learnable skill, not innate talent. It requires investing in training and practice that develops inclusive leadership through deliberate effort. Good intentions aren't enough—you need good techniques and regular practice to overcome a lifetime of biased conditioning.

FOR FURTHER READING

U.S. military integration efforts including deliberate contact programs

MacGregor, Morris J. (1981). Integration of the Armed Forces, 1940-1965. Washington, D.C.: Center of Military History.

South Africa's Truth and Reconciliation Commission recognizing need for active dialogue

Truth and Reconciliation Commission of South Africa Report (1998). Cape Town: Truth and Reconciliation Commission.

Patricia Devine's work on bias interruption and prejudice reduction

Devine, Patricia G. (1989). "Stereotypes and Prejudice: Their Automatic and Controlled Components." Journal of Personality and Social Psychology 56(1): 5-18.

Psychology research on how biased patterns form through repetition

Greenwald, Anthony G. and Mahzarin R. Banaji (1995). "Implicit social cognition: Attitudes, self-esteem, and stereotypes." Psychological Review 102(1): 4-27.

Refusing to see race **prevents** addressing racism.

Claiming not to see race/color constitutes a perceptual defect that prevents addressing racial injustice. Accurate perception requires acknowledging differences and their social meanings.

This statement exposes how being "colorblind" can prevent addressing racism—when you refuse to see race, you can't identify or fix racial disparities. However, the colorblind approach often stems from genuine belief that treating everyone identically regardless of race promotes equality. Many parents teach colorblindness hoping to raise unprejudiced children. The challenge is that both race-conscious and colorblind approaches carry risks: one may perpetuate division while the other may ignore injustice.

Historically, colorblind rhetoric has had complex origins and effects. The Civil Rights Movement itself promoted judging people "not by the color of their skin but by the content of their character." Many interpreted this as calling for colorblindness. Since the 1980s, colorblind constitutionalism has indeed dismantled programs addressing racial inequalities.[1] Yet many supporters genuinely believe that any race-based distinctions, even remedial ones, perpetuate the racial thinking that created problems initially.

Parents teaching colorblindness often come from admirable motivations. They want children who don't prejudge based on race, who have diverse friendships, who see humanity before color. These parents often experienced or witnessed explicit racism and believe that not "seeing" race prevents racist thinking. Their lived experience tells them that emphasizing racial differences creates division. They point to their own diverse friendships as evidence that colorblindness works.

Modern research presents a nuanced picture. Studies show colorblind attitudes can correlate with missing racial discrimination and resisting equity efforts. Eduardo Bonilla-Silva's work[2] reveals how colorblind racism enables opposition to racial equity while maintaining non-racist self-image. However, other research suggests that emphasizing racial categories can increase essentialist thinking and intergroup anxiety, particularly among children. Some studies find that multicultural approaches that celebrate differences work better than either colorblindness or silence about race.

The lived experience includes people harmed by both approaches. Black professionals describe the exhaustion of colleagues who "don't see race" missing the daily microaggressions they face. Asian Americans report that colorblindness erases their experiences of both discrimination and cultural identity. Yet others describe feeling reduced to their race when well-meaning diversity initiatives constantly emphasize racial categories, making them representatives of their race rather than individuals.

Some communities report that constant racial focus increases tension and division. They experience diversity training that seems to create racial self-consciousness where little existed before. Parents in diverse schools worry when racial affinity groups separate children who previously played together. They fear that emphasizing differences undermines the common humanity that brings people together.

Practically, this suggests a both/and approach: teaching children to value diversity while emphasizing shared humanity; tracking disparities to identify problems while avoiding reducing individuals to statistics; addressing systemic racism while building cross-racial coalitions based on common interests; celebrating cultural differences without essentializing racial categories; and recognizing that different contexts may require different approaches.

The deeper challenge involves competing goods. Colorblindness aims to treat everyone with equal dignity but can ignore unequal realities. Race-consciousness aims to address inequality but can reinforce categorical thinking. Perhaps the path forward involves "race-cognizance"—seeing race as one important factor among many, neither ignoring it nor making it all-defining.

Some argue we must choose: either see race or don't. But lived experience suggests most people operate situationally—seeing race when it matters for understanding inequality, not seeing it when evaluating individual merit. The problem comes when either approach becomes absolute: never seeing race blinds us to injustice, always seeing race can reduce people to categories.

This connects to principles about systemic racism requiring visible remedies while also connecting to principles about judging individuals by their actions, not their group. The tension between these principles reflects genuine philosophical complexity.

For today's leaders, this demands sophisticated approaches that can identify and address racial disparities without reducing individuals to racial representatives. It means teaching children both to recognize inequality and to see common humanity. It means acknowledging that parents teaching colorblindness and parents teaching race-consciousness often share the same goal—raising children who treat others with dignity—even as they disagree on methods. Most importantly, it means recognizing that the choice between colorblindness and race-consciousness may be false: we need the ability to see race when it matters and to see past race when it doesn't.

FOR FURTHER READING

Justice Antonin Scalia's assertion about colorblind Constitution

Scalia, Antonin (1995). Adarand Constructors, Inc. v. Peña, 515 U.S. 200 (concurring opinion).

Eduardo Bonilla-Silva's work on colorblind racism

Bonilla-Silva, Eduardo (2003). Racism Without Racists: Color-Blind Racism and the Persistence of Racial Inequality in the United States. Lanham, MD: Rowman & Littlefield.

True equality means **equal opportunity**, not just outcomes.

True equality requires equal opportunity, though outcomes may vary. However, vastly unequal outcomes indicate unequal opportunities, demanding correction.

This statement navigates a complex truth: real equality means equal opportunity, not forcing identical outcomes. But here's the catch—when outcomes are vastly unequal, that's usually a sign that opportunities weren't really equal either. However, implementing this principle creates genuine conflicts between competing legitimate interests: families who see their high-achieving children denied opportunities, communities still facing systemic barriers, and the challenge of defining merit itself when different groups have faced different obstacles.

Classical philosophy reveals that this distinction has sparked major debates. The Great Society programs (1964-1968) tried to provide real equal opportunity through compensatory education, job training, and community development.[1] They recognized that just removing "Whites Only" signs doesn't fix generations of accumulated disadvantage. Yet decades later, the debate has evolved into something more complex than either side anticipated.

The lived experience of Asian American families illustrates the painful complexity. Many immigrant parents sacrificed everything for their children's education—working multiple jobs, living in cramped conditions, spending savings on tutoring. When their children with near-perfect grades and test scores are rejected from elite universities while seemingly less qualified students are admitted, they experience this as profound injustice. They came to America believing in meritocracy and feel betrayed when their children's achievements seem penalized. The accusation that they're "privileged" rings hollow when they remember arriving with nothing and building success through sacrifice.

Simultaneously, Black and Latino families face ongoing discrimination that standardized tests don't capture. Their children navigate under-resourced schools, stereotype threat, and systemic barriers that affect performance. When a Black student achieves a 1400 SAT score while attending an underfunded school, working part-time, and lacking test prep resources, this may represent greater achievement than a 1600 from a student with private tutors and every advantage. The "merit" comparison isn't straightforward.

The philosophy involves what economists call "equality of initial conditions."[2] But here's the problem: we can't actually equalize initial conditions without time travel. We're trying to run a fair race when some runners are starting miles behind, others are wearing ankle weights, and still others have been training with professional coaches since childhood. No adjustment can make this race perfectly "fair" to everyone.

Practically, different institutions have tried different approaches. Some use socioeconomic factors rather than race, helping first-generation college students regardless of ethnicity. Others maintain racial considerations arguing that race affects experience independent of class. Some have eliminated standardized tests entirely. Each approach helps some while potentially disadvantaging others.

The deeper tension involves competing values that can't be simultaneously maximized. Individual merit matters—students who work hard deserve recognition. Historical justice matters—communities subjected to centuries of discrimination deserve repair. Diversity matters—educational environments benefit from varied perspectives. Proportional representation matters—dramatic demographic disparities suggest systemic problems. These are all legitimate values that sometimes conflict.

Real families are caught in this conflict. The Asian American student who scored perfectly on every metric but was rejected from every Ivy League school—their pain is real. The Black student who got in with lower scores but overcame extraordinary obstacles—their achievement is real. The white student from Appalachia who had no advantages but doesn't fit diversity categories—their frustration is real. The Native American student whose entire community has been systematically excluded from higher education—their need is real.

Some argue for pure meritocracy based on test scores and grades. But this ignores how opportunities to develop those metrics are unequally distributed. Others argue for proportional representation by demographics. But this can feel like collective punishment to individuals who had no role in creating historical injustices. Still others propose class-based affirmative action, but this can miss how race affects experience independent of income.

The uncomfortable truth is that any system will feel unfair to someone because we're trying to solve centuries of injustice through individual college admissions or job applications. We're asking eighteen-year-olds to bear the weight of historical repair or exclusion. No perfect solution exists that doesn't involve someone paying a price for problems they didn't create.

This connects to principles about systemic advantages and historical justice while also connecting to principles about individual merit and achievement. The tension between these principles reflects genuine moral complexity, not simple right versus wrong.

For today's leaders, this demands honest acknowledgment that we're managing trade-offs, not implementing perfect solutions. It means transparency about what values are being prioritized and why. It means supporting those who lose out in any system—whether that's talented Asian Americans facing higher bars or underrepresented minorities still facing barriers. Most importantly, it means recognizing that behind every statistic is a family with legitimate hopes and real pain when those hopes are disappointed, regardless of which side of the debate they're on.

FOR FURTHER READING

The Great Society programs attempting to provide equal opportunity through compensatory measures

Johnson, Lyndon B. (1964). "The Great Society." Speech at University of Michigan, May 22, 1964. Presidential Archives.

Economic and philosophical discussion of equality of initial conditions

Roemer, John E. (1998). Equality of Opportunity. Cambridge, MA: Harvard University Press.

Multicultural environments increase **collective strength**.

Multicultural environments increase collective capacity. Diversity enhances rather than diminishes organizational and societal strength.

This statement establishes that diversity is a source of strength, not a problem to manage. It directly challenges those who claim multiculturalism weakens organizations or societies. Drawing from systems theory, it shows that diverse systems outperform uniform ones in adaptability, innovation, and resilience. It's like having a toolbox containing multiple and varied tools—the more such tools you have, the better equipped you are to address problems as they arise. Multicultural environments create what experts call "requisite variety"—the diversity needed to handle complex challenges.

History consistently illustrates this principle. The Islamic Golden Age[1] (8th-13th centuries) flourished because it brought together Arab, Persian, Greek, and Indian traditions. This cultural mixing produced breakthroughs in mathematics, medicine, and philosophy that wouldn't have happened in isolation. The Venetian Republic dominated trade for centuries (9th-18th centuries) partly because its multicultural approach incorporated diverse perspectives and skills from across the Mediterranean.

Modern research strongly validates this. Scott Page's work[2] shows that diverse groups consistently outperform uniform groups on complex problem-solving. McKinsey's research[3] found that companies with ethnic and cultural diversity are 35% more likely to beat industry averages. Countries with greater cultural diversity show higher rates of innovation and economic growth.

The science involves "cognitive diversity"—different cultural backgrounds give people different problem-solving approaches, knowledge bases, and creative insights. When teams include people from various cultures, they can use a much broader range of strategies than single-culture teams. It's like having multiple GPS systems that know different routes—you're less likely to get stuck.

Practically, this means actively seeking cultural diversity in hiring, team building, and decision-making. Organizations that leverage cultural differences rather than suppress them consistently show better innovation, market adaptation, and crisis response. Multicultural competency is a competitive advantage, not just a compliance checkbox. Some worry about coordination challenges. But there's a key difference between diversity and fragmentation. Effective multicultural environments keep shared purposes and values while embracing different approaches to reaching goals. Think of jazz bands—they create beautiful harmony through coordinated improvisation, not uniformity. This connects to principles like "diversity is nature's fundamental principle" and "excluding any group diminishes society's virtue." Together, they show multiculturalism as strength, not weakness.

This means seeing cultural diversity as an organizational asset, not a management headache. Multicultural environments enhance institutional effectiveness—they don't threaten it. When you bring together different cultural perspectives around common goals, you get innovation and resilience that uniform groups simply can't match.

FOR FURTHER READING

The Islamic Golden Age flourishing through cultural synthesis

Saliba, George (2007). Islamic Science and the Making of the European Renaissance. Cambridge, MA: MIT Press.

Scott Page's work on diverse groups outperforming homogeneous groups

Page, Scott E. (2007). The Difference: How the Power of Diversity Creates Better Groups, Firms, Schools, and Societies. Princeton: Princeton University Press.

McKinsey research on diversity and company performance

Hunt, Vivian, Dennis Layton, and Sara Prince (2015). "Why Diversity Matters." McKinsey & Company Report.

Systems theory concept of requisite variety

Ashby, W. Ross (1956). An Introduction to Cybernetics. London: Chapman & Hall.

Like music, society needs **multiple voices.***

Just as music requires multiple notes to create harmony, society requires multiple voices. Homogeneity impoverishes culture; diversity enriches it.

|| ॐ ||

This statement uses music as a perfect metaphor for why diversity creates social harmony rather than threatens it. Just as a symphony needs different instruments playing different parts to create beauty, society needs diverse voices contributing unique perspectives. The principle challenges those who think multiculturalism undermines unity. Real harmony comes from coordinated difference, not everyone singing the same note. A single note repeated endlessly isn't music—it's just noise.

* *Timeless Principle: Social harmony, like musical harmony, results from different voices and other components working together—not from monotone repetition.*

From East to West, societies reached their cultural peaks by embracing diversity, not suppressing it. The Harlem Renaissance[1] (1918-1940) showed how cultural mixing creates artistic breakthroughs. African American traditions blended with European forms to create jazz, blues, and modern literature that changed the world. China's Tang Dynasty[2] (618-907 CE) flowered culturally because it welcomed Persian, Indian, and Central Asian influences rather than shutting them out.

Modern research illustrates this principle. Cities with more cultural diversity consistently show higher rates of patents, artistic achievement, and economic energy. Richard Florida's research[3] reveals that creative professionals move to diverse environments, while uniform regions lose talent and stagnate culturally. It's like the difference between a vibrant music scene with many genres versus a town where everyone plays the same three songs.

The philosophy involves what experts call "aesthetic complexity"—beauty comes from unity within variety, not simple sameness. Complex harmonies create richer, more sustainable experiences than monotones. Diverse social environments provide deeper cultural and intellectual stimulation than uniform ones. Think about food—a meal with varied flavors and textures satisfies more than eating the same thing repeatedly.

Practically, this means designing institutions that encourage cultural expression rather than suppress it. Organizations that celebrate diverse holidays, languages, and traditions create more engaging environments that attract talent from all backgrounds. Schools that include multiple cultural perspectives produce graduates ready for our interconnected world. Some worry about creating "cacophony" or chaos. But there's a key difference between coordinated diversity and noise. Good multicultural environments need shared purposes and mutual respect, like orchestras achieving harmony through disciplined collaboration. Each musician plays their part while listening to others.

This connects to principles like "diversity is nature's fundamental principle" and "including everyone maintains social harmony." Together, they show how unity comes through diversity, not despite it.

This means seeing cultural differences as instruments in an orchestra, not disruptions to eliminate. Real social harmony needs multiple voices working together, not forced uniformity. When we let different cultural "instruments" play together with respect and coordination, we create social music far richer than any single voice could produce alone.

FOR FURTHER READING

The Harlem Renaissance exemplifying cultural cross-pollination

Lewis, David Levering (1981). When Harlem Was in Vogue. New York: Knopf.

Tang Dynasty's cultural flowering through cosmopolitan openness

Lewis, Mark Edward (2009). China's Cosmopolitan Empire: The Tang Dynasty. Cambridge, MA: Harvard University Press.

Richard Florida's work on creative professionals gravitating toward diverse environments

Florida, Richard (2002). The Rise of the Creative Class. New York: Basic Books.

Denying **qualified people** opportunities is unjust.

Denying qualified people opportunities based on identity constitutes unrighteousness. Merit blocked by prejudice violates cosmic order.

|| ॐ ||

This statement reframes diversity as protecting merit, not compromising it. It shows that discrimination prevents true meritocracy by denying opportunities to qualified people based on their identity rather than their abilities. When we exclude talented individuals because of race, gender, or other characteristics, we commit a fundamental injustice that hurts everyone. The principle is clear: blocking merit with prejudice violates the natural order where talent should be recognized regardless of who possesses it.

History repeatedly shows how excluding qualified people wastes talent and perpetuates injustice. When Jackie Robinson integrated baseball in 1947, it revealed how racial barriers had denied opportunities to countless skilled athletes for decades.[1] As women entered previously male-only fields, their success proved that gender exclusion had wasted enormous human potential. Each breakthrough exposed the injustice of judging people by identity rather than ability.

Current research shows that discrimination still blocks qualified people today. Studies prove that identical résumés get different responses based on the perceived race or gender of applicants. Performance evaluations often reflect reviewer bias rather than actual achievement. These patterns show that our systems often fail to recognize merit when it comes from underrepresented groups.

The philosophy involves what moral philosophers call "desert theory"—people deserve opportunities based on their qualifications and achievements, not their demographics. When qualified people face exclusion based on identity, it violates basic fairness principles that legitimate institutions depend on. It's like a race where some runners are disqualified for their shoe color, not their speed.

Practically, this means creating evaluation systems focused on actual capability rather than demographics or cultural signals. Organizations using structured assessments consistently find more diverse talent than those relying on "gut feelings" or personal networks. Diversity initiatives serve merit recognition, not merit compromise. Some claim diversity efforts deny opportunities to "more qualified" candidates. But this often rests on biased definitions of qualification that favor certain backgrounds while ignoring others. Real qualification assessment must account for different opportunities people had to develop credentials. A student who excels despite attending underfunded schools may show more merit than one with identical grades from elite institutions. This connects to principles like "pure meritocracy ignores systemic advantages" and "equal or comparable achievement demonstrates equal rights." Together, they show that protecting merit requires eliminating discrimination.

This means seeing inclusion efforts as talent identification, not social engineering. Discrimination prevents merit-based selection—it doesn't protect it. When we deny opportunities to qualified people based on identity, we don't just hurt them; we rob our organizations and society of their contributions.

FOR FURTHER READING

Jackie Robinson's baseball integration revealing previously excluded talent

Robinson, Jackie (1972). I Never Had It Made: An Autobiography. New York: G.P. Putnam's Sons.

Diversity **programs** often lack genuine commitment.

Programs lacking authentic dedication produce hollow results. Righteousness requires sincere intention behind institutional efforts.

This statement exposes a harsh truth: many diversity programs are just for show, lacking real commitment to change. It distinguishes between performative initiatives designed to look good and genuine efforts to achieve equity. However, even well-intentioned programs face complex challenges: organizational resistance, resource limitations, unintended consequences, and the difficulty of changing entrenched cultures. The line between insufficient commitment and genuine struggle with implementation isn't always clear.

History is full of diversity initiatives that failed for various reasons. After civil rights laws passed, many corporate diversity programs became compliance checkboxes. Yet the picture is more complex than simple insincerity. Organizations often face competing pressures: legal requirements, shareholder expectations, employee resistance, customer reactions, and genuine uncertainty about what works.[1] What looks like lack of commitment might sometimes be paralysis in the face of complexity.

The lived experience of diversity practitioners reveals profound challenges. Chief Diversity Officers often describe being hired with fanfare but given minimal budgets, no real authority, and impossible expectations.[3] They're asked to transform centuries-old cultures with PowerPoint presentations and lunch workshops. When programs fail, they become scapegoats. Many burn out, creating revolving doors that further undermine progress.

Meanwhile, employees experience diversity initiatives differently based on their position. Underrepresented minorities may see token efforts that don't address real barriers. White male employees may experience programs as accusatory or threatening, creating backlash.[6] Middle managers tasked with implementation often lack training and support.[4] Everyone ends up frustrated for different reasons.

Current research reveals gaps between stated goals and actual practice,[5] but also shows why. Studies find that even when leadership genuinely commits resources, middle management resistance can sabotage implementation. Cultural change takes years or decades, but leadership changes every few years, disrupting continuity. Metrics that would show real progress take time, while pressure for immediate results pushes toward visible but superficial changes.

Some programs create unintended consequences despite good intentions. Mandatory diversity training can increase bias by making people defensive.[2] Aggressive hiring targets can lead to tokenism that undermines the very people programs aim to help. Public diversity commitments can trigger backlash that makes workplace climates worse. Even successful programs in one context may fail when transplanted elsewhere.

The challenge of measurement adds complexity. What constitutes success? Demographic numbers? Climate surveys? Retention rates? Business outcomes? Different stakeholders prioritize different metrics. A program showing numerical diversity might hide toxic culture. One improving culture might not move numbers quickly. Organizations struggle to define success, let alone achieve it.

Philosophically, this involves distinguishing between moral sincerity and practical capability. Some organizations genuinely want change but lack knowledge, resources, or skills for implementation. Others have resources but face entrenched resistance. Still others make symbolic gestures knowing they're insufficient but believing something is better than nothing. Pure cynicism exists but may be less common than inadequate execution of genuine intentions.

You can identify genuine commitment through several factors, though none are definitive: sustained investment over leadership changes; willingness to acknowledge and learn from failures; transparent communication about challenges; integration of diversity goals into core business metrics; and patience with long-term culture change over quick fixes. But even these indicators can mislead—well-resourced programs can fail while scrappy efforts succeed.

Practically, this suggests approaching diversity efforts with both healthy skepticism and recognition of genuine challenges. It means distinguishing between organizations making excuses and those facing real obstacles. It means supporting practitioners trying to create change within resistant systems. It means recognizing that even imperfect efforts might represent genuine struggle rather than mere performance.

Some argue that intent doesn't matter—only results count. But this ignores how understanding why programs fail helps fix them. If we assume all failure stems from insincerity, we miss opportunities to address real implementation challenges. Conversely, accepting all excuses enables continued inaction. The balance is difficult.

This connects to principles about systemic change requiring sustained effort and the complexity of transforming entrenched cultures. Real change is harder than either critics or champions often acknowledge.

For today's leaders, this demands honest assessment of both commitment and capability. Are diversity initiatives failing because of lack of will or lack of way? Do you need more sincerity or more strategy? Are you prepared for the long, difficult work of cultural change, or are you hoping for quick wins? Most importantly, can you acknowledge both the reality that many programs are performative AND the reality that even genuine efforts face enormous challenges? True transformation requires not just deep commitment but also patience, resources, skill, and acceptance that progress will be imperfect and sometimes painful for everyone involved.

FOR FURTHER READING

Research on ineffective diversity training and potential backlash

Dobbin, Frank and Alexandra Kalev (2016). Why Diversity Programs Fail. Harvard Business Review, 94(7), 52-60.

Study on how mandatory diversity training can increase bias

Kalev, Alexandra, Frank Dobbin, and Erin Kelly (2006). Best Practices or Best Guesses? Assessing the Efficacy of Corporate Affirmative Action and Diversity Policies. American Sociological Review, 71(4), 589-617.

Research on Chief Diversity Officer challenges and turnover

Leon, Raul A. (2014). The Chief Diversity Officer: An Examination of CDO Models and Strategies. Journal of Diversity in Higher Education, 7(2), 77-91.

Analysis of middle management resistance to diversity initiatives

Thomas, Kecia M. and Victoria C. Plaut (2008). The Many Faces of Diversity Resistance in the Workplace. In K.M. Thomas (Ed.), Diversity Resistance in Organizations (pp. 1-22). New York: Lawrence Erlbaum.

Research on the gap between diversity rhetoric and practice

Ahmed, Sara (2012). On Being Included: Racism and Diversity in Institutional Life. Durham, NC: Duke University Press.

Study on unintended consequences of diversity initiatives

Dover, Tessa L., Brenda Major, and Cheryl R. Kaiser (2016). Members of High-Status Groups Are Threatened by Pro-Diversity Organizational Messages. Journal of Experimental Social Psychology, 62, 58-67.

Justice requires substantive, **not just formal**, equality.

True justice requires substantive equality, not formal equality that preserves actual inequality. Treating unequals equally perpetuates injustice.

This statement reveals why treating everyone exactly the same can actually maintain injustice. It distinguishes between formal equality (identical treatment) and substantive equality (fair outcomes). When we give identical treatment to people in very different situations, we often preserve inequality rather than fix it. It's like giving everyone the same size shoes—it seems fair but actually hurts those who need different sizes. Real justice requires recognizing and correcting for different starting points and ongoing barriers.

Throughout history, thinkers have recognized this distinction. Aristotle understood that treating unequals equally is itself a form of injustice.[1] The U.S. Supreme Court's journey from Plessy v. Ferguson (1896) declaring "separate but equal" to Brown v. Board (1954) rejecting it showed movement from formal to substantive equality.[2] After the Civil Rights era, we learned that colorblind policies often preserved racial disparities rather than eliminating them.

Today, we see how formal equality masks real inequality everywhere. Universities that ignore preparation gaps from unequal K-12 education perpetuate advantage, not create fairness. Workplaces with identical policies for everyone fail to accommodate different cultural communication styles or family responsibilities, maintaining bias rather than eliminating it. Same treatment often produces unequal outcomes.

The philosophy comes from what John Rawls called "fair equality of opportunity"—ensuring not just identical procedures but genuine access to advancement.[3] When systematic barriers create unequal starting positions, identical treatment preserves injustice. It's like a race where some start at the starting line while others begin miles back—same rules don't create a fair race.

In practice, this means affirmative action policies, targeted mentorship, flexible work arrangements accommodating diverse needs, and resource allocation addressing historical deficits. Organizations achieving real equality show improved outcomes over time, not just procedural compliance. Some claim different treatment violates equality. But they misunderstand justice as uniformity rather than fairness. True equality sometimes requires different treatment for equivalent outcomes, just as doctors give different treatments for different conditions while serving the same goal of health.

This connects to principles like "invisible barriers need visible remedies" and "equal treatment serves the common good." Together, they show that authentic equality serves genuine fairness.

This means examining whether policies produce fair outcomes, not just following identical procedures. Substantive justice may require different approaches to achieve truly equal opportunity. When we insist on identical treatment regardless of circumstances, we often perpetuate the very inequalities we claim to oppose.

FOR FURTHER READING

Aristotle's concept of distributive justice recognizing treating unequals equally as injustice

Aristotle (350 BCE). Nicomachean Ethics, Book V. Translated by Terence Irwin. Indianapolis: Hackett Publishing, 1999.

Supreme Court's evolution from Plessy v. Ferguson to Brown v. Board of Education

Plessy v. Ferguson, 163 U.S. 537 (1896) and Brown v. Board of Education, 347 U.S. 483 (1954).

John Rawls's concept of 'fair equality of opportunity'

Rawls, John (1971). A Theory of Justice. Cambridge, MA: Harvard University Press.

Discriminatory traditions must yield to justice.

When tradition embeds discrimination, new practices must replace old ones. Virtue evolves to meet justice; unjust traditions lack authority.

|| ॐ ||

This statement establishes a clear hierarchy: justice always outranks tradition when they conflict. It declares that discriminatory customs must give way to moral principles, no matter how old or deeply rooted they are. The key insight is that tradition gets its authority from being righteous, not from being ancient. When traditional practices violate justice, they lose all legitimate authority. True virtue means evolving beyond inherited patterns of discrimination.

History shows repeatedly how justice triumphs over discriminatory traditions. Abolishing slavery meant abandoning economic and social traditions centuries old. Women's suffrage required overturning political exclusions that many claimed were essential to social order. Racial integration challenged segregation practices that defenders said preserved important cultural traditions. Each transformation proved that justice ultimately beats traditional authority.

Today, we see this conflict playing out in many areas. Universities dropping legacy admissions that favor wealthy families show tradition yielding to merit-based fairness. Companies eliminating "old boys' networks" that excluded women and minorities demonstrate evolution toward inclusive excellence. Religious organizations ordaining women or welcoming LGBTQ+ members show tradition adapting to universal dignity principles.

The philosophy involves what's called "dharmic evolution"—the idea that righteous action adapts to serve eternal values rather than preserving temporary forms. When traditional practices violate universal justice, continuing them perpetuates harm rather than preserves virtue. Real tradition serves timeless values, not outdated customs that hurt people.

Practically, this means distinguishing between valuable cultural preservation and discriminatory practice. Successful organizations keep cultural elements that promote inclusion while eliminating exclusionary aspects. This preserves what's authentically valuable in tradition while advancing justice. Some claim that justice-oriented changes "destroy tradition." But they're confusing discriminatory practices with valuable cultural elements. Real cultural preservation means eliminating unjust aspects while strengthening inclusive values that represent tradition's true spirit. It's like renovating a historic building—you preserve the beautiful architecture while updating dangerous wiring.

This connects to principles like "discriminatory traditions have no moral authority" and "universal acceptance protects existence itself (see below)." Together, they show justice as tradition's proper goal.

This means evaluating whether traditional practices serve universal dignity or just preserve historical discrimination. Authentic tradition evolves to embody justice principles rather than violate them. When tradition conflicts with justice, tradition must change—not the other way around.

Universal acceptance protects existence itself.*

Universal acceptance and inclusion protect the cosmic order itself. Exclusion threatens not just individuals but the fabric of existence. Yet this principle requires wisdom to apply: accepting human dignity while maintaining boundaries against actions that would destroy acceptance itself.

This powerful teaching elevates inclusion from a nice social policy to a cosmic necessity. It says that universal acceptance preserves the fundamental order that keeps existence itself intact. When we exclude others, we don't just hurt individuals—we create disorder that threatens the whole fabric of reality. It's like removing threads from a tapestry; eventually the whole thing unravels. However, the principle distinguishes between accepting people's inherent dignity and enabling destructive ideologies. True universal acceptance paradoxically requires protecting inclusive systems from those who would destroy them.

* *Timeless Principle: The universe maintains itself through embracing all its parts—yet preservation of the whole sometimes requires boundaries against forces that would destroy its inclusive nature.*

Research confirms that major philosophical and spiritual traditions have recognized this truth. Buddhist concepts of dependent origination show how everything exists through mutual dependence—nothing stands alone. Indigenous wisdom traditions teach that excluding any part of creation disrupts the whole system. Even modern ecology shows this: when we lose biodiversity, entire ecosystems collapse. This shows that exclusion endangers survival itself.

Yet wisdom traditions also recognize a crucial paradox: unlimited tolerance can enable its own destruction. Karl Popper's 'paradox of tolerance' reveals that if we tolerate the intolerant without limit, tolerance itself disappears.[1] The Bhagavad Gita shows Krishna explaining to Arjuna that sometimes protecting dharma (righteous order) requires opposing those who would destroy it.[2] This isn't exclusion based on identity but rather boundary-setting against destructive actions.

Today, we see how exclusion creates cascading problems that threaten everyone. Social systems that exclude large populations become unstable and eventually collapse. Inclusive societies show greater resilience, innovation, and prosperity. Yet we also see how movements that exploit tolerance to spread intolerance can destroy inclusive systems from within. Climate change itself is a form of exclusion—treating the environment as separate from human systems rather than integral to them—and it threatens all life on Earth.

The philosophy involves what systems theorists call "emergent properties"—qualities that arise from diverse parts interacting, not from any single element. Think of water: hydrogen and oxygen separately can't quench thirst, but together they create something essential for life. When systems exclude essential diversity, they lose abilities needed for adaptation and survival. But systems also need immune responses—ways to identify and respond to elements that would destroy the system itself.

Practically, this creates challenging applications. Economic systems that exclude major populations become unstable and crash—yet they also need protection from exploitation and fraud. Schools that embrace diverse perspectives produce better thinkers—yet they must maintain boundaries against ideologies that deny others' humanity. Democracies including all voices prove more resilient—yet they must guard against anti-democratic movements that would use democratic means to end democracy.

The key distinction: We accept people's inherent human dignity while maintaining boundaries against ideologies and actions that threaten others' existence or dignity. A person who holds racist views still possesses human dignity deserving of basic respect, but their racist ideology itself deserves no acceptance, and their discriminatory actions require active opposition. Someone raised in a supremacist movement deserves compassion and opportunity for transformation, but the supremacist ideology itself must be excluded from acceptable discourse.

This connects to principles like "excluding any group diminishes society's virtue" and ideas about unity through diversity, while also connecting to principles about protecting the vulnerable and maintaining conditions for human flourishing. Together, they establish inclusion as essential to cosmic order—but inclusion with wisdom, not naivety.

This means seeing inclusion not as unlimited permissiveness but as existential necessity guided by protective wisdom. We need diverse participation to maintain the systemic health that all existence depends on, while also maintaining boundaries that protect this very diversity from those who would destroy it. When we exclude based on identity, we damage the interconnected web that sustains us all. When we exclude destructive ideologies and harmful actions, we protect that web. The wisdom lies in knowing the difference.

FOR FURTHER READING

Karl Popper's formulation of the paradox of tolerance

Popper, Karl. The Open Society and Its Enemies. Vol. 1. London: Routledge, 1945.

The Bhagavad Gita's discussion of protecting dharma through righteous action

The Bhagavad Gita. Translated by Eknath Easwaran. 2nd ed. Tomales, CA: Nilgiri Press, 2007. Chapter 2, verses 31-38.

True unity emerges through, not despite, diversity.*

True unity emerges through, not despite, diversity. The vision of cosmic harmony requires all voices, not enforced uniformity.

This final teaching reveals the ultimate truth: real unity comes from embracing diversity, not suppressing it. It exposes the fundamental error of thinking diversity divides us. Instead, it shows that genuine social cohesion requires integrating differences, not eliminating them. It's like a chorus—harmony comes from different voices singing together, not everyone singing the same note. Forced uniformity creates fake harmony; inclusive diversity creates real unity.

* *Timeless Principle: E pluribus unum—from many, one. Unity without diversity is uniformity; true unity celebrates difference.*

Across human societies, diverse societies achieved remarkable unity through inclusion, not exclusion. Ancient Athens reached its golden age by welcoming diverse populations and ideas. The Islamic Golden Age flourished by embracing scholars from multiple traditions. America's greatest periods of innovation and prosperity came with waves of diverse immigration. Each example shows how diversity generates national strength rather than threatening it.

Modern research consistently shows that diverse teams, organizations, and societies outperform uniform ones across every measure. Companies with diverse leadership show higher profits. Diverse schools produce better learning. Multicultural societies demonstrate more innovation and resilience. These patterns reveal how diversity creates abilities that uniformity simply can't achieve.

The philosophy involves what complexity theorists call "heterogeneity advantage"—diverse systems generate novel solutions and adaptations that uniform systems can't. Just as ecosystems need species diversity for stability, social systems need human diversity to function well. Unity through diversity produces strong harmony; unity through uniformity creates brittle conformity that breaks under pressure.

Practical examples are everywhere. Orchestras achieve musical unity through different instruments, not identical sounds. Democracies create governance through multiple competing voices, not single-party rule. Successful organizations build culture through shared values while celebrating individual differences. Each shows unity through diversity, not despite it. Some claim diversity necessarily creates conflict. But they ignore how skillful integration transforms difference into strength.

Conflict comes from exclusion and suppression, not from inclusion and celebration of diversity. Real unity requires learning to harmonize differences, not eliminate them. It's the difference between a garden with one type of plant versus a thriving ecosystem.

This connects to principles like "diversity is nature's fundamental principle" and "excluding any group diminishes society's virtue." Together, they establish diversity as essential to authentic unity.

For today's leaders, this final principle demands seeing diversity initiatives not as threats to cohesion but as pathways to genuine unity that goes beyond surface uniformity. Lasting harmony comes from celebrating, not suppressing, the magnificent diversity through which existence expresses itself. The ancient motto "E pluribus unum"—from many, one—captures this perfectly. Unity without diversity is just uniformity; true unity celebrates difference.

ON GUN CONTROL

Weapons should **protect, not enable violence.***

The legitimate purpose of weapons is protection, not enabling violence. When weapons primarily enable harm rather than defense, their proliferation violates virtue.

This foundational teaching establishes that weapons have a proper moral purpose: protection, not enabling violence. It says that tools carry moral weight based on their primary function—protective tools serve virtue while violence-enabling tools violate it. When weapons mainly facilitate aggression rather than defense, spreading them violates the natural order. The key is examining whether gun policies actually enhance protection or primarily enable harm. A weapon's virtue depends on what it accomplishes in society, not individual intentions.

* *Timeless Principle: Tools have inherent purposes—using them contrary to their protective purpose violates their virtue.*

Throughout history, societies have distinguished between protective and aggressive weapon uses. Ancient rulers controlled weapons to maintain order. Medieval guilds regulated dangerous tools to prevent misuse. Even America's Second Amendment mentions a "well-regulated militia," showing that weapons serve collective defense, not individual violence. History consistently shows societies regulating weapons to enhance protection while minimizing harm.

Modern research shows that widespread gun availability increases violence rather than protection. Studies show more guns in circulation mean higher rates of homicide, domestic violence deaths, and accidents. Countries with stricter gun laws have lower violent crime despite having effective self-defense options. Police data reveals guns are more often used to intimidate and harm than to protect victims.

The philosophy works through the principle that tools must fulfill their stated purpose to maintain moral legitimacy. Since weapons claim to protect but statistically enable more harm than protection, current gun policies violate their own stated purpose. It's like medicine that causes more illness than it cures—it fails its essential function.

Practically, this means evaluating all gun policies by asking: do they protect or enable violence? It means restricting weapon types that mainly serve offense rather than defense. It means implementing regulations that enhance real protection while minimizing violence. Some claim individual responsibility, not weapon availability, determines violence. But this ignores why societies with restricted weapon access achieve better protective outcomes than those with unrestricted access. Individual virtue works within structural constraints—a peaceful person in a weapons-saturated environment faces more danger than a violent person in a weapons-restricted one.

This connects to principles like "self-defense doesn't require mass-casualty weapons." Together, they establish how to distinguish legitimate defensive tools from violence-enabling weapons.

For today's leaders, this demands measuring gun policies by actual outcomes: do they protect or harm? When weapons primarily enable violence rather than protection, their proliferation violates both practical wisdom and moral principle.

Unrestricted weapon access endangers society.

Unrestricted access to weapons creates danger for society. The principle of public welfare requires reasonable restrictions on dangerous items.

This statement establishes that unlimited weapon access violates the basic principle of collective welfare. It recognizes that while self-defense is legitimate, unrestricted access to dangerous weapons threatens the broader community's safety. However, implementing this principle must acknowledge legitimate defensive needs. rural communities with hour-long police response times, vulnerable individuals facing specific threats, and communities that historically couldn't rely on law enforcement for protection. The challenge is balancing genuine safety needs with preventing societal harm.

Across civilizations, every organized society has regulated dangerous items to protect public welfare. Even frontier communities, despite their gun culture, typically banned firearms in town limits and required weapons to be checked with the sheriff. This pattern shows that social organization inherently requires balancing individual access with collective safety. Current evidence shows that societies with unrestricted weapon access suffer higher rates of violence, accidents, and suicides.

Yet the lived experience of many Americans includes legitimate reliance on firearms for protection. Rural families may live 45 minutes from the nearest sheriff's deputy. Women facing stalkers or domestic abusers often can't rely on restraining orders for protection—paper doesn't stop bullets. Communities that have faced racial violence, from Black Americans during Reconstruction to Korean Americans during the L.A. riots, learned that police protection isn't guaranteed when you need it most. Native Americans on remote reservations, Jewish communities facing rising antisemitism, LGBTQ people in hostile areas—many vulnerable groups reasonably view firearms as essential protection.

The philosophy recognizes that individual rights exist within social order, not in opposition to it. But this creates complex tensions. Urban communities devastated by gun violence have different needs than rural communities where guns are tools for both protection and sustenance. A single mother in a high-crime neighborhood faces different risks than a suburban family in a gated community. One-size-fits-all policies fail to acknowledge these disparities.

The data on defensive gun use is contested and politicized. Estimates range from 60,000 to 2.5 million defensive uses annually, depending on methodology and definitions.[2] What's clear is that some people have successfully defended themselves and their families with firearms. Their lived experience of survival is as real as the experience of gun violence victims. Both truths coexist uncomfortably.

International comparisons are complex. Countries with strict gun laws generally have lower gun deaths but may have different crime patterns, police response times, and social safety nets. Switzerland has high gun ownership with low gun crime, suggesting culture and implementation matter as much as laws themselves. Rural Australia faced backlash after gun restrictions because firearms served essential functions on remote properties—controlling dangerous wildlife, euthanizing injured livestock, and protection where police might be hours away.

Practically, this suggests differentiated approaches: universal background checks that don't burden law-abiding citizens; red flag laws with due process protections; safe storage requirements that still allow quick access for self-defense; training requirements that improve safety without creating prohibitive barriers; recognition that different communities may need different solutions; and focus on keeping guns from demonstrably dangerous people rather than limiting law-abiding citizens.

Some advocate for complete civilian disarmament, trusting only police with firearms. But this ignores both American cultural realities and the fact that police have no legal duty to protect individuals (as established in Castle Rock v. Gonzales)[3]. Others advocate for unlimited access, arguing that armed societies are polite societies. But this ignores the clear correlation between gun availability and gun deaths, including suicides and accidents.

The deeper challenge is trust. Gun rights advocates don't trust that reasonable regulations will stop there, fearing a slippery slope to confiscation. Gun control advocates don't trust that gun owners will be responsible, fearing the next mass shooting. Both fears have some historical justification, creating a cycle of maximalist positions that prevent pragmatic solutions.

This connects to principles about balancing individual liberty with collective welfare while acknowledging that different communities face different threats and have different relationships with both firearms and law enforcement.

For today's leaders, this demands moving beyond urban-rural divides to create nuanced policies that address both gun violence and legitimate protection needs. It means acknowledging that a Black family in rural Mississippi, a rancher in Montana, and a domestic violence survivor in Chicago all have valid but different relationships with firearms. Most importantly, it means recognizing that both "I survived because I had a gun" and "my child died because someone else had a gun" are true statements that policy must somehow reconcile.

FOR FURTHER READING

John Stuart Mill's principle balancing individual liberty with collective harm prevention

Mill, John Stuart (1859). On Liberty. London: John W. Parker and Son.

National Research Council report discussing the wide range of defensive gun use estimates

National Research Council (2013). Priorities for Research to Reduce the Threat of Firearm-Related Violence. Washington, DC: The National Academies Press.

Supreme Court case establishing that police have no constitutional duty to protect individuals

Castle Rock v. Gonzales, 545 U.S. 748 (2005).

Easy access to lethal force **increases violence**.

Easy access to lethal force increases violent outcomes. The principle of non-violence requires making violence difficult, not easy. Gun proliferation facilitates harm.

This statement establishes a simple but crucial truth: when deadly weapons are easy to get, more people die. It's based on the principle of non-violence (ahimsa) and observable patterns of cause and effect. When lethal tools are readily available, moments of anger, despair, or poor judgment can become irreversible tragedies. It's like leaving matches near gasoline—you're creating conditions for disaster. The principle says virtuous societies should make it harder, not easier, to act on violent impulses.

From antiquity to today, societies have known that easy access to lethal force increases its use. Ancient military strategists controlled weapon distribution to prevent internal conflicts. Medieval communities restricted the deadliest weapons to maintain peace. Even frontier towns developed informal rules for managing dangerous tools during disputes. Modern data shows countries with easier gun access have higher rates of homicide, suicide, and accidental death. The pattern is consistent across all cultures: availability directly influences usage.

Current research overwhelmingly shows that gun accessibility increases lethal violence. States with higher gun ownership have higher gun death rates. Studies on domestic violence show that gun presence increases intimate partner murder risk by 500%. International comparisons reveal that similar societies with different gun availability have vastly different violence rates. Even accounting for other factors, easier firearm access correlates with more deaths, not fewer crimes prevented.

The philosophy recognizes that tools shape behavior by creating or removing barriers to action. Since humans experience emotional states that can lead to poor decisions, easy access to lethal force during these states produces predictably tragic outcomes. It's not about assuming people are bad—it's about recognizing that good people make terrible decisions in bad moments. Virtue means structuring society to support good choices while creating obstacles to harmful ones.

Practically, this means waiting periods that create cooling-off time between buying and getting weapons. It means secure storage requirements to prevent impulsive access. It means background checks to identify high-risk individuals. It means licensing systems ensuring deliberate rather than casual weapon acquisition. Some argue that determined criminals will always find weapons. But this misses how access barriers save lives in suicide prevention, domestic violence, and accidental deaths—areas where criminal intent isn't even involved. It's like saying seatbelt laws don't matter because determined speeders will speed anyway.

This connects to principles like "weapons plus emotional volatility produce deadly outcomes" and "regulating weapon sales saves lives." Together, they establish the empirical foundation for access controls.

For today's leaders, this demands creating deliberate barriers between emotional states and lethal capabilities while preserving legitimate defensive access for responsible people. When we make violence easy, we get more violence—it's that simple.

FOR FURTHER READING

The principle of non-violence (ahimsa) in ancient Eastern philosophy

Chapple, Christopher Key (1993). Nonviolence to Animals, Earth, and Self in Asian Traditions. Albany: State University of New York Press.

Self-defense doesn't require **mass-casualty weapons**.

Self-defense rights don't extend to weapons designed for mass casualties. Military-grade weapons exceed legitimate self-protection needs, serving only offensive purposes.

|| ॐ ||

This statement distinguishes between legitimate self-defense weapons and mass-casualty instruments. It says that while self-defense is a valid right, the weapons used must match that purpose. Tools designed to kill many people quickly serve military offensive purposes, not individual protection. It's like saying you need a sledgehammer to crack a nut—the mismatch reveals the real intent. When people claim they need military weapons for defense, they're using defensive language to acquire offensive capabilities.

Throughout history, societies have distinguished between defensive and offensive weapons based on their capabilities. Ancient military texts separated personal protection arms from siege weapons. Medieval laws restricted the most dangerous weapons to armies while allowing defensive tools for citizens. Modern military doctrine explicitly designs certain weapons to inflict maximum casualties in warfare, not for personal protection. This shows that classifying weapons by capability rather than claimed intent is standard practice across civilizations.

Current evidence shows that military-style assault weapons far exceed defensive needs while enabling mass casualties. Self-defense typically involves close-range encounters with single attackers, requiring accuracy and stopping power—not rapid-fire capability against multiple targets. Data from actual defensive gun uses shows that high-capacity magazines and automatic features are rarely necessary for protection but consistently used in mass shootings. Countries that restrict military-style weapons maintain effective self-defense while preventing mass casualties.

The philosophy involves proportionality—tools must match legitimate goals. Since real self-defense means stopping individual threats, not killing multiple people rapidly, weapons designed for mass casualties exceed defensive purposes. They serve only offensive or intimidation functions that violate the principle of restraint. It's like claiming you need a flamethrower for home heating.

Practically, this means banning civilian access to military weapons, distinguishing between hunting rifles and assault weapons based on capability not appearance, limiting magazine capacities to reasonable defensive needs, and ensuring available defensive weapons can protect without enabling mass violence. Some claim citizens need military weapons to resist government tyranny. But modern militaries win through tactics, training, and coordination, not individual firepower. Historical resistance movements succeed through asymmetric strategies, not direct firepower confrontations. The "tyranny" argument often masks the desire for offensive capability.

This connects to principles like "weapons should protect, not enable violence" and "excessive arsenals suggest offensive intent." Together, they establish capability-based weapon classification.

For today's leaders, this demands distinguishing between legitimate defensive tools and offensive weapons that enable mass casualties. When someone says they need a weapon that can kill dozens quickly for "self-defense," the mismatch between means and ends reveals the truth.

Regulating dangerous items **protects public virtue**.

Regulating dangerous items protects virtue by reducing harm potential. Just as ritual regulations exist for safety, weapon regulations serve protective purposes.

This statement establishes that regulating dangerous items serves virtue by preventing harm. It draws a parallel to ritual safety protocols—just as religious practices include rules to prevent contamination or injury, society must regulate dangerous items to protect innocent life. When lethal instruments circulate without safeguards, society fails its moral duty. The principle extends ritual purity logic (maintaining conditions that support virtue) to civil regulation of dangerous materials and tools.

Legal traditions demonstrate that every organized society has regulated dangerous items as a basic function of governance. Ancient civilizations controlled poisons, explosives, and military weapons to maintain order. Medieval guilds regulated dangerous tools and materials to prevent accidents. Modern governments routinely regulate chemicals, pharmaceuticals, vehicles, and other potentially harmful items while preserving legitimate uses. This universal pattern shows regulation serves protective, not oppressive purposes when applied to genuinely dangerous items.

Today's successful regulations prove this works. Pharmaceutical controls prevent drug abuse while ensuring medical access. Chemical regulations prevent industrial accidents while maintaining commercial use. Vehicle licensing reduces traffic deaths while preserving transportation freedom. Building codes prevent collapses while allowing architectural innovation. Each shows that thoughtful regulation enhances legitimate use while preventing foreseeable harms.

The philosophy recognizes that preventing harm is a positive moral duty, not negative restriction. Since dangerous items inherently risk innocent lives, society must manage those risks through appropriate frameworks. Regulation serves the same function as ritual safety protocols—maintaining conditions that support virtue while preventing accidental or intentional harm. It's proactive care, not reactive punishment.

Practically, this means licensing systems ensuring competency before access, storage requirements preventing unauthorized use, background checks identifying high-risk individuals, and periodic renewals maintaining safety standards. These aren't restrictions on freedom—they're protections of life. Some claim regulation infringes freedom. But they must explain why we regulate countless other dangerous items without controversy. We require licenses for cars, prescriptions for powerful drugs, permits for explosives. The principle applies consistently—dangerous items need proportional safeguards regardless of type.

This connects to principles like "unrestricted weapon access endangers society" and "without training, weapon eligibility is lost." Together, they establish regulation as virtue protection.

For today's leaders, this demands implementing comprehensive safety frameworks for all dangerous items, including firearms, that protect public welfare while preserving legitimate uses. When we regulate danger, we protect virtue.

Society bears **collective fault** for preventable deaths.*

When children die from gun violence, society bears collective fault for failing to protect them. This collective responsibility demands policy change.

This statement establishes that we all share moral responsibility when preventable deaths occur, especially children's deaths. It says that when we have the knowledge and means to prevent deaths but fail to act, we violate our fundamental duty to protect innocent life. This is particularly true for children, who depend entirely on adults for protection and can't influence the policies affecting their safety. It's like knowing a bridge is unsafe but not fixing it—when someone falls, the community that ignored the danger shares the blame.

* *Timeless Principle: A society that fails to protect its children from preventable death has failed its most basic virtue.*

For centuries, societies have recognized collective responsibility for preventable deaths as a basic moral principle. Ancient legal codes held communities liable for crimes that happened due to inadequate protection. Medieval guilds accepted responsibility for workplace accidents from insufficient safety measures. Modern public health acknowledges society's duty to prevent epidemics through collective action. Recognizing that preventable deaths create collective moral obligation, not just individual tragedy, represents consistent moral reasoning across all cultures.

Current evidence shows that gun violence deaths, especially involving children, are preventable through policies successfully implemented elsewhere. Countries with comprehensive gun regulations have dramatically lower child gun death rates while maintaining legitimate defense capabilities. Research shows specific policies—universal background checks, assault weapon restrictions, safe storage requirements—directly reduce child fatalities. When effective solutions exist but remain unused, the resulting deaths become societal choices, not natural disasters.

The philosophy recognizes that knowledge creates obligation. When communities understand the connection between policies and outcomes, they bear responsibility for choosing policies that protect or endanger life. Since we know empirically that gun availability correlates with child deaths, continued inaction constitutes a collective decision to accept preventable child mortality. It's not ignorance—it's negligence.

Practically, this means implementing policies proven to reduce gun violence elsewhere, establishing systems prioritizing child safety over political convenience, creating accountability for policymakers who block evidence-based safety measures, and recognizing that child protection is a non-negotiable societal obligation. Some claim individual responsibility, not social policy, determines outcomes. But this ignores that children bear consequences for adult policy decisions they can't influence. A five-year-old can't vote, lobby, or protect themselves from adults' policy choices. Children depend entirely on adult protective systems.

This connects to principles like "weapons in schools constitute grave moral failure" and "mass shootings reflect societal, not just individual, failure." Together, they establish collective accountability for preventable deaths.

For today's leaders, this demands prioritizing child protection over political considerations when implementing gun safety policies. When we know how to prevent deaths but choose not to, we share moral responsibility for every preventable tragedy.

Greater weapon power requires **greater responsibility**.

Weapon ownership requires corresponding responsibility. The greater the weapon's power, the greater the required demonstration of responsibility through training and screening.

This statement establishes that more dangerous weapons require more proof of responsibility to own them. It recognizes that rights and responsibilities exist in balance—as tools become more lethal, the requirements for using them must become more rigorous. It's like how we require more training to fly a plane than drive a car. The principle says that greater capability demands greater demonstration of competence and character to handle that capability safely.

Ethical philosophy shows that all societies have required more qualifications for more dangerous roles and tools. Ancient warrior traditions demanded extensive training and character evaluation before granting military weapons. Medieval guilds required years of apprenticeship before allowing use of dangerous tools. Today we continue this pattern—doctors need more training than nurses, pilots more certification than drivers, demolition experts more qualifications than construction workers. This universal principle shows that danger level determines qualification requirements.

Modern examples prove this works well. We require stricter licensing for commercial trucks than personal cars, more extensive background checks for security clearances than basic jobs, more rigorous training for heavy machinery than simple tools. Countries with graduated firearms licensing—basic permits for simple weapons, advanced licenses for powerful guns—achieve better safety while preserving legitimate use. Proportional requirements enhance rather than restrict legitimate access.

The philosophy recognizes that competence must match responsibility to maintain order. Since more powerful weapons create greater potential for harm, their users must demonstrate greater capability to handle that responsibility. This prevents dangerous mismatches between tool capability and user qualification that lead to tragedies. It's common sense—you wouldn't give a formula one race car to someone who just got their learner's permit.

Practically, this means graduated licensing systems with more requirements for more powerful weapons. It means requiring advanced training for assault-style weapons, periodic competency testing for high-capacity firearms, and character evaluation for weapons capable of mass casualties. The more damage a tool can do, the more we need to ensure the user can handle it responsibly. Some claim any training or screening requirements violate constitutional rights. But they must explain why we accept such requirements for driving, flying, practicing medicine, and countless other activities involving public safety. Constitutional rights have always operated within frameworks of reasonable regulation based on public risk.

This connects to principles like "without training, weapon eligibility is lost" and "self-defense doesn't require mass-casualty weapons." Together, they establish graduated responsibility systems.

For today's leaders, this demands implementing comprehensive training and evaluation requirements that scale with weapon lethality while preserving access for qualified individuals. The more powerful the weapon, the more proof we need that its owner can handle it responsibly.

Weapons plus emotional volatility produce **deadly outcomes**.

The presence of weapons during emotional disturbance increases lethal outcomes. This observable pattern justifies cooling-off periods and red flag laws.

|| ॐ ||

This statement identifies a deadly equation: emotional volatility + weapon access = tragic outcomes. It recognizes that while emotions are natural human experiences, combining them with lethal instruments creates disproportionate tragedy compared to emotional episodes without weapons. When rage, despair, fear, or intoxication meet immediate weapon availability, momentary feelings produce permanent consequences. It's like driving while emotionally impaired—dangerous becomes deadly when powerful tools are involved.

Throughout history, wisdom traditions have recognized the danger of mixing emotional states with dangerous instruments. Ancient military codes banned weapon access during certain emotional conditions. Traditional societies created cooling-off periods before important decisions during grief or anger. Medical traditions have long known that emotional disturbance impairs judgment with dangerous substances. Modern psychology documents how emotions alter risk assessment and impulse control. This universal recognition shows that emotions and dangerous tools create hazardous combinations.

Current research overwhelmingly shows that weapon access during emotional crises dramatically increases deaths. Suicide attempts with guns succeed at much higher rates than other methods, often during brief crisis periods. Domestic violence turns deadly when weapons are easily accessible during conflicts. Road rage becomes homicide when firearms are present. Studies on waiting periods show significant drops in both murders and suicides when delays exist between buying and getting weapons.

The philosophy recognizes that temporary states need temporary protective measures to prevent permanent harm. Since emotional disturbance temporarily impairs judgment while death is permanent, moral duty requires creating barriers between volatile emotional states and lethal capabilities. It's not about judging people for having emotions—it's about preventing irreversible decisions during temporary crises.

Practically, this means mandatory waiting periods between purchasing and receiving weapons, extreme risk protection orders that temporarily remove weapons during crises, secure storage requirements preventing impulsive access during emotional episodes, and systems for families to seek temporary weapon removal during mental health crises. Some claim determined individuals will find weapons anyway. But suicide and domestic violence rates drop significantly when immediate weapon access is reduced, proving many violent outcomes result from impulsive decisions, not determined planning. It's the difference between a momentary urge and a calculated plan.

This connects to principles like "mental health conditions necessitate weapon restrictions" and "easy access to lethal force increases violence." Together, they establish the need for temporal barriers.

For today's leaders, this demands implementing policies that create deliberate delays between emotional crises and weapon access. When we separate temporary emotions from permanent consequences, we save lives.

Without training, **weapon eligibility is lost.**

Without proper training, one loses eligibility to use weapons and other potentially deadly devices and products such as vehicles and medicine.

This statement establishes that you must be trained before you can use dangerous tools—period. It says competence must come before authorization to prevent harm through ignorance. Just as we require training for driving cars, practicing medicine, flying planes, or handling chemicals, weapons require demonstrated skill to use safely. When people lack proper training in handling, safety, laws, and tactics, they endanger themselves and everyone around them. It's not optional—training is a fundamental requirement for legitimate access to dangerous tools.

In human experience, warrior traditions universally required extensive training before granting weapon access. Ancient military systems demanded years of preparation before soldiers got full armaments. Medieval knighthood required mastery of weapons, tactics, and codes of conduct. Traditional hunting cultures passed down generations of training in safety, marksmanship, and ethical use. Today's military and police continue with intensive training programs. This universal recognition that weapons require training reflects practical wisdom accumulated over centuries.

Untrained weapon owners create significantly higher risks of accidents, misuse, and tragedy. States with mandatory training requirements have lower rates of accidental shootings, domestic violence deaths, and improper storage. Countries requiring comprehensive firearms training achieve better safety while maintaining robust sporting and defensive use. Research shows even brief training programs dramatically improve safety outcomes and responsible use.

The philosophy recognizes that authority comes from competence, not from desire or claims of rights. Since weapon use affects not just the owner but potentially innocent others, society has a moral duty to ensure weapon access correlates with demonstrated competence. This prevents foreseeable harm through ignorance or poor training. It's like requiring a pilot's license—the stakes are too high for untrained operation.

Practically, this means mandatory training covering safety, legal requirements, marksmanship, and situational awareness before weapon purchase. It means periodic refresher training to maintain licenses, competency standards that must be demonstrated not assumed, and specialized training for different weapons based on their complexity and danger level. Some claim training requirements create barriers to constitutional rights. But they must explain why we accept training requirements for driving, professional licensing, and countless other activities without controversy. Rights operate within frameworks of competent exercise—you have the right to practice medicine, but only after proving competence.

This connects to principles like "greater weapon power requires greater responsibility" and "regulating dangerous items protects public virtue." Together, they establish competence requirements.

For today's leaders, this demands comprehensive training systems ensuring weapon competence before access while providing accessible pathways for responsible citizens to demonstrate qualification. No training, no access—it's that simple.

Public spaces require protection from weapons.

Public spaces require special protection from weapons. The principle of public safety supersedes individual preferences and even rights with respect to possession and use of weapons.

This statement establishes that public spaces need special protection from weapons because shared environments demand collective safety measures that override individual preferences. It recognizes that places like schools, government buildings, houses of worship, and entertainment venues serve community functions that require security from weapon threats. When weapons proliferate in public spaces, they transform environments meant for learning, governance, worship, and gathering into potential conflict zones. It's like allowing smoking in hospitals—individual preference can't override collective health needs.

Social evolution reveals that societies have recognized that certain spaces need to be weapon-free to fulfill their purposes. Ancient temples banned weapons to maintain sacred sanctity. Medieval courts restricted arms to preserve judicial proceedings. Traditional places of learning excluded weapons to protect scholarly discourse. Even frontier societies established weapon-free zones around churches, schools, and government buildings. This universal pattern shows that community spaces need protection from armed conflict potential.

Today's successful weapon-free public spaces prove this works. Airports, courthouses, government buildings, and many schools successfully exclude weapons while remaining accessible for legitimate purposes. Countries with strict public carry restrictions maintain vibrant public life without increased crime. Research shows weapon-free policies in sensitive locations reduce both accidental and intentional violence while preserving these spaces' primary functions.

The philosophy recognizes that collective spaces serve community purposes requiring protection from individual actions that could compromise those purposes. Since public spaces exist for education, governance, worship, and culture, individual weapon carry preferences can't override the collective need for security that enables these functions. It's about preserving the character and accessibility of shared spaces.

Practically, this means establishing weapon-free zones around schools, government buildings, places of worship, and entertainment venues. It means implementing security screening at sensitive locations, creating clear legal frameworks defining prohibited carry areas, and ensuring law enforcement can effectively maintain weapon-free environments while preserving accessibility. Some claim weapon-free zones create vulnerability. But they must explain why highly secured weapon-free areas like airports and federal buildings experience lower violence rates, not higher. Countries with extensive public carry restrictions maintain excellent public safety. The evidence shows protection works.

This connects to principles like "weapons in schools constitute grave moral failure" and "society bears collective fault for preventable deaths." Together, they establish public space protection as moral imperative.

For today's leaders, this demands implementing comprehensive weapon-free zone policies that protect community spaces while ensuring effective enforcement. When we prioritize collective security in shared spaces, we preserve their essential community functions.

Mental health conditions **necessitate weapon restrictions**.

Mental health conditions that impair judgment require weapon restrictions for everyone's safety, including the affected person. This is protective, not punitive.

This statement says that mental health conditions affecting judgment require temporary weapon restrictions as protective measures, not punishment. It recognizes that certain conditions can temporarily compromise decision-making, impulse control, and risk assessment in ways that make weapon access dangerous for everyone involved. It's like temporarily taking car keys from someone who's impaired—it's about preventing tragedy during vulnerable periods while preserving long-term rights. The goal is compassionate protection, not discrimination.

Throughout history, societies have recognized that impaired mental states require protective interventions with dangerous activities. Ancient legal codes provided temporary guardianship during mental incapacity. Traditional communities developed protocols for managing dangerous tools during emotional crises. Modern medicine routinely restricts access to potentially harmful items during certain treatments. This consistent pattern shows that temporary incapacity requires temporary protection.

Current research clearly shows connections between certain mental health conditions and increased weapon-related harm, particularly suicide during depression and violence during psychotic episodes. Studies prove that temporary weapon removal during crisis periods significantly reduces both suicide attempts and violent incidents. Countries with robust mental health screening for weapon access achieve better outcomes while maintaining pathways for rights restoration when conditions stabilize.

The philosophy operates through the duty to protect life during periods of impaired judgment, similar to preventing intoxicated driving. Since mental health conditions can temporarily compromise the judgment needed for safe weapon use, protective restrictions serve virtue, not discrimination. It's about capability, not stigma.

Practically, this means extreme risk protection orders allowing temporary weapon removal during crises, mandatory reporting by mental health professionals when patients pose imminent risks, background check systems identifying disqualifying conditions while protecting privacy, and clear restoration procedures when individuals demonstrate stability. Some worry about stigmatization. But physical health conditions also create temporary restrictions on dangerous activities without stigma—we don't let people with seizures fly planes until controlled. The principle applies to capacity, not identity. It's protective healthcare, not discrimination.

This connects to principles like "weapons plus emotional volatility produce deadly outcomes." Together, they establish capacity-based restrictions as protective measures.

For today's leaders, this demands implementing mental health-informed weapon policies that protect vulnerable individuals while avoiding discrimination. When someone's judgment is temporarily impaired, removing access to lethal means saves lives—including their own.

Regulating weapon sales **saves lives**.

Regulating weapon sales protects lives. The acceptance of marketplace regulation for public good extends to deadly weapons trade.

This statement establishes that regulating weapon sales protects lives by applying standard commercial oversight to deadly weapons. It recognizes that while legitimate weapon trade serves valid purposes—sporting, hunting, self-defense—unregulated sales create pathways for dangerous people to get lethal weapons. When weapon sales take place without safeguards, it enables preventable deaths through sales to prohibited persons, straw purchases, and inadequate verification. It's like regulating pharmaceuticals—we control dangerous products to protect public health while preserving legitimate access.

Observation confirms that societies have regulated dangerous item sales as basic public safety measures. Ancient markets controlled poisons and military weapons. Medieval guilds regulated tool sales to prevent misuse by unqualified people. Modern governments routinely regulate explosives, pharmaceuticals, chemicals, and other potentially harmful items while preserving legitimate commerce. This universal pattern shows that dangerous item regulation protects rather than restricts legitimate trade by ensuring responsible distribution.

Comprehensive weapon sales regulation significantly reduces gun deaths while preserving legal access. States with universal background checks have lower homicide and suicide rates. Countries with robust licensing and sales oversight achieve dramatic reductions in gun violence while maintaining sporting and defensive use. Research shows that closing sales loopholes—gun shows, private sales, online transactions—prevents prohibited persons from acquiring weapons through unregulated channels.

The philosophy recognizes that commercial activity must serve, not threaten, social welfare. Since unregulated weapon sales demonstrably increase preventable deaths, regulation serves the moral duty to protect life while preserving legitimate commerce for qualified individuals. It's basic marketplace ethics applied to deadly products.

Practically, this means universal background checks covering all sales venues, requiring licensed dealers for all weapon transactions, establishing waiting periods to prevent impulsive purchases, creating tracking systems to prevent illegal trafficking, and ensuring private sales meet the same standards as commercial ones. Some claim criminals will circumvent regulations. But they must explain why regulation works for other dangerous items and why states with comprehensive sales regulation have lower, not higher, crime rates. Evidence shows regulation works when properly implemented.

This connects to principles like "dangerous weapons require registration and tracking" and "unrestricted weapon access endangers society." Together, they establish commercial oversight as life-saving necessity.

For today's leaders, this demands implementing comprehensive weapon sales regulation that protects public safety while preserving legitimate commerce. When we regulate dangerous product sales, we save lives—it's proven by data from every jurisdiction that's tried it.

Excessive arsenals suggest **offensive intent**.

Massive weapon stockpiling raises legitimate suspicions about intent. Beyond reasonable self-defense needs, arsenals suggest offensive purposes.

This statement says that accumulating weapons far beyond reasonable needs indicates potential offensive rather than defensive intent. It applies proportionality reasoning—while someone might legitimately own multiple weapons for hunting, sport, and home defense, collections reaching military-scale quantities suggest preparation for offensive action. It's like someone buying 50 fire extinguishers; at some point, you have to wonder what they're really planning. When weapon collections exceed any reasonable defensive justification, they warrant investigation.

Through generations, societies have monitored large weapon accumulations as potential threats. Ancient kingdoms tracked private armories that could challenge state authority. Medieval lords regulated castle armaments to prevent rebellions. Modern law enforcement investigates unusual weapon stockpiling as indicators of planned violence. Intelligence agencies monitor arms accumulation patterns to identify security threats. This consistent pattern shows that excessive weapon collection raises legitimate suspicions about intent.

Current evidence shows correlations between large weapon collections and planned violence. Mass shooting perpetrators often accumulate far more weapons than single incidents require, suggesting premeditation and potential for multiple attacks. Domestic terrorists frequently stockpile weapons and ammunition beyond any defensive need. Research reveals that individuals planning violence often acquire weapons systematically over time, creating observable patterns that could enable intervention.

The philosophy applies means-ends proportionality—when means exceed stated ends significantly, we must consider alternative purposes. Since legitimate self-defense has practical limits while offensive capabilities can scale indefinitely, disproportionate accumulation suggests offensive intent. It's reasonable to question why someone needs military-scale firepower for home defense.

Practically, this means establishing thresholds for weapon ownership that trigger investigation, requiring justification for large-scale purchases, monitoring acquisition patterns exceeding normal use categories, creating reporting requirements for dealers observing unusual buying patterns, and implementing early warning systems for potential threats. Some claim collecting is a legitimate hobby. But they must explain why collectors need operational weapons rather than deactivated models, and why collection rights should override public safety when accumulations reach military scales. Stamp collectors don't need functioning post offices.

This connects to principles like "self-defense doesn't require mass-casualty weapons" and "mass shootings reflect societal failure." Together, they establish prevention frameworks.

For today's leaders, this demands monitoring excessive weapon accumulation as a potential threat indicator while respecting legitimate collection and sporting interests. When someone's "collection" could arm a small militia, it's reasonable to ask why.

Weapons in schools constitute **grave moral failure**.

Weapons in educational spaces constitute great sin by threatening children and learning. Schools must remain sanctuaries from violence.

|| ॐ ||

This statement declares that weapons in schools represent profound moral failure because they violate the sacred nature of educational spaces. It recognizes schools as sanctuaries for learning, growth, and protecting young minds, making weapon presence a fundamental violation of their purpose. It's like bringing weapons into a church or hospital—it destroys the essential character of the space. When schools become potential violence sites, they can't fulfill their primary purpose of nurturing intellectual and moral development.

History teaches that educational institutions have been recognized as protected spaces requiring sanctuary from violence. Ancient schools operated under divine protection in many traditions. Medieval universities claimed sanctuary rights that even kings respected. Traditional societies consistently recognized that learning environments needed protection from armed conflict to function. This universal pattern reveals that education and violence are fundamentally incompatible—weapons destroy the trust, openness, and vulnerability necessary for real learning.

Current evidence shows that weapon presence in schools creates fear, trauma, and educational disruption even without actual violence. Students can't learn effectively when they fear for their safety. Teachers can't create open, supportive environments when worried about potential violence. Increased security measures, including armed personnel, often worsen educational outcomes by creating prison-like atmospheres. Countries with strict gun control keeping weapons out of schools consistently achieve better educational results.

The philosophy recognizes that spaces dedicated to sacred purposes—and education is sacred activity—must be protected from elements that corrupt their function. Since weapons represent potential violence while education requires trust and openness, their presence in schools violates the essential nature of educational space. It's like trying to meditate in a war zone—the environments are fundamentally incompatible.

Practically, this means establishing absolute weapon-free zones around schools with strong enforcement, implementing threat assessment programs to identify risks early, creating support systems for troubled students rather than armed deterrence, and designing security that protects without militarizing schools. Some claim armed teachers or guards improve safety. But they must explain why countries with weapon-free schools have fewer school violence incidents, and why educational experts consistently oppose classroom weapons. The evidence shows that weapons in schools create danger, not safety.

This connects to principles like "society bears collective fault for preventable deaths" and "public spaces require protection from weapons." Together, they establish educational sanctuary as moral imperative.

For today's leaders, this demands absolute commitment to keeping weapons out of schools while addressing root causes of youth violence. When we allow weapons where children learn, we commit a grave moral failure that corrupts education's sacred purpose.

Even constitutional rights include **'well-regulated.'**

Even constitutional gun rights include "well-regulated" language. Original intent included regulation, not unrestricted access. Regulation fulfills, not violates, constitutional principles.

This statement points out that the Second Amendment itself includes the words "well-regulated militia," showing that the founders intended regulation as part of gun rights, not opposed to them. When people quote only the "right to bear arms" part while ignoring "well-regulated," they violate basic principles of reading—you must consider the whole text, not just fragments. It's like quoting "Congress shall make no law" while ignoring "respecting an establishment of religion." The Constitution itself establishes that gun rights exist within a regulatory framework.

Throughout American history, constitutional interpretation has recognized that rights exist within regulatory frameworks, not as absolute licenses. The founders themselves regulated gun ownership in early communities, including storage requirements, registration, and restrictions on certain groups. Colonial and early state laws commonly regulated gunpowder storage, weapon inspection, and militia service obligations. Supreme Court precedents consistently recognize that constitutional rights have boundaries—free speech doesn't protect threats, religious freedom doesn't excuse lawbreaking, property rights accept zoning restrictions.

Constitutional scholarship shows that "well-regulated" had specific meaning in the 18th century—it meant properly functioning and trained forces subject to rules and discipline. Legal analysis reveals the amendment's structure (explaining purpose, then granting right) indicates that regulation serves rather than contradicts the amendment's purpose. Even individual rights interpretations acknowledge that regulation can fulfill constitutional intent when serving protective purposes.

The philosophy involves comprehensive textual interpretation—all parts of a statement must be considered to understand its complete meaning. Since the Second Amendment includes regulatory language alongside rights language, constitutional compliance requires implementing appropriate regulation, not rejecting it. You can't cherry-pick the parts you like.

Practically, this means designing gun regulations that fulfill constitutional intent, emphasizing training and competency requirements aligning with "well-regulated" language, creating licensing systems mirroring the amendment's militia structure, and ensuring regulations serve protective rather than prohibitive purposes. Some claim any regulation violates constitutional rights. But they must explain why the Constitution itself includes regulatory language and why other constitutional rights accept reasonable limitations without controversy. The text itself refutes their argument.

This connects to principles like "without training, weapon eligibility is lost" and "greater weapon power requires greater responsibility." Together, they establish constitutional basis for regulation.

For today's leaders, this demands implementing comprehensive regulatory frameworks that fulfill rather than violate constitutional intent. When the Constitution says "well-regulated," it means what it says.

FOR FURTHER READING

The Second Amendment's text including 'well-regulated militia' language

U.S. Const. amend. II.

Dangerous weapons require **registration and tracking**.

Tracking dangerous weapons through registration serves public safety. Just as other dangerous items require documentation, so should lethal weapons.

|| ॐ ||

This statement says dangerous weapons need registration and tracking systems, applying the same logic we use for other dangerous items. When instruments capable of significant harm circulate in society, public safety demands knowing their location, ownership, and transfer patterns. We track vehicles, chemicals, pharmaceuticals, and other potentially dangerous items without controversy—weapons capable of killing multiple people require similar oversight. It's about accountability: both preventing misuse and enabling investigation when crimes occur.

Throughout history, societies have tracked dangerous items as basic administrative functions. Ancient civilizations tracked military equipment for security. Medieval authorities registered private weapons to prevent rebellions and solve crimes. Early American colonies maintained militia rolls including weapon inventories. Modern governments routinely track explosives, radioactive materials, controlled substances, and vehicles without constitutional challenges. This pattern shows registration serves protective, not confiscatory purposes when properly implemented.

Current evidence shows that weapon registration enhances public safety while preserving legitimate ownership. Countries with comprehensive firearm registries have lower illegal weapon trafficking, faster crime solving, and reduced theft-related violence. Studies show registration deters straw purchases and illegal transfers while minimally burdening law-abiding owners. States with better tracking systems solve more gun crimes and have fewer weapons flowing to criminals.

The philosophy recognizes that authority over dangerous items requires corresponding accountability. Since weapon ownership affects not just the owner but potentially innocent others, society has a duty to maintain systems enabling accountability when weapons cause harm or threaten safety. It's basic responsibility—if you own something dangerous, society needs to know.

Practically, this means comprehensive registration databases tracking ownership and transfers, requiring documentation for all sales including private ones, creating systems for law enforcement to trace crime weapons, implementing secure storage requirements preventing unauthorized access, and ensuring registration serves public safety not confiscation. Some claim registration enables government confiscation. But they must explain why registration works for countless other dangerous items without confiscation, and why countries with weapon registration maintain robust civilian ownership. Cars are registered—has the government confiscated all cars?

This connects to principles like "regulating weapon sales saves lives" and "regulating dangerous items protects public virtue." Together, they establish tracking infrastructure as public safety necessity.

For today's leaders, this demands implementing comprehensive registration systems that enhance public safety while protecting legitimate ownership rights. When we track dangerous items, we create accountability that protects everyone.

Mass shootings reflect **societal, not just individual, failure**.

Mass shootings reflect societal failure, not just individual evil. Systemic solutions, not just individual blame, must address systemic problems.

|| ॐ ||

This statement reflects that mass shootings represent systemic rather than just individual failures. While perpetrators bear direct responsibility, the consistent occurrence of mass violence across different people and places points to underlying societal conditions that enable these tragedies. It's like a disease outbreak—while individuals get sick, recurring patterns indicate environmental factors. When similar societies have vastly different mass shooting rates based on their policies, it reveals that individual evil operates within systems that either prevent or facilitate violence.

Evidence demonstrates that societies have recognized that recurring problems need structural solutions beyond individual punishment. Ancient legal codes addressed underlying conditions leading to crimes, not just punishing criminals. Medieval societies made systemic changes to address violence patterns. Modern public health doesn't just treat sick individuals—it changes conditions that cause illness. This pattern shows that persistent social problems require systemic analysis and solutions.

Current evidence reveals clear patterns distinguishing societies with frequent mass shootings from those without. Countries with similar mental health issues, violent media, and social problems have dramatically different mass shooting rates based on gun availability and regulation. Research shows mass shootings correlate with weapon accessibility, not mental illness rates or violent culture. International comparisons prove that policy changes can virtually eliminate mass shootings while addressing underlying problems through other means.

The philosophy recognizes that effects with common patterns require examining common causes. Since mass shootings occur across different individuals and contexts but follow similar patterns within societies, their causation must include systemic elements addressable through policy. Individual evil exists everywhere—but only some systems enable it to become mass violence.

Practically, this means implementing comprehensive threat assessment in schools and workplaces, addressing social isolation and grievance patterns leading to violence, restricting access to mass-casualty weapons, creating intervention programs for those showing warning signs, and building community resilience against radicalization. Some claim evil individuals, not social systems, cause mass shootings. But they must explain why similar rates of disturbed individuals in different societies produce vastly different mass violence rates, and why policy changes in specific locations lead to measurable violence reductions.

This connects to principles like "society bears collective fault for preventable deaths" and "weapons in schools constitute grave moral failure." Together, they establish systemic responsibility for recurring tragedies.

For today's leaders, this demands comprehensive approaches addressing both individual and systemic factors enabling mass violence. When we treat mass shootings as only individual evil, we guarantee they'll continue. Systemic problems require systemic solutions.

Life preservation outweighs unlimited weapon access.*

When rights conflict, preserving life takes precedence over unrestricted weapon access. The hierarchy of values places existence before convenience.

|| ॐ ||

This final teaching establishes the ultimate hierarchy: when different rights conflict, preserving life must come first. It recognizes that while self-defense and weapon ownership are valid rights, they can't override the more basic right to life that makes all other rights possible. It's like a foundation—without life, no other rights matter. When weapon policies serve convenience or ideology rather than genuine protection, they violate the principle that places survival above secondary considerations.

* *Timeless Principle: The right to life supersedes all lesser rights—a principle that subordinates weapon access to survival.*

Wisdom traditions affirm that legal and moral systems have consistently recognized life preservation as the highest earthly value. Ancient legal codes prioritized preventing death over protecting property or convenience. Religious traditions across cultures establish preserving life as overriding other considerations. Constitutional frameworks recognize life as the first and most fundamental right from which others derive meaning. Modern international law places the right to life as a supreme norm that can't be violated. This universal pattern shows that life preservation is the foundational value making all other rights meaningful.

Societies prioritizing life preservation over unlimited weapon access achieve better outcomes for both safety and freedom. Countries with evidence-based gun policies that restrict access for dangerous individuals while preserving legitimate use have lower violence rates without sacrificing democracy or liberty. Research shows reasonable weapon regulations enhance genuine security by reducing threats to innocent life. International comparisons reveal that life-prioritizing policies create environments where other rights flourish more fully.

The philosophy recognizes value hierarchy—when competing goods conflict, the more fundamental must take precedence. Since life constitutes the foundation for all other human goods and rights, policies must be evaluated based on their actual effect on life preservation, not abstract claims divorced from outcomes. Dead people can't exercise any rights.

Practically, this means designing all weapon policies to maximize life preservation, accepting reasonable restrictions when they protect life, implementing evidence-based rather than ideologically driven policies, and recognizing that genuine security serves rather than opposes individual freedom. Some claim unlimited weapon access is more important than life preservation. But they must explain how dead people exercise freedom, and why societies with reasonable gun laws have both lower death rates and robust freedoms. The evidence shows that protecting life enhances rather than diminishes liberty.

This principle culminates the gun control argument by establishing that authentic rights protection requires prioritizing life preservation over unlimited access claims that threaten the very existence rights are meant to protect. When we must choose, life comes first.

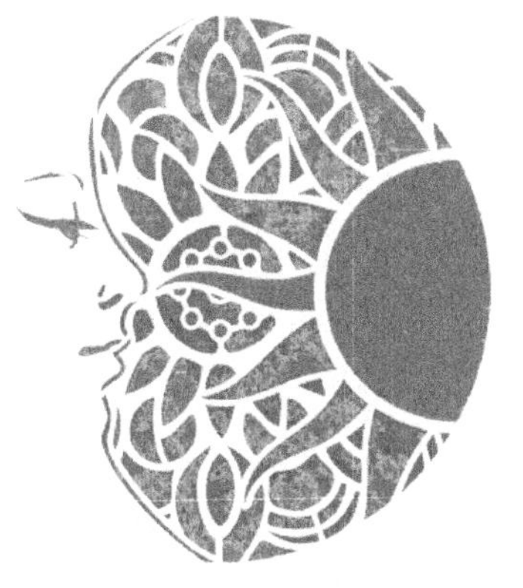

ON REPRODUCTIVE FREEDOM

Control over one's body is **the foundation of autonomy**.*

Control over one's own body constitutes the foundation of all autonomy. Denying reproductive choice violates the most fundamental authority—that over one's own physical existence.

This foundational teaching establishes that controlling your own body is the prerequisite for all other freedoms. It says reproductive choice isn't just one right among many—it's the fundamental authority without which no other autonomy matters. It's like owning your house versus owning the land it sits on; without the land, the house ownership means nothing. True human dignity requires individual sovereignty over bodily functions and reproductive decisions, not external control over them.

* *Timeless Principle: Self-ownership of the body is the foundation of all freedom—a principle that predates and transcends political systems.*

Throughout history, philosophers have recognized the body as the first domain of legitimate authority. John Locke's theory of self-ownership says you own yourself before anything else.[1] Immanuel Kant's concept of human dignity centers on self-determination over your own existence.[2] Indigenous traditions emphasize bodily sovereignty as sacred. All these converge on one truth: physical autonomy is foundational to human freedom. Legal systems that deny bodily autonomy invariably restrict other freedoms too.

Current evidence shows how reproductive restrictions lead to broader autonomy violations. Countries severely restricting reproductive choice typically also limit women's education, economic participation, and political engagement. This correlation reveals how bodily control serves as the foundation for comprehensive self-determination across all life areas. You can't be free in society if you're not free in your own body.

The philosophy recognizes that the body is the instrument through which all conscious action occurs. When external authorities control bodily functions, they effectively control the person's entire capacity for autonomous action. Reproductive autonomy thus becomes not just personal preference but essential precondition for human agency. It's the difference between being a person and being property.

Practically, this means legal frameworks recognizing reproductive decisions as fundamental rights needing the highest protection, healthcare systems prioritizing patient autonomy in reproductive choices, and social policies supporting rather than coercing reproductive decisions. Some claim reproductive decisions affect others. But forced reproduction or forced pregnancy termination equally involve third-party interference in personal autonomy. True concern for others supports individual bodily sovereignty, not undermines it. You can't protect life by enslaving bodies.

This connects to principles like "self-determination is a universal human right" and "no one else may control your bodily functions." Together, they establish comprehensive bodily autonomy as the foundation of freedom.

For today's leaders, this demands recognizing reproductive choice as foundational rather than peripheral to human rights. Bodily sovereignty constitutes the prerequisite for all other meaningful freedoms. Without control over your own body, no other rights matter.

FOR FURTHER READING

John Locke's theory of self-ownership

Locke, John (1689). Two Treatises of Government. London: Awnsham Churchill.

Immanuel Kant's concept of human dignity as self-determination

Kant, Immanuel (1785). Groundwork of the Metaphysics of Morals. Translated by Mary Gregor. Cambridge: Cambridge University Press, 1997.

Those who bear pregnancy's burden **hold its authority**.*

Since only women bear the physical burden and risk of pregnancy, only they possess unique authority over reproductive decisions. Those who don't bear the burden cannot claim the authority.

This statement establishes that unique burdens create unique authorities. Since women alone bear the physical, emotional, and life-threatening risks of pregnancy, they alone possess the corresponding decision-making authority. It's like saying the person who carries the heavy load gets to decide how fast to walk. When others try to control pregnancy decisions without bearing pregnancy risks, it violates basic justice by separating authority from responsibility. True ethical decision-making aligns power with consequences.

* *Timeless Principle: Authority rightfully belongs to those who bear the burden.*

Ethical traditions teach that burden-bearing establishes legitimate authority. Military commanders who share battlefield risks with troops earn moral authority that distant politicians lack. Parents who sacrifice for children gain parental authority through demonstrated commitment. These examples show how authentic authority comes from shared stakes, not external imposition.

Today, pregnancy involves unique burdens that can't be equally shared. Women face risks of death, permanent disability, career disruption, economic hardship, and profound life changes that partners, while affected, don't directly experience. Morning sickness, labor pain, bodily transformation, potential complications—these aren't equally distributed. This asymmetry creates corresponding asymmetry in decision-making authority.

The philosophy recognizes that those bearing consequences of actions should have primary authority over those actions. When others control decisions whose burdens they don't share, it violates the fundamental relationship between responsibility and authority that makes governance just. It's like letting someone else decide if you'll climb a dangerous mountain while they stay safely at home.

Practically, this means legal frameworks recognizing women's ultimate authority in reproductive decisions, healthcare systems prioritizing pregnant women's autonomy over family or partner preferences, and social norms respecting rather than overriding women's reproductive choices. Some cite male genetic contribution or emotional investment. But these factors, while significant, don't create equivalent physical burdens or life risks. Emotional stakes don't equal decision-making authority when physical burdens remain unequal. Both parents may care about a child, but only one risks death in childbirth.

This connects to principles like "control over one's body is the foundation of autonomy" and "actual persons take precedence over potential ones." Together, they establish that pregnancy burden creates unique authority.

For today's leaders, this demands recognizing that reproductive decision-making authority corresponds to pregnancy burden-bearing. Authentic justice requires alignment between those who face consequences and those who make choices. You can't separate power from responsibility without creating injustice.

Without consciousness, **personhood is not established**.

Without developed consciousness, full life status is not established. Early pregnancy involves potential life, not actual personhood, making termination different from ending conscious life. However, this consciousness-based view of personhood is contested. Many people hold deeply sincere beliefs that human life begins at conception, grounded in religious teachings, philosophical reasoning, or intuitive conviction. For them, the presence of unique human DNA and developmental potential establishes personhood regardless of consciousness. Research shows that views on when life begins correlate strongly with religious and cultural backgrounds, suggesting multiple legitimate frameworks exist for understanding personhood.

This statement addresses when personhood begins by establishing consciousness as the essential criterion. It distinguishes between potential and actual life in early pregnancy. While embryonic and early fetal life has potential for personhood, it lacks the developed consciousness that makes someone an actual person. It's like the difference between an acorn and an oak tree—one has potential, the other is actualized. This distinction is crucial for understanding why early pregnancy termination differs qualitatively from ending established conscious life. Yet studies reveal that 38% of Americans believe human life begins at conception, viewing the embryo as possessing inherent dignity and rights from fertilization. Many report experiencing profound grief after early miscarriage, suggesting their lived experience treats early pregnancy as meaningful human life. These perspectives challenge purely consciousness-based definitions of personhood.

Since time immemorial, philosophers and religions have grappled with when meaningful life begins. Ancient Greek philosophy emphasized consciousness and rationality as defining human characteristics. Medieval scholars debated when the soul entered the body. Buddhist thought traditionally focuses on consciousness as the essential life principle. Even some Christian traditions historically distinguished between formed and unformed fetal life, not treating early miscarriage the same as infant death. However, other religious traditions, particularly within Catholicism and many Protestant denominations, teach that ensoulment occurs at conception, making the embryo a full human person deserving protection.[6] Islamic jurisprudence offers varied views, with some scholars marking personhood at 40 days, others at 120 days.[7]

Modern neuroscience supports this consciousness-based approach. The neural structures necessary for awareness don't develop until well into pregnancy. The cerebral cortex required for conscious experience doesn't begin functioning until at least 20-24 weeks gestation. Many consciousness researchers argue meaningful awareness requires even later development. Before this, there's biological activity but not conscious experience. Yet critics argue that consciousness represents only one dimension of personhood. They point to humans in comas or with severe cognitive disabilities who lack consciousness but retain personhood.[8] Some philosophers argue for a substance view where humans possess inherent dignity by virtue of their nature, not their current capacities.[9]

The philosophy recognizes that consciousness constitutes the essential characteristic of persons. Without developed consciousness, biological life lacks the essential quality granting full moral status as a person. Potential consciousness differs fundamentally from actual consciousness in moral consideration. It's why we don't hold funerals for miscarriages the way we do for infant deaths—we intuitively recognize the difference. However, this claim is complicated by growing movements for miscarriage recognition and grief support. Many parents report experiencing their pregnancy loss as the death of their child, not merely potential life.[10] Some cultures and religions do conduct funeral rites for miscarried fetuses, challenging assumptions about universal intuitions.[11]

Practically, this means legal frameworks recognizing gradual development of personhood rather than assuming full personhood from conception, medical ethics considering consciousness development in treatment decisions, and public policies distinguishing between early pregnancy termination and later interventions. Some claim genetic uniqueness or biological development establishes personhood. But they must explain why these factors should override consciousness as the defining criterion. Biology provides necessary but not sufficient conditions for personhood. A brain-dead body has unique DNA and biological functions but isn't a person. Conversely, those holding conception-based views argue that consciousness-based criteria must explain why temporary absence of consciousness (sleep, coma) doesn't eliminate personhood, and why potential for consciousness in the fetus differs morally from potential recovery of consciousness in coma patients.[12]

This connects to principles like "actual persons take precedence over potential ones" and "inner knowledge supersedes external observation." Together, they establish consciousness as the personhood criterion. Yet this framework itself reflects particular philosophical assumptions that many reasonably reject. Surveys of women who have had abortions reveal diverse beliefs about fetal status—some viewing it as tissue, others as life but not yet a person, still others as a person whose life they ended for compelling reasons.[13]

For today's leaders, this demands recognizing that early pregnancy involves potential rather than actual personhood. Consciousness development creates graduated rather than absolute moral status during pregnancy. This isn't about devaluing life but about honestly assessing what makes someone a person. However, leaders must also acknowledge that sincere, thoughtful people disagree fundamentally about these assessments, and that lived experiences of pregnancy, loss, and decision-making reveal profound complexity in how people understand nascent human life.

FOR FURTHER READING

Aristotle's concept of consciousness and rationality as defining human characteristics

Aristotle (350 BCE). De Anima (On the Soul). Translated by Hugh Lawson-Tancred. London: Penguin Classics, 1986.

Survey research on American beliefs about when life begins

Pew Research Center (2022). America's Abortion Quandary: Majority of Americans say abortion should be legal in some cases, illegal in others.

Cross-cultural analysis of personhood concepts and religious influences

Morgan, Lynn M. (1989). When does life begin? A cross-cultural perspective on the personhood of fetuses and young children. Abortion Rights and Fetal Personhood, 97-114.

Polling data on beliefs about when human life begins

Gallup (2023). Abortion Trends and Attitudes in America. Gallup Historical Trends.

Qualitative research on experiences of early pregnancy loss

Layne, Linda L. (2003). Motherhood Lost: A Feminist Account of Pregnancy Loss in America. Routledge.

Catholic theological perspective on ensoulment and personhood

Congregation for the Doctrine of the Faith (1987). Donum Vitae: Instruction on Respect for Human Life.

Islamic jurisprudential views on ensoulment and fetal development

Atighetchi, Dariusch (2007). Islamic Bioethics: Problems and Perspectives. Springer.

Philosophical critique of consciousness-based personhood criteria

Lee, Patrick & George, Robert P. (2008). Body-Self Dualism in Contemporary Ethics and Politics. Cambridge University Press.

Substance view of human dignity and personhood

Kaczor, Christopher (2014). The Ethics of Abortion: Women's Rights, Human Life, and the Question of Justice. Routledge.

Anthropological study of miscarriage grief and recognition practices

Van der Sijpt, Erica (2018). The Pain and Pride of 'Repeat Pregnancy Loss' in Cameroon. Medical Anthropology Quarterly, 32(2), 241-259.

Cross-cultural funeral and memorial practices for pregnancy loss

Murphy, Fiona & Merrell, Jean (2009). Negotiating the transition: caring for women through the experience of early miscarriage. Journal of Clinical Nursing, 18(11), 1583-1591.

Arguments about potentiality and consciousness in bioethics debates

Beckwith, Francis J. (2007). Defending Life: A Moral and Legal Case Against Abortion Choice. Cambridge University Press.

Women's diverse beliefs about fetal status in abortion decisions

Foster, Diana Greene, et al. (2012). Attitudes and decision making among women seeking abortions at one U.S. clinic. Perspectives on Sexual and Reproductive Health, 44(2), 117-124.

Life-threatening pregnancies justify **emergency exceptions**.

The principle of emergency exceptions especially applies to life-threatening pregnancies. Preserving the mother's life takes precedence over potential life.

This statement establishes that life-threatening pregnancies are emergency situations requiring special ethical consideration. When continuing pregnancy threatens the mother's life, preserving her established life takes precedence over protecting potential life. It's like medical triage—you save the patient who can be saved rather than losing both. Absolute prohibition of pregnancy termination in these cases violates life-protection principles by requiring sacrifice of actual life for potential life. True respect for life means saving, not sacrificing, those whose lives are threatened.

Throughout history, medical ethics across cultures have recognized emergencies require exceptional responses. Ancient Greek medical ethics, medieval Islamic law, and traditional Catholic moral theology all acknowledged situations where saving the mother's life justified pregnancy termination. Even the most restrictive traditions typically included exceptions for maternal life preservation. They understood that rigid rules causing death violate the principles behind those rules.

Modern medicine reveals numerous conditions where pregnancy continuation threatens maternal life: ectopic pregnancy (where the embryo implants outside the uterus), severe preeclampsia, certain cardiac conditions, and pregnancy-related cancers needing immediate treatment. In these cases, delaying intervention to protect fetal life often results in losing both mother and fetus. Absolute restrictions become counterproductive to life-preservation goals.

The philosophy recognizes emergency modification principles—extreme circumstances require different ethical responses than normal conditions. When standard rules produce outcomes contradicting their underlying purposes (preserving life), emergency exceptions serve rather than violate fundamental principles. It's like speed limits—normally important for safety, but ambulances can exceed them to save lives.

Practically, this means medical protocols prioritizing maternal life preservation, legal frameworks guaranteeing emergency reproductive care, and healthcare systems ensuring immediate access to life-saving interventions regardless of abortion restrictions. Some claim all pregnancy termination constitutes killing. But forcing women to die in childbirth equally constitutes killing—of actual rather than potential persons. True pro-life positions preserve existing life, not sacrifice it. You can't protect life by mandating death.

This connects to principles like "actual persons take precedence over potential ones" and "society bears collective fault for preventable deaths." Together, they establish emergency intervention as necessity.

For today's leaders, this demands ensuring life-saving medical care remains available regardless of general abortion policies. Emergency situations require exceptional responses to preserve rather than sacrifice human life. When the choice is saving one life or losing two, the moral answer is clear.

Fertilized eggs **lack the characteristics of persons.**

A fertilized egg lacks the characteristics of personhood — consciousness, form, viability. Potential is not actuality in this metaphysics. However, many people sincerely believe that fertilized eggs are human beings deserving full moral status, pointing to unique human DNA, self-directed development, and continuity of identity from conception through adulthood. For them, the absence of current capacities doesn't diminish inherent human dignity, just as it doesn't for newborns or people with severe disabilities.

|| ॐ ||

This statement establishes that fertilized eggs lack the essential characteristics that make someone a person—consciousness, developed form, and ability to exist independently. It distinguishes between biological life and personal existence. The key insight is that potential personhood differs fundamentally from actual personhood. It's like saying a blueprint isn't a house—having the plans doesn't mean you have a place to live. This makes early pregnancy termination qualitatively different from ending established personal life. Yet for those who view fertilization as the beginning of human life, this analogy misrepresents the reality—they see the embryo not as a blueprint but as a human being in its earliest stage of development, like an infant is a human in an early stage, not a potential human. Research shows that healthcare workers who view embryos as persons experience moral distress when involved in procedures affecting embryonic life.

Philosophical inquiry reveals that philosophers have distinguished between different stages of life development. Ancient Greek thought emphasized form and function in determining what something actually is. Medieval philosophy distinguished between vegetative life (like plants), animal life, and rational human life, seeing these as progressive developments. Even traditional Jewish law historically recognized different pregnancy stages with different ethical implications—they didn't treat early miscarriage the same as losing a born child. However, other philosophical traditions argue for substantial continuity of identity—that the same individual exists from fertilization through natural death, merely at different developmental stages.[5] Some point to the immediate genetic completeness and self-directed development beginning at fertilization as evidence of individual human existence.[6]

Modern embryology confirms this gradual development. Fertilized eggs lack nervous systems, organs, consciousness, and capacity for independent existence. The embryonic stage involves cellular division and basic differentiation but not the integrated systems necessary for personhood. A microscopic cluster of cells doesn't think, feel, or exist as an independent being. Scientific understanding supports rather than contradicts philosophical distinctions between potential and actual persons. Yet embryologists also document the remarkable continuity and self-direction of human development from fertilization onward. The embryo actively directs its own development, exhibiting what some scientists describe as organismal behavior from the earliest stages.[7] This biological evidence is interpreted differently—some see mere cellular processes, others see the earliest manifestation of human life.[8]

The philosophy distinguishes between potential and actual existence. While fertilized eggs possess potential for developing into persons, they lack the actualized characteristics—consciousness, integrated form, and independent existence—that constitute complete personhood. Conflating potential with actual violates logical categories. An acorn isn't an oak tree, even though it might become one. Critics of this view argue the acorn analogy is flawed—an acorn that naturally develops will become an oak unless prevented, but more importantly, humans develop through stages while maintaining identity. A toddler lacks many adult capacities but remains the same individual who will later possess them.[9] Studies of parents experiencing IVF show complex attitudes—some view unused embryos as potential children deserving respect, others as cellular material, still others struggle with uncertainty.[10]

Practically, this means embryo research policies recognizing gradual development of moral status, contraception access preventing fertilization without moral controversy, and early pregnancy care prioritizing women's health without assuming full personhood conflicts. Some claim genetic uniqueness establishes personhood. But they must explain why DNA should determine moral status rather than consciousness, development, or viability. Every cancer cell has unique DNA too—that doesn't make it a person. Genetic potential provides necessary but not sufficient conditions for full moral consideration. Those holding fertilization-based views respond that the embryo, unlike cancer cells, is a complete, self-integrating organism of the human species, not merely human tissue.[11] They argue their position isn't about controlling women but protecting what they genuinely perceive as the most vulnerable members of the human family.[12] Women in the pro-life movement report that their advocacy stems from beliefs about protecting life rather than restricting women's autonomy.[13]

This connects to principles like "without consciousness, personhood is not established" and "full personhood rights begin at birth." Together, they establish graduated development rather than instant personhood. Yet surveys reveal that beliefs about embryonic status don't follow simple patterns—many people hold intermediate positions, viewing early embryos as deserving some moral consideration without full personhood status.[14]

For today's leaders, this demands recognizing that early pregnancy involves potential rather than actual personhood. Ethical evaluation must acknowledge developmental realities rather than imposing artificial absolutes that ignore biological facts. However, leaders must also recognize that sincere, thoughtful people interpret these biological facts through different philosophical and religious lenses, leading to fundamentally different conclusions about the moral status of embryonic life.

FOR FURTHER READING

Philosophical argument for embryonic personhood based on substantial identity

George, Robert P. & Tollefsen, Christopher (2008). Embryo: A Defense of Human Life. Doubleday.

Analysis of inherent dignity arguments in bioethics

Kittay, Eva Feder (2005). At the Margins of Moral Personhood. Ethics, 116(1), 100-131.

Perspectives on continuous human identity from conception

Condic, Maureen L. (2014). Totipotency: What it is and what it is not. Stem Cells and Development, 23(8), 796-812.

Healthcare worker experiences with embryo-related procedures

Ehrich, K., et al. (2010). Embryo futures and stem cell research: The management of informed uncertainty. Sociology of Health & Illness, 32(1), 1-17.

Thomistic philosophy on continuous human identity

Oderberg, David S. (2008). Applied Ethics: A Non-Consequentialist Approach. Blackwell.

Scientific argument for organismal behavior from fertilization

Condic, Maureen L. (2008). When does human life begin? A scientific perspective. Westchester Institute White Paper, 1(1), 1-18.

Embryological perspectives on early human development

Gilbert, Scott F. (2017). When 'personhood' begins in the embryo: Avoiding a syllabus of errors. Birth Defects Research, 109(8), 553-562.

Varied scientific interpretations of embryonic development

Hurlbut, William B. (2017). Biology and Being: The Emerging Science of Human Nature. Notre Dame Press.

Critique of potentiality arguments and defense of developmental view

Marquis, Don (1989). Why abortion is immoral. Journal of Philosophy, 86(4), 183-202.

IVF patients' complex attitudes toward embryo status

Provoost, V., et al. (2009). Infertility patients' beliefs about their embryos and their disposition preferences. Human Reproduction, 24(4), 896-905.

Organismic view of embryonic life versus tissue view

Austriaco, Nicanor (2002). On Static Eggs and Dynamic Embryos. National Catholic Bioethics Quarterly, 2(4), 659-683.

Pro-life perspectives on protecting vulnerable life

Camosy, Charles (2015). Beyond the Abortion Wars: A Way Forward for a New Generation. Eerdmans.

Women's motivations in pro-life advocacy

Munson, Ziad (2009). The Making of Pro-life Activists: How Social Movement Mobilization Works. University of Chicago Press.

Public opinion research on graduated views of embryonic status

Evans, John H. & Hudson, Kathy (2007). Religion and reproductive genetics: Beyond views of embryonic life? Journal for the Scientific Study of Religion, 46(4), 565-581.

No one else may control your bodily functions.*

Others controlling one's bodily functions violates fundamental autonomy. Forced pregnancy or forced abortion equally violate this principle of self-determination over one's own body.

This statement establishes absolute sovereignty over bodily functions as a fundamental human right. It says that external control of reproductive processes violates essential autonomy, regardless of who's trying to control you or why. Both forced pregnancy and forced abortion violate bodily sovereignty equally. It's like saying no one else can force you to donate organs, even to save lives—your body, your choice. True respect for human dignity means recognizing individual authority over physical existence, not overriding it.

* *Timeless Principle: The body as the first property establishes all other property rights—no authority can justly override bodily self-ownership.*

For ages, philosophers have emphasized self-ownership and bodily integrity. Classical liberal theory from John Locke forward recognized the body as the first property—you own yourself before you own anything else.[1] Various human rights frameworks acknowledge bodily autonomy as foundational. Legal systems that let others control reproductive functions violate human dignity, regardless of their justifications.

Today, we see how reproductive control extends beyond individual pregnancy decisions to comprehensive bodily sovereignty. Forced sterilization programs targeting ethnic minorities or disabled individuals violate this principle just as much as forced pregnancy continuation. China's one-child policy showed how state control over reproduction violates fundamental human rights regardless of population concerns. Whether forcing pregnancy or preventing it, external control over bodies is wrong.

The philosophy recognizes that the self has inherent authority over its own body. When external authorities override individual control of bodily functions, they deny personhood by treating conscious beings as objects rather than subjects. It's the difference between being a person and being property. Bodily sovereignty becomes prerequisite for all other rights—without it, you have no real freedom.

Practically, this means legal frameworks recognizing reproductive autonomy as fundamental right, healthcare systems prioritizing patient consent in all reproductive decisions, and international human rights standards prohibiting forced reproductive interventions regardless of justifications. Some claim fetal rights or social interests override bodily autonomy. But they must address how forced physical use of women's bodies violates basic principles of human dignity and consent that underpin all legitimate authority. You can't protect rights by violating the most fundamental right of all.

This connects to principles like "control over one's body is the foundation of autonomy" and "self-determination is a universal human right." Together, they establish comprehensive bodily sovereignty.

For today's leaders, this demands recognizing that reproductive decisions remain within individual rather than collective authority. Bodily sovereignty constitutes the foundation rather than obstacle to human rights. No one—not partners, not families, not governments—can justly control another person's bodily functions.

FOR FURTHER READING

John Locke's classical liberal theory recognizing the body as first property

Locke, John (1689). Two Treatises of Government. London: Awnsham Churchill.

Ending one's own suffering is **legitimate self-care**.

Ending one's own suffering constitutes legitimate virtue. Women experiencing unwanted pregnancy suffer physically and mentally; alleviating this suffering is righteous action.

This statement establishes that alleviating your own suffering is inherently virtuous. It recognizes that unwanted pregnancy creates legitimate suffering—physical, emotional, economic—that justifies seeking relief. However, this framing confronts profound moral complexity: many genuinely believe abortion involves ending human life, not just alleviating suffering. The conflict between relieving women's suffering and protecting what many see as innocent life creates genuine moral anguish that transcends simple categorization as self-care.

Throughout history, medical traditions have recognized suffering relief as a primary goal. Ancient Greek medical ethics prioritized patient welfare. Buddhist medicine emphasized ending suffering as central to healing. The principle that reducing suffering constitutes virtuous action appears consistently across ethical systems. Today we understand how unwanted pregnancy creates multidimensional suffering: physical discomfort, emotional distress, economic hardship, social stigma, and life disruption.

Yet the lived experience around abortion involves profound moral complexity rarely captured by simple frameworks. Many people—including those who ultimately choose abortion—experience deep moral conflict because they genuinely believe or fear that abortion ends a human life. This isn't just religious indoctrination but often comes from intuitive responses to ultrasound images, fetal development knowledge, or philosophical beliefs about when morally significant life begins.

Women facing unwanted pregnancies often navigate competing moral considerations. They may simultaneously experience their pregnancy as a source of suffering AND feel moral weight about ending it. Studies show many women who have abortions report mixed emotions—relief alongside sadness, certainty alongside moral questioning.[1] The phrase "self-care" may not capture this complexity for those who feel they're making the least bad choice among difficult options.

For those who believe life begins at conception, opposing abortion isn't about controlling women or dismissing their suffering—it's about what they genuinely see as preventing killing. They often acknowledge women's suffering while believing that ending another life isn't morally acceptable suffering relief. They might point to other contexts where we don't accept ending life to relieve suffering—we don't generally support killing born children with severe disabilities to end parental suffering, for instance.

Different ethical frameworks weigh these considerations differently. Utilitarian approaches might calculate overall suffering reduction. Deontological ethics might focus on duties and rights. Virtue ethics might ask what a compassionate person would do. Religious frameworks often emphasize the sanctity of life.[2] These aren't simply right vs. wrong perspectives but different ways of navigating genuine moral complexity.

The philosophy recognizes that righteous action serves welfare. But here we face competing welfare concerns: the pregnant woman's immediate suffering vs. what many see as the fetus's right to life. Even those who prioritize women's autonomy often acknowledge this isn't simple "healthcare" like removing a tumor—there's something morally significant about ending potential human life, even if they ultimately support that choice.[3]

Practically, this suggests need for nuanced approaches: acknowledging the real suffering of unwanted pregnancy while respecting moral complexity; providing compassionate support for women regardless of their choice; recognizing that women choosing abortion may need space to process complex emotions, not just celebration of "self-care"; and understanding that those opposing abortion on life grounds aren't necessarily dismissing women's suffering.

Some argue that calling abortion "self-care" appropriately normalizes it and reduces stigma. Others feel this language minimizes the moral weight many women themselves feel about their decisions. The reality is that different women experience abortion differently—for some it may feel like straightforward self-care, for others like a tragic necessity, for still others like a complex moral compromise.[4]

The deeper challenge involves how we talk about abortion in ways that neither minimize women's suffering nor dismiss genuine beliefs about fetal life. Can we acknowledge that unwanted pregnancy causes real suffering deserving relief while also acknowledging that many people—including many women who have abortions—experience moral weight about ending potential life?

This connects to principles about bodily autonomy and compassion while also intersecting with principles about life preservation and moral complexity. The tension between these principles reflects genuine ethical difficulty, not simple misogyny versus feminism.

For today's leaders, this demands creating space for moral complexity while still ensuring access to abortion for those who need it. It means acknowledging that women's suffering is real and deserves relief while also acknowledging that many people—including women having abortions—experience this as more morally complex than routine self-care. Most importantly, it means recognizing that behind every abortion decision is often a woman navigating profound moral complexity, not simply accessing healthcare, and she deserves support for that full experience.

FOR FURTHER READING

Research on emotional complexity following abortion

Rocca, Corinne H., et al. (2020). Emotions and decision rightness over five years following an abortion: An examination of decision difficulty and abortion stigma. Social Science & Medicine, 248, 112704.

Philosophical frameworks for approaching abortion ethics

Hursthouse, Rosalind (1991). Virtue Theory and Abortion. Philosophy & Public Affairs, 20(3), 223-246.

Research on moral perspectives and abortion

Foster, Diana Greene (2020). The Turnaway Study: Ten Years, a Thousand Women, and the Consequences of Having—or Being Denied—an Abortion. New York: Scribner.

Study on diverse women's experiences of abortion

Kimport, Katrina, et al. (2012). Social Sources of Women's Emotional Difficulty After Abortion: Lessons from Women's Abortion Narratives. Perspectives on Sexual and Reproductive Health, 44(2), 103-109.

Forced pregnancy from rape **extends the violence**.

Forced continuation of unwanted pregnancy, especially from rape or incest, perpetuates the original violence. Denying abortion in such cases extends rather than prevents harm.

|| ॐ ||

This statement establishes that forcing rape victims to continue pregnancies constitutes continuation of the violence, not prevention of it. It reveals how reproductive restrictions perpetuate sexual assault rather than address it. Requiring women to bear their rapists' children extends the violation of bodily autonomy and adds institutional trauma to personal trauma. It's like forcing someone to wear their attacker's chains permanently. True protection of victims means ending their suffering, not prolonging it through forced pregnancy.

Throughout history, societies that denied abortion access to rape victims showed how institutional policies compound individual trauma. Medieval legal systems requiring rape victims to marry their attackers exemplified how supposedly protective measures actually extended victimization. These weren't protections—they were additional punishments for victims. Today's examples reveal how pregnancy from assault creates ongoing psychological trauma that forced continuation significantly amplifies.

Modern understanding of trauma shows how pregnancy from rape creates complex psychological injury: loss of control, body violation, and forced connection to the assault. Studies prove that rape victims who can't access abortion experience higher rates of depression, anxiety, and PTSD. Forcing pregnancy continuation demonstrably increases suffering rather than decreases it. The pregnancy becomes a daily reminder of the violence.

The philosophy recognizes that actions producing harmful results contradict their stated protective purposes. When policies claiming to protect life actually increase suffering and trauma, they violate their fundamental goals. It's like claiming to help someone while actively harming them. True protection requires alleviating victim suffering, not extending it.

Practically, this means legal frameworks guaranteeing abortion access for sexual assault victims, healthcare systems prioritizing victim welfare over abstract principles, and social policies focusing on survivor healing rather than forced pregnancy continuation. Some claim pregnancy termination constitutes additional violence. But they must address how forced pregnancy demonstrably creates greater trauma than abortion access. Ask rape survivors—they'll tell you which causes more suffering. Victim welfare rather than theoretical concerns should determine appropriate responses.

This connects to principles like "ending one's own suffering is legitimate self-care" and "rape victims have no duty to accept its consequences." Together, they establish trauma prevention as moral imperative.

For today's leaders, this demands recognizing that reproductive restrictions can extend rather than prevent violence. True victim protection requires supporting survivor choices about pregnancy continuation, not overriding them. When we force rape victims to bear their attackers' children, we become complicit in the violence.

Personal virtue choices **supersede state authority**.

The state lacks authority to dictate individual ethical choices. Personal reproductive decisions fall under individual, not collective, virtue determination. However, for those who believe abortion involves ending another human life, this framing fundamentally mischaracterizes the issue. They argue it's not merely a personal ethical choice but involves duties to protect vulnerable others, similar to laws against assault or neglect. Research shows that abortion opponents primarily frame their position around protecting fetal life rather than controlling women's choices.

|| ॐ ||

This statement establishes clear limits on governmental authority over personal moral decisions. It says reproductive choices fall within individual rather than state jurisdiction for determining what's virtuous. It's like saying the government can't dictate your religious beliefs—some moral decisions are simply beyond state authority. When governments control personal reproductive decisions, they violate the proper relationship between collective authority and individual conscience. True governance serves personal moral agency rather than replacing it. Yet those who view the fetus as a person argue this analogy fails—they contend that just as religious freedom doesn't permit human sacrifice, personal autonomy doesn't extend to harming what they perceive as another human being. Legal scholars debate whether pregnancy involves one entity making autonomous choices or two entities whose interests must be balanced.

Classical thought demonstrates that the most oppressive regimes have sought control over reproductive functions for population control and social engineering. Nazi reproductive policies forced some to breed while sterilizing others. Soviet family planning mandates controlled when and how many children people could have. Today's authoritarian restrictions on childbearing show how reproductive control serves totalitarian, not legitimate governmental purposes. Democratic traditions typically recognize reproductive decisions as personal, not political. However, critics note that democratic societies routinely legislate to protect vulnerable populations, including laws requiring parents to provide for their children, prohibiting neglect, and mandating medical care in certain circumstances.[5] They argue that if the fetus is a person, protecting it falls within legitimate governmental authority, not totalitarian overreach.[6]

Modern constitutional theory in many democracies recognizes reproductive autonomy as within zones of privacy limiting governmental authority. The principle that personal decisions affecting primarily yourself fall outside legitimate state control appears in various legal traditions emphasizing individual liberty against governmental overreach. Your body isn't state property. Yet competing constitutional theories argue that when another life is involved, the state has legitimate interests. Some legal scholars contend that pregnancy inherently involves relational rather than purely individual considerations.[7] International human rights documents reveal tensions—some emphasize reproductive autonomy while others assert rights beginning at conception.[8]

The philosophy recognizes that moral decisions require individual rather than external authority. Since reproductive choices primarily affect the decision-maker and involve personal moral evaluation, external authorities lack both the knowledge and authority necessary for valid judgment. It's like the government deciding what career you should pursue—they lack the intimate knowledge of your life needed for such decisions. Those who oppose abortion rights respond that this misunderstands their position—they argue the state regularly intervenes to protect those who cannot protect themselves, from child abuse laws to elder care regulations.[9] They contend that if the fetus is a person, the state's role isn't imposing virtue but preventing harm, similar to laws against domestic violence that override family privacy.[10]

Practically, this means constitutional frameworks limiting governmental authority over reproductive decisions, legal principles requiring compelling state interests to override reproductive autonomy, and political philosophies distinguishing between legitimate collective concerns and improper governmental overreach. Some claim reproductive decisions affect society. But they must demonstrate compelling collective interests justifying overriding individual autonomy. General social preferences don't constitute adequate justification for controlling personal reproductive choices. The government's opinion about your family planning doesn't override your own moral judgment. However, those viewing abortion as involving another life argue the compelling interest is protecting human beings from being killed.[11] Studies of abortion opponents reveal they often support social programs for mothers and children, suggesting their motivation extends beyond controlling women to what they perceive as protecting life.[12]

This connects to principles like "individual conscience governs personal moral choices" and "self-determination is a universal human right." Together, they establish governmental limits on controlling personal decisions. Yet surveys reveal that even among those supporting abortion rights, many acknowledge moral complexity when potential life is involved—with majorities supporting some restrictions based on gestational age, suggesting recognition that purely individualistic frameworks may not capture the full ethical dimensions.[13]

For today's leaders, this demands recognizing reproductive decisions as falling within personal rather than governmental authority. Democratic governance requires respecting individual moral agency, not controlling it. The state that dictates personal virtue choices has exceeded its legitimate authority. However, leaders must grapple with the sincere convictions of citizens who view this not as personal virtue regulation but as basic protection of human life, similar to other laws protecting vulnerable populations. The challenge lies in governing societies with fundamentally incompatible views about what pregnancy involves and what justice requires.

FOR FURTHER READING

Analysis of pro-life framing around protecting life versus controlling women

Luker, Kristin (1984). Abortion and the Politics of Motherhood. University of California Press.

Survey research on abortion opponents' primary motivations

Jelen, Ted G. & Wilcox, Clyde (2003). Causes and consequences of public attitudes toward abortion. Annual Review of Political Science, 6, 489-518.

Legal argument about limits of autonomy when others are affected

Finnis, John (1973). The rights and wrongs of abortion. Philosophy & Public Affairs, 2(2), 117-145.

Comparative analysis of state duties regarding fetal versus born life

Glendon, Mary Ann (1987). Abortion and Divorce in Western Law. Harvard University Press.

Democratic theory and protection of vulnerable populations

Arkes, Hadley (1986). First Things: An Inquiry into the First Principles of Morals and Justice. Princeton University Press.

Arguments for legitimate state interest in potential life

Rubenfeld, Jed (1989). The Right of Privacy. Harvard Law Review, 102(4), 737-807.

Relational autonomy theory in reproductive ethics

Mackenzie, Catriona & Stoljar, Natalie (2000). Relational Autonomy: Feminist Perspectives on Autonomy, Agency, and the Social Self. Oxford University Press.

Analysis of competing human rights frameworks on abortion

Zampas, Christina & Gher, Jaime M. (2008). Abortion as a human right. Human Rights Law Review, 8(2), 249-294.

State intervention to protect vulnerable populations

Callahan, Daniel & Callahan, Sidney (1984). Abortion: Understanding Differences. Plenum Press.

Comparison of abortion restrictions to other protective laws

Beckwith, Francis J. (1993). Politically Correct Death: Answering Arguments for Abortion Rights. Baker Books.

Arguments about state interest in protecting human life

Tollefsen, Christopher (2008). Biomedical Research and Beyond: Expanding the Ethics of Inquiry. Routledge.

Research on pro-life support for social welfare programs

Shields, Jon A. (2009). The Democratic Virtues of the Christian Right. Princeton University Press.

Public opinion on abortion restrictions and moral complexity

Saad, Lydia (2023). Broader Support for Abortion Rights Continues Post-Dobbs. Gallup Poll Social Series.

Biological contribution **doesn't create control rights**.

Male reproductive intention alone doesn't create fatherhood-related rights over women's bodies. Fatherhood begins with birth and acceptance of responsibility, not with conception.

This statement establishes that biological contribution to conception doesn't create authority over pregnancy decisions. It distinguishes between genetic participation and actual parental responsibility that begins with birth and voluntary commitment. Sperm contribution alone doesn't grant control rights over women's bodies during pregnancy, just as egg donation doesn't grant women control over surrogate mothers. It's like saying that donating building materials doesn't give you ownership of the house. True fatherhood emerges through commitment and responsibility, not mere biological participation.

Throughout history, legal systems granting men authority over pregnancy decisions based solely on genetic contribution violated women's bodily autonomy while failing to establish meaningful paternal responsibility. Traditional patriarchal systems often claimed male reproductive authority without corresponding obligations. This revealed how control-focused rather than responsibility-focused approaches to fatherhood serve neither children nor families.

Today we understand that meaningful fatherhood involves ongoing emotional, financial, and practical commitment beginning after birth, not at conception. Men who oppose abortion but abandon resulting children demonstrate how genetic contribution alone doesn't establish authentic parental commitment. True father-child relationships develop through sustained engagement, not biological connection. Being a father is about showing up, not just showing up once.

The philosophy recognizes that authority must correspond to responsibility and consequences. Since men don't bear pregnancy's physical burdens or risks, they lack corresponding decision-making authority. Biological participation creates potential rather than actual paternal responsibility until voluntary commitment occurs. You can't claim control without accepting consequences.

Practically, this means legal frameworks recognizing women's pregnancy autonomy while establishing paternal responsibility after birth, social norms emphasizing commitment over control in fatherhood concepts, and support systems encouraging rather than mandating male involvement in reproductive decisions. Some claim genetic contribution establishes equal parental rights. But they must address how pregnancy involves unequal physical investment creating corresponding decision-making asymmetry. Equal ultimate parental rights don't require equal pregnancy authority. Both parents may love a born child equally, but only one risks death bringing it to birth.

This connects to principles like "those who bear pregnancy's burden hold its authority" and "marriage means partnership, not ownership." Together, they establish reproductive decision authority based on burden-bearing.

For today's leaders, this demands recognizing that biological contribution alone doesn't create control rights. Authentic fatherhood emerges through commitment rather than reproductive authority. Real fathers support mothers' choices rather than trying to control them.

Moral duties vary with developmental stages.

Moral duties regarding potential life vary with developmental stage. What applies to viable fetuses doesn't apply to embryos—temporal distinctions matter ethically.

This nuanced teaching acknowledges that abortion ethics change with fetal development. It establishes that moral obligations vary according to developmental stages rather than remaining static throughout pregnancy. Early pregnancy involves fundamentally different ethical considerations than late pregnancy. It's like how we have different rules for toddlers than teenagers—development matters. This framework allows for graduated moral assessment rather than black-and-white judgments about pregnancy termination.

Across traditions, most moral traditions have recognized developmental distinctions in reproductive ethics. Ancient Jewish law established ensoulment at quickening (felt movement), typically around 18-20 weeks. Medieval Christian theology debated when the soul entered the body. Islamic jurisprudence traditionally allowed early pregnancy termination before 120 days, recognizing different developmental stages. Even secular bioethics acknowledges viability, consciousness, and sentience as meaningful milestones affecting moral status.

Modern understanding confirms that fetal development involves gradual acquisition of personhood characteristics—neural development, consciousness capacity, viability outside the womb, and pain sensitivity. Early embryonic stages lack nervous systems, consciousness, or capacity for independent existence. Later stages progressively develop these characteristics. This biological reality supports ethical frameworks recognizing graduated moral status rather than absolute positions.

The philosophy recognizes that different situations require different moral applications. Just as ritual obligations vary with circumstances and capacity, reproductive ethics must acknowledge developmental realities. What's appropriate regarding an eight-week embryo differs from decisions about a thirty-week fetus because they possess fundamentally different characteristics. It's not hypocrisy—it's nuance.

Practically, this means legal frameworks allowing early abortion while restricting late-term procedures except for serious medical reasons, medical guidelines adjusting procedures based on gestational age, and counseling approaches acknowledging the emotional complexity of decisions at different developmental stages. Some claim moral status begins at conception. But they must address how identical obligations can apply to vastly different developmental stages. A microscopic fertilized egg and a viable fetus aren't the same thing morally any more than they are physically. If moral duties vary with capacity and circumstances, then reproductive ethics must acknowledge developmental distinctions.

This connects to principles like "without consciousness, personhood is not established" and "full personhood rights begin at birth." Together, they establish developmental gradualism rather than absolutism.

For today's leaders, this demands nuanced approaches to reproductive ethics acknowledging developmental realities rather than imposing absolute positions. Moral complexity requires sophisticated rather than simplistic responses. One size doesn't fit all trimesters.

FOR FURTHER READING

Thomas Aquinas's theory of delayed ensoulment distinguishing developmental stages

Aquinas, Thomas (1273). Summa Theologica. Translated by Fathers of the English Dominican Province. New York: Benziger Brothers, 1947.

Full personhood rights **begin at birth**.

Full rights of living beings commence after birth when independent existence begins. Pre-birth existence remains dependent and potential, not independently rights-bearing.

|| ॐ ||

This statement establishes birth as the decisive threshold for full personhood rights. It says independent existence constitutes the meaningful criterion for complete legal and moral status. The principle distinguishes between dependent potential life during pregnancy and independent actual life after birth. It's like the difference between being a passenger on a plane and being the pilot—dependency matters. This creates a clear philosophical foundation for reproductive rights while acknowledging genuine development toward personhood.

Legal philosophy shows that birth has served as the universal legal threshold for personhood across cultures. Roman law established birth as the beginning of legal personality, requiring a child be "born alive" to possess rights. English common law's "born alive" rule became foundational to American law. Even religious traditions valuing prenatal life typically distinguish between pre-birth and post-birth moral status—baptism, naming ceremonies, and mourning practices generally occur after birth, reflecting implicit recognition of birth's significance.

Modern understanding supports birth as a meaningful biological and social threshold. Birth involves fundamental physiological transitions—independent breathing, circulation, and metabolic function—constituting genuine independence from maternal life support. Legally, birth certificates, citizenship, inheritance rights, and social security all begin at birth. Medical care shifts from maternal-fetal medicine to pediatrics at birth, acknowledging emergence of an independent patient needing separate medical advocacy.

The philosophy recognizes that rights correspond to independent existence and capacity for autonomous action. Before birth, fetal existence depends entirely on maternal bodily systems, making true independence impossible. Birth establishes the physical independence necessary for separate rights claims while acknowledging the gradual development that pregnancy represents. You can't have independent rights without independent existence.

Practically, this means legal frameworks protecting pregnancy while maintaining women's decision-making authority until birth, medical protocols balancing fetal welfare with maternal autonomy, and social policies supporting both pregnant women and children after birth without conflating their separate interests. Some claim birth is an arbitrary line. But they must address why physical independence doesn't constitute a meaningful threshold for rights. If dependence doesn't affect rights status, then all dependency relationships would require similar rights modifications. We don't grant power of attorney to everyone caring for dependent adults.

This connects to principles like "those who bear pregnancy's burden hold its authority" and "actual persons take precedence over potential ones." Together, they establish birth as the clear demarcation for full personhood.

For today's leaders, this demands legal frameworks acknowledging birth as the threshold for independent rights while protecting the developmental process leading there. Clear boundaries enable rather than restrict appropriate moral consideration.

FOR FURTHER READING

English common law's 'born alive' rule as legal foundation

Blackstone, William (1765-1769). Commentaries on the Laws of England. Oxford: Clarendon Press.

Fetal welfare **depends entirely on maternal welfare**.

Fetal welfare depends entirely on maternal welfare. Harming pregnant women through restrictive laws undermines the stated goal of protecting potential life.

|| ॐ ||

This pragmatic teaching exposes a fundamental contradiction: policies claiming to protect fetal life while undermining maternal health defeat their own purpose. It recognizes the biological reality that fetal development depends entirely on maternal health. It's like trying to save a plant by poisoning the soil—you can't help one while harming what sustains it. This creates irrefutable logic: policies genuinely concerned with fetal welfare must prioritize maternal welfare.

Throughout history, societies providing comprehensive maternal healthcare, nutrition support, and social services achieved better fetal outcomes than those focused on restrictive laws. Countries with legal abortion access plus strong maternal healthcare consistently show lower infant mortality than nations with abortion bans but inadequate healthcare. The United States, despite restrictive abortion laws in many states, has higher maternal and infant mortality rates than European nations with legal abortion and comprehensive healthcare.

Current research overwhelmingly shows that maternal stress, poverty, malnutrition, and inadequate healthcare directly impact fetal development and birth outcomes. Restrictive abortion laws create additional stress, delay prenatal care, and force women into dangerous situations—all harmful to fetal welfare. States with the most restrictive abortion laws often have the highest infant mortality rates, revealing the practical contradiction between restrictive policies and fetal welfare claims.

The philosophy recognizes that means must align with stated ends to be valid. If the genuine goal is fetal welfare, then policies must actually improve rather than worsen conditions for fetal development. Restrictive laws that increase maternal stress, delay healthcare, or force dangerous procedures contradict their stated protective purpose. You can't claim to protect life while creating conditions that harm it.

Practically, this means comprehensive prenatal healthcare, nutritional support programs, paid family leave, affordable childcare, and poverty reduction initiatives that actually support fetal development. Healthcare systems prioritizing maternal wellness achieve better fetal outcomes than punitive legal systems. Some claim restriction plus support would be ideal. But they must address why restriction remains necessary if comprehensive support eliminates factors driving abortion decisions. If maternal welfare truly determines fetal welfare, then supporting mothers becomes the logical priority.

This connects to principles like "control over one's body is the foundation of autonomy" and "true compassion respects autonomous decisions." Together, they establish maternal primacy in determining fetal outcomes.

For today's leaders, this demands policies that actually improve rather than worsen maternal conditions. Authentic pro-life positions must prioritize the life and welfare of the woman whose body sustains potential life. You can't separate fetal welfare from maternal welfare—they're one system.

Rape victims have **no duty** to accept its consequences.

No moral obligation exists to accept the results of sexual violence. Forcing rape victims to bear pregnancies compounds the original violation of consent and autonomy.

This statement establishes that rape victims bear no moral obligation to accept pregnancy resulting from sexual violence. It asserts that forced continuation of such pregnancies extends victimization rather than fulfills moral duty. The principle recognizes that consent violations can't create moral obligations for victims. It's like saying a robbery victim has no duty to let the thief keep what was stolen. Forced pregnancy from rape continues the original assault rather than being a separate moral issue.

Human societies have recognized that most legal and religious traditions have recognized rape as a fundamental violation creating no legitimate obligations for victims. Ancient Hebrew law protected rape victims and didn't require them to bear children from assault. Medieval European law, despite limiting women's rights, generally recognized rape as violence creating no paternal rights or maternal duties. Even restrictive religious traditions often included rape exceptions, acknowledging the moral distinction between consensual and violent conception.

Modern understanding confirms that forced pregnancy from rape creates additional trauma beyond the initial assault. Psychological research shows that carrying a rapist's pregnancy can trigger ongoing PTSD, prevent healing, and create lasting psychological damage. Medical evidence reveals that rape victims who can't access abortion experience higher rates of depression, anxiety, and suicide. Countries denying abortion to rape victims show increased maternal mortality and suicide among sexual assault survivors.

The philosophy recognizes that violence can't create valid moral obligations. Since rape violates consent and autonomy, it can't generate legitimate consequences that victims must accept. Forcing pregnancy continuation transfers violence's burden from perpetrator to victim, compounding the original injustice. You can't create moral duties through immoral acts.

Practically, this means legal frameworks providing immediate abortion access for rape victims, trauma-informed healthcare prioritizing victim autonomy, and judicial systems recognizing forced pregnancy as continued victimization rather than neutral consequence. Some claim "innocent babies shouldn't pay for rapists' crimes." But they must address why victims should pay instead. This statement reframes the issue entirely—ending forced pregnancy isn't punishing fetuses but stopping ongoing victimization. The victim didn't choose this situation and bears no moral duty to continue it.

This connects to principles like "forced pregnancy from rape extends the violence" and "no one else may control your bodily functions." Together, they establish rape exceptions as moral necessity.

For today's leaders, this demands immediate abortion access for sexual assault survivors. Justice requires ending rather than extending the consequences of violence. Forcing rape victims to bear their attackers' children is unconscionable cruelty disguised as morality.

True compassion **respects autonomous decisions**.

True compassion requires respecting women's autonomous decisions about their bodies and lives. Forced birth lacks compassion for the unwilling mother. However, lived experiences reveal complexity: some individuals report feeling empowered by autonomous choice while others describe feeling isolated by pure emphasis on individual decision-making without adequate support. Research shows that people facing reproductive decisions often simultaneously value their autonomy while seeking connection and guidance from trusted others.

|| ॐ ||

This statement reframes compassion by establishing that authentic care requires respecting rather than overriding autonomous decisions. It asserts that forced pregnancy lacks genuine concern for women's welfare and constitutes false compassion that prioritizes external moral positions over individual suffering. It's like forcing medicine on someone who knows it will harm them—that's not compassion, it's control. The principle distinguishes between sentimental compassion imposing predetermined outcomes and genuine compassion honoring the complexity of individual circumstances. Yet research also reveals that 60% of those making reproductive decisions experience simultaneous conflicting emotions, suggesting that compassionate support must acknowledge ambivalence rather than assuming straightforward autonomy. Some individuals from collectivist cultures report that family involvement in decision-making represents care rather than intrusion.

From ancient wisdom, authentic compassion has been distinguished from paternalistic control. Buddhist compassion emphasizes skillful means respecting individual wisdom rather than imposing external solutions. Christian charity at its best honors recipients' dignity and agency rather than treating them as objects of pity. Secular humanistic traditions emphasize empathy that seeks understanding rather than judging individual circumstances. True helpers recognize that outsiders can't fully comprehend others' complex situations.

Modern psychology confirms genuine support requires respecting individual autonomy. Trauma recovery research shows that restoring agency and choice promotes healing, while removing choice recreates traumatic powerlessness. Studies of complex moral decision-making demonstrate that individuals facing difficult circumstances possess insights unavailable to external observers. Forcing predetermined outcomes, regardless of good intentions, often increases suffering rather than decreases it. However, research also documents how structural barriers—poverty, lack of healthcare access, absence of family support—can constrain what choices are genuinely available, complicating ideals of pure autonomy.[6]

The philosophy recognizes that virtue must respect individual agency. Since autonomy constitutes fundamental human dignity, authentic compassion can't justify removing decision-making authority from those directly affected by consequences. True care seeks to support rather than replace individual judgment. It's the difference between holding someone's hand and tying their hands. Yet healthcare providers report complex realities: many describe providing compassionate care as offering comprehensive information while respecting that patients are experts on their own lives, while also navigating situations where patients face coercion or lack resources for genuine choice.[7]

Practically, this means counseling approaches providing information while respecting client decisions, support systems offering resources without imposing outcomes, and policies ensuring access to all options rather than limiting choices based on external moral judgments. Some claim certain decisions require external override. But they must explain why paternalistic control constitutes compassion rather than convenience for the controllers. If genuine concern exists, supporting rather than constraining choice becomes the compassionate response. Real compassion trusts people to know their own lives. Research indicates that both those who continue and terminate pregnancies report highest satisfaction when they felt their decision was truly their own, made with adequate support and information.[8] This suggests compassion requires not just respecting choice but ensuring conditions where genuine choice is possible.

This connects to principles like "personal virtue choices supersede state authority" and "individual conscience governs personal moral choices." Together, they establish what authentic compassion looks like, while acknowledging the complex interplay between individual autonomy and social support systems.

For today's leaders, this demands respecting rather than overriding individual decision-making in reproductive matters. True compassion honors human dignity by supporting people's choices, not replacing their judgment with ours. Yet it also requires addressing structural inequalities and ensuring comprehensive support systems that make authentic choice possible for all.

FOR FURTHER READING

Buddhist concept of compassion (karuna) emphasizing skillful means respecting individual wisdom

Harvey, Peter (2000). An Introduction to Buddhist Ethics. Cambridge: Cambridge University Press.

Qualitative research on support needs and autonomy during reproductive decision-making

Altshuler, A. L., et al. (2017). Male partners' involvement in abortion care: A mixed-methods systematic review. Perspectives on Sexual and Reproductive Health, 49(2), 71-84.

Study on autonomy and relational decision-making in reproductive choices

Foster, D. G. (2020). The Turnaway Study: Ten Years, a Thousand Women, and the Consequences of Having—or Being Denied—an Abortion. Scribner.

Research on emotional complexity and ambivalence in abortion decisions

Rocca, C. H., et al. (2015). Decision rightness and emotional responses to abortion in the United States. PLOS One, 10(7), e0128832.

Cross-cultural perspectives on family involvement in reproductive decision-making

Mumtaz, Z., et al. (2014). Unintended pregnancy in Pakistan: The role of gender and empowerment. International Journal of Gynecology & Obstetrics, 124(3), 250-253.

Analysis of structural barriers to reproductive autonomy

Roberts, D. (1997). Killing the Black Body: Race, Reproduction, and the Meaning of Liberty. Pantheon Books.

Healthcare provider perspectives on balancing autonomy and care

Lipp, A. (2011). Self-preservation in abortion care: A grounded theory study. Journal of Clinical Nursing, 20(5-6), 892-900.

Long-term outcomes and decision satisfaction research

Biggs, M. A., et al. (2017). Women's mental health and well-being 5 years after receiving or being denied an abortion. JAMA Psychiatry, 74(2), 169-178.

Actual persons take precedence over potential ones.

Fully developed human life takes precedence over potential life. When interests conflict, the complete person's rights override those of the incomplete potential person. However, many people assign significant moral status to potential life without equating it to born persons. Research shows that most Americans hold layered views—seeing fetal life as deserving increasing protection as it develops, while still prioritizing maternal life in conflicts. Some argue that vulnerability itself creates moral obligations, even if the vulnerable entity lacks full personhood.

This statement establishes the fundamental hierarchy between actual and potential personhood. When reproductive conflicts arise, the interests of the fully realized person must take precedence over those of potential life. It's like prioritizing a built house over blueprints when you can only save one—both have value, but one is actualized while the other is potential. This creates a clear philosophical framework for resolving competing claims while acknowledging the value of both. Yet many ethical frameworks reject simple binaries, arguing for graduated moral status where potential life deserves significant (though not equal) protection. Studies of women making reproductive decisions reveal they often assign moral weight to fetal life while still prioritizing their own circumstances and existing responsibilities.

Throughout history, most moral and legal traditions have implicitly recognized this hierarchy. Medical practices prioritize maternal life in emergencies. Inheritance laws begin at birth. Social customs treat pregnancy loss differently from child death. Ancient medical traditions, including the Hippocratic Oath, directed physicians to save mothers when forced to choose. Even restrictive religious traditions typically include exceptions for maternal life, acknowledging the precedence of actual over potential existence. However, these same traditions often assign significant moral status to fetal life—Catholic doctrine, for instance, prohibits direct abortion even while permitting procedures that save maternal life with fetal death as an unintended consequence.[5] This double-effect reasoning suggests recognition of fetal moral status even when maternal life takes precedence.[6]

Modern bioethics consistently applies this principle across medical contexts. Organ transplant protocols prioritize existing patients over potential future recipients. Medical research ethics protects actual research subjects over hypothetical future benefits. Emergency medicine, when resources are limited, prioritizes patients with the greatest chance of survival—typically those already born and viable. This consistent pattern confirms the principle's broad applicability. Yet bioethicists increasingly recognize proportional approaches—many argue that late-term fetuses deserve greater moral consideration than early embryos, even if neither equals born persons.[7] Neonatal intensive care practices reveal complex judgments about viability and moral status at the margins of life.[8]

The philosophy recognizes that complete actualization carries greater moral weight than incomplete potential. Since actual persons possess fully developed consciousness, autonomy, and social relationships, their interests necessarily outweigh those of potential persons lacking these complete characteristics. This doesn't diminish potential life's value but establishes appropriate priorities when conflicts arise. It's about recognizing degrees of development and corresponding moral weight. Critics argue this framework oversimplifies—pointing to humans with severe cognitive disabilities who lack full autonomy but retain personhood.[9] They contend that potential for relationship and development, not just current capacities, generates moral obligations. Some philosophers argue for a "future-like-ours" account where what matters is the valuable future that abortion prevents.[10]

Practically, this means medical guidelines prioritizing maternal life in emergencies, legal frameworks protecting women's autonomy while acknowledging fetal interests, and healthcare policies ensuring pregnant women receive full personhood recognition rather than being treated as fetal containers. Some claim equal status for potential and actual persons. But they must address why completion and potentiality should carry identical moral weight. If potential and actual were truly equivalent, then all potential persons—including unconceived ones—would have equal claims to resources and protection. That's clearly unworkable. However, those assigning significant (not equal) status to fetal life argue this slippery slope misrepresents their position—they distinguish between actual potential life (existing fetuses) and merely possible life (unconceived), arguing the former deserves protection even if the latter doesn't.[11] Legal frameworks in many nations reflect this complexity through gestational limits that increase fetal protection over time.[12]

This connects to principles like "full personhood rights begin at birth" and "those who bear pregnancy's burden hold its authority." Together, they establish clear moral priorities. Yet lived experiences reveal more complexity—parents who choose abortion for wanted pregnancies with fatal abnormalities report simultaneously viewing their fetus as their child while prioritizing maternal health and family wellbeing.[13] These experiences suggest that real-world moral reasoning often transcends simple hierarchies.

For today's leaders, this demands policies recognizing the precedence of actual over potential persons while seeking to support both when possible. Clear hierarchies enable rather than prevent appropriate moral consideration. When we must choose, actual persons come first. However, leaders must also recognize that many citizens assign significant moral weight to potential life, leading them to support policies that protect fetal interests when they don't directly conflict with maternal wellbeing. The challenge lies in crafting policies that respect both the priority of actual persons and the moral significance many assign to potential life.

FOR FURTHER READING

Public opinion research on gradated views of fetal moral status

Pew Research Center (2022). Public Opinion on Abortion: Views on abortion by trimester. Pew Research Center Religion & Public Life.

Philosophical argument about vulnerability creating moral obligations

MacIntyre, Alasdair (1999). Dependent Rational Animals: Why Human Beings Need the Virtues. Open Court.

Analysis of gradated moral status in reproductive ethics

Warren, Mary Anne (1997). Moral Status: Obligations to Persons and Other Living Things. Oxford University Press.

Women's moral reasoning in abortion decisions

Kjelsvik, M. & Gjengedal, E. (2011). First-trimester abortion: Women's experiences of the decision and the procedure. Scandinavian Journal of Caring Sciences, 25(3), 449-457.

Catholic doctrine on double effect and maternal life exceptions

Kaczor, Christopher (2011). The Ethics of Abortion: Women's Rights, Human Life, and the Question of Justice. Routledge, pp. 165-178.

Analysis of double-effect reasoning in medical ethics

Cavanaugh, T.A. (2006). Double-Effect Reasoning: Doing Good and Avoiding Evil. Oxford University Press.

Gradated approaches to fetal moral status in bioethics

Steinbock, Bonnie (2011). Life Before Birth: The Moral and Legal Status of Embryos and Fetuses, 2nd ed. Oxford University Press.

Neonatal care and moral status at margins of viability

Wilkinson, Dominic (2013). Death or Disability?: The 'Carmentis Machine' and Decision-making for Critically Ill Children. Oxford University Press.

Cognitive disability and personhood debates

McMahan, Jeff (2002). The Ethics of Killing: Problems at the Margins of Life. Oxford University Press.

Future-like-ours account of abortion ethics

Marquis, Don (1989). Why abortion is immoral. Journal of Philosophy, 86(4), 183-202.

Distinguishing actual potential from merely possible life

Stone, Jim (1987). Why potentiality matters. Canadian Journal of Philosophy, 17(4), 815-830.

International comparison of gestational limits in abortion law

Center for Reproductive Rights (2021). The World's Abortion Laws. Center for Reproductive Rights Global Maps.

Parents' experiences with abortion for fetal abnormalities

Lafarge, C., Mitchell, K., & Fox, P. (2013). Women's experiences of coping with pregnancy termination for fetal abnormality. Qualitative Health Research, 23(7), 924-936.

Individual conscience governs personal moral choices.

Each person serves as their own authority in determining their virtue regarding reproduction. External religious or state authorities cannot override personal moral judgment.

This statement establishes individual conscience as the supreme authority in personal reproductive decisions. It asserts that each person has the exclusive right and responsibility to determine their own moral choices regarding pregnancy and childbearing. The principle recognizes that these decisions involve intimate knowledge of personal circumstances, values, and capacity that no external authority can adequately assess. It's like saying only you can know if a shoe fits your foot—others can guess, but only you feel the truth.

Moral philosophy teaches that the primacy of individual conscience has been recognized across diverse traditions. Protestant Reformation theology emphasized the individual's direct relationship with divine authority without institutional intermediaries.[1] Enlightenment philosophy, particularly through Kant, established personal moral autonomy as fundamental to human dignity.[2] Even traditional religious frameworks, through private confession and personal spiritual direction, acknowledge that moral decision-making ultimately occurs within individual consciousness rather than through external dictation.

Modern understanding confirms that moral decision-making requires personal knowledge unavailable to external observers. Psychological research shows individuals facing complex moral situations possess insights about their circumstances, capacity, and values that outsiders can't fully comprehend. Bioethics consistently recognizes patient autonomy in medical decisions precisely because personal knowledge exceeds external assessment. Forcing predetermined moral conclusions violates this reality.

The philosophy recognizes that valid moral action requires proper knowledge of circumstances and capacity. Since reproductive decisions involve intimate knowledge of personal situation, health, relationships, and values, only the individual involved possesses sufficient information for authentic moral choice. External authorities lack this essential knowledge base. They're making decisions blindfolded.

Practically, this means legal frameworks protecting individual decision-making rather than imposing external moral standards, healthcare systems providing information while respecting patient autonomy, and social policies supporting rather than constraining individual moral discernment. Some claim certain moral choices require external guidance. But they must explain why reproductive decisions would be exempt from individual moral authority while other personal choices aren't. If conscience governs other intimate moral decisions—whom to marry, whether to have surgery, how to die—reproductive choices can't be logically excluded.

This connects to principles like "personal virtue choices supersede state authority" and "true compassion respects autonomous decisions." Together, they establish conscience as supreme in personal matters.

For today's leaders, this demands protecting rather than overriding individual moral authority in reproductive matters. Authentic morality emerges from personal conscience, not external imposition. Each person must live with their choices—therefore, each person must make them.

FOR FURTHER READING

Protestant Reformation theology emphasizing individual's direct relationship with divine authority

Luther, Martin (1520). On the Freedom of a Christian. Wittenberg: Melchior Lotter.

Kant establishing personal moral autonomy as fundamental to human dignity

Kant, Immanuel (1785). Groundwork of the Metaphysics of Morals. Translated by Mary Gregor. Cambridge: Cambridge University Press, 1997.

Reproduction must be **chosen, not coerced**.*

The desire for or against bearing children must originate from one's own will. Forced pregnancy or forced sterilization equally violate this fundamental reproductive autonomy.

This culminating teaching establishes voluntary choice as the essential foundation of ethical reproduction. It asserts that both forced pregnancy and forced sterilization violate fundamental human autonomy by imposing external will over individual reproductive decisions. Whether forcing someone to have children or preventing them from having children, coercion violates the same principle. It's like forcing someone to marry or forbidding them to marry—both violate the fundamental requirement that such intimate decisions must come from personal choice.

* *Timeless Principle: Reproduction by choice, not coercion, aligns with virtue—forced breeding or forced barrenness equally violate natural law.*

Through the centuries, coercive reproductive policies have consistently produced suffering rather than flourishing. Nazi Germany's forced sterilization programs violated human dignity while failing to achieve their eugenic goals. China's one-child policy created massive social disruption, gender imbalances, and individual trauma while failing to achieve sustainable population balance. The United States' own history of forced sterilization of "undesirable" populations demonstrates how reproductive coercion serves political rather than moral purposes. Countries supporting voluntary family planning through education, healthcare access, and economic opportunity achieve better outcomes while respecting autonomy.

Modern evidence overwhelmingly supports choice-based reproductive policies. Nations with comprehensive reproductive healthcare, including both contraception and abortion access, show lower unintended pregnancy rates, better maternal health outcomes, and more sustainable population trends than countries with restrictive policies. Research consistently demonstrates that voluntary family planning leads to healthier families, better child outcomes, and greater social stability than coercive approaches.

The philosophy recognizes that authentic virtue requires voluntary action rather than forced compliance. Since reproduction involves the most intimate aspects of human existence—body, relationships, future planning, and values—external coercion violates the autonomy essential to moral action. True reproductive virtue emerges from careful consideration of circumstances, capacity, and values rather than submission to external authority. You can't force virtue.

Practically, this means policies expanding rather than restricting reproductive options, healthcare systems providing comprehensive services while respecting patient decisions, and social support enabling rather than constraining individual choice. Some might argue that certain reproductive outcomes serve social good. But they must explain why violating individual autonomy in reproduction differs from forced organ donation or mandatory medical procedures—all might serve collective interests but violate fundamental human rights.

This connects to the entire reproductive freedom sequence, from "control over one's body is the foundation of autonomy" through all subsequent principles. Together, they establish choice as paramount in reproduction.

For today's leaders, this demands protecting reproductive autonomy from all forms of coercion. Authentic reproductive ethics emerges through individual freedom, not despite it. Whether the coercion aims to increase or decrease reproduction, it violates the same fundamental principle: reproduction must be chosen, not commanded.

ON TRANSGENDER RIGHTS

External body differs from **internal identity**.*

Physical sex characteristics are external while gender identity constitutes internal self-nature. The principle that internal knowledge supersedes external observation applies here.

This foundational teaching distinguishes between external physical characteristics and internal identity. It asserts that gender identity represents authentic self-knowledge that transcends external bodily appearance. The principle recognizes that consciousness and self-awareness constitute the essential aspects of human identity, while physical form is merely external manifestation that may or may not align with internal truth. It's like the difference between knowing you're left-handed versus what others assume from seeing you write—internal knowledge trumps external observation.

* *Timeless Principle: The eternal self transcends physical form—a truth recognized across spiritual traditions that validates gender diversity.*

Throughout history, numerous traditions have recognized the distinction between essential identity and physical form. Hindu concepts of the eternal soul (atman) transcending bodily characteristics, Buddhist teachings about the illusory nature of physical identity, and Platonic philosophy distinguishing between essential forms and material manifestations all acknowledge that authentic identity exists beyond physical appearance. Many indigenous cultures worldwide have recognized gender roles and identities transcending simple biological categories, demonstrating cross-cultural acknowledgment of this fundamental distinction.

Modern neuroscience increasingly supports that gender identity originates in brain development and neural patterns rather than external genital configuration. Research shows transgender individuals have brain structure patterns more consistent with their identified gender than their assigned sex, confirming that internal gender knowledge reflects authentic neurological reality. Medical understanding recognizes gender dysphoria as distress from mismatch between internal identity and external form, not mental illness regarding the identity itself.

The philosophy recognizes that direct internal knowledge carries greater validity than external inference. Since individuals have direct access to their internal gender experience while others can only infer gender from external characteristics, self-knowledge must supersede external observation. This framework invalidates attempts to deny transgender identity based on external physical evidence. You know your own mind better than others know your body.

Practically, this means legal recognition of gender identity regardless of birth assignment, medical approaches affirming rather than pathologizing transgender identity, and social policies prioritizing self-identification over external assessment in gender determination. Some claim biology determines gender absolutely. But they must address why external physical characteristics would override internal consciousness and self-knowledge. If consciousness represents the essential human characteristic, then conscious gender identity necessarily supersedes physical form.

This connects to principles like "self-knowledge of gender identity is supreme authority" and "inner knowledge supersedes external observation." Together, they establish the foundational understanding of gender diversity.

For today's leaders, this demands recognizing transgender identity as authentic self-knowledge rather than confusion or disorder. When internal identity differs from external body, the internal truth takes precedence.

Self-knowledge of gender identity is **supreme authority**.*

One's internal experience of gender identity constitutes the highest form of direct knowledge. External observers cannot invalidate this self-knowledge through their limited perception.

|| ॐ ||

This statement establishes self-knowledge of gender identity as the highest authority. It asserts that individuals have supreme authority regarding their own gender experience, and external observers lack the access necessary to override this internal knowledge. Gender identity exists as immediate, first-person experience that can't be validated or contradicted from outside. It's like pain—only you can know if you're in pain; others can guess but can't feel it for you. This makes self-identification the most reliable source of gender knowledge.

* *Timeless Principle: While applied to gender here, this represents a broader universal principle that direct, first-person knowledge of internal states supersedes external observation - a fundamental epistemological truth.*

Wisdom traditions worldwide have recognized that philosophical traditions have recognized the authority of first-person experience in matters of internal states. Descartes' "I think, therefore I am" established the primacy of self-knowledge over external observation.[1] Buddhist epistemology recognizes direct experience as superior to inference or testimony regarding internal states. Even empirical science acknowledges that subjective experiences like consciousness, pain, and identity can't be definitively assessed by external observers—we need self-report as primary data.

Modern psychology and neuroscience confirm gender identity represents genuine internal experience rather than choice or confusion. Research shows gender identity typically manifests early in childhood, remains consistent over time, and resists external attempts at modification. Brain development studies show neurological correlates of gender identity aligning with self-reported experience rather than assigned sex. Attempts to override or change gender identity through therapy or social pressure consistently fail and cause psychological harm.

The philosophy recognizes that direct knowledge supersedes all other forms of evidence. Since only the individual experiencing gender identity has direct access to this internal reality, their testimony constitutes the most valid available evidence. External observers can only infer gender from secondary indicators, making their assessments necessarily less reliable than direct self-knowledge. It's the difference between knowing and guessing.

Practically, this means legal frameworks prioritizing self-identification over external assessment in gender determination, medical protocols affirming rather than questioning patient-reported gender identity, and social policies respecting individual gender knowledge rather than imposing external verification requirements. Some claim external observers can better assess gender identity. But they must address why internal experience would be less reliable than external inference. If self-knowledge lacks authority in gender matters, then all subjective experience becomes questionable. Can others know your thoughts better than you do?

This connects to principles like "external body differs from internal identity" and "inner knowledge supersedes external observation." Together, they establish epistemic supremacy of self-knowledge.

For today's leaders, this demands treating transgender self-identification as authoritative rather than questionable. Authentic knowledge comes from individual experience, not external assessment. When someone tells you their gender, they're the expert—not you.

FOR FURTHER READING

Descartes establishing the primacy of self-knowledge

Descartes, René (1637). Discourse on Method. Translated by Donald A. Cress. Indianapolis: Hackett Publishing, 1998.

Medical transition aligns body with **inner truth**.

Just as ritual modifications of the body serve virtuous purposes, medical transitions align external form with internal truth, constituting legitimate virtuous action.

This statement establishes medical transition as virtuous action that aligns external physical form with internal authentic identity. It asserts that body modification for gender affirmation serves the same legitimate purposes as ritual body modifications and is therefore righteous rather than harmful. It's like correcting a birth defect—restoring what should have been rather than creating something artificial. The principle recognizes that achieving harmony between internal truth and external manifestation represents spiritual and psychological virtue.

Across cultures and centuries, body modification for spiritual, social, and identity purposes has been recognized across cultures as legitimate and often sacred. Hindu traditions include various body modifications for spiritual purposes. Many indigenous cultures practice body modification as part of coming-of-age ceremonies or spiritual transformation. Even restrictive religious traditions accept body modifications for health, spiritual purification, or social integration when they serve recognized virtuous purposes. The principle that aligning external form with internal truth constitutes legitimate action appears consistently across human cultures.

Modern medical understanding recognizes gender transition as medically necessary treatment for gender dysphoria, not elective cosmetic procedure. Major medical organizations—the American Medical Association, World Health Organization, and American Psychological Association—recognize transition-related healthcare as essential medical treatment. Research consistently shows that access to transition healthcare dramatically improves mental health outcomes, reduces suicide risk, and enables psychological flourishing for transgender individuals.

The philosophy recognizes that actions serving authentic virtue constitute righteous action regardless of conventional appearances. Since medical transition serves the fundamental virtue of aligning external reality with internal truth, it fulfills rather than violates moral principles. Achieving harmony between inner and outer reality represents a highest spiritual aspiration, not a violation of nature.

Practically, this means healthcare systems providing transition-related medical services, insurance coverage for medically necessary transition procedures, and medical protocols affirming rather than gatekeeping transition healthcare. Some claim medical transition violates natural order. But they must address why achieving alignment between internal truth and external form would constitute violation rather than restoration of harmony. If authenticity represents virtue, then enabling authentic self-expression serves natural law rather than contradicting it.

This connects to principles like "external body differs from internal identity" and "transition healthcare serves righteous purposes." Together, they establish medical transition as virtuous action.

For today's leaders, this demands treating transition healthcare as medically necessary rather than optional. Supporting authentic self-expression serves moral imperatives rather than violating them. When we help people align their bodies with their true selves, we enable flourishing.

Everyone has the right to **change name and form**.

The right to change name and form to match identity is fundamental. Just as spiritual initiation involves new names, gender transition includes naming rights.

This statement establishes the fundamental right to modify both name and physical form to align with authentic identity. It asserts that changing external markers to match internal truth is a basic human right, not a social privilege. Names and physical appearance are primary means of expressing identity, so the ability to modify them is essential to authentic self-presentation. It's like immigrants changing their names to fit their new lives—external changes that reflect internal transformation have always been recognized as legitimate.

Throughout history, name changes have been recognized across cultures for various reasons: marriage, adoption, spiritual transformation, and social integration. Many religious traditions include formal name-changing ceremonies—Christian confirmation, Jewish bar/bat mitzvah, Hindu sannyasa initiation—acknowledging personal transformation through new names. Legal systems have long permitted name changes for legitimate purposes, recognizing that names serve social rather than biological functions. Physical modifications for cultural, spiritual, or personal reasons have similarly been accepted.

Today, progressive legal frameworks increasingly recognize the right to gender marker and name changes as fundamental civil rights. Countries like Argentina, Ireland, and Malta have implemented self-identification laws allowing individuals to change legal gender markers based on self-determination rather than medical gatekeeping. These policies recognize that accurate identity documents constitute basic civil rights necessary for employment, education, healthcare, and social participation.

The philosophy recognizes that individuals have authority over their own social presentation and identity expression. Since names and appearance serve primarily social functions rather than biological ones, individuals must retain the right to modify these elements for authentic self-presentation. Denying this right violates fundamental autonomy over self-expression. It's about being able to present yourself truthfully to the world.

Practically, this means streamlined legal processes for name and gender marker changes, reduced requirements for medical documentation in identity changes, and recognition of chosen names in educational, employment, and healthcare settings regardless of legal status. Some claim name and form changes threaten social order. But they must address why accommodating authentic identity expression would be more disruptive than forcing people to live with inaccurate identity markers. Clear processes for identity changes typically enhance rather than threaten social stability—people function better when their documents match their reality.

This connects to principles like "name changes follow established traditional precedent" and "self-knowledge of gender identity is supreme authority." Together, they establish comprehensive change rights.

For today's leaders, this demands accessible processes for legal name and gender marker changes. Accurate identity documents constitute basic civil rights rather than special privileges. When people can't change their documents to match their reality, they're forced to live a lie every time they show ID.

Multiple genders exist across cultures and history.*

Ancient texts acknowledge non-binary genders, proving gender diversity is traditional, not modern. Denying this reality contradicts established scriptural authority.

This statement establishes that gender diversity represents universal human reality rather than modern invention. Multiple gender categories have existed across cultures and throughout history, making contemporary non-binary and transgender identities part of traditional rather than revolutionary human experience. Ancient Hindu texts acknowledge hijras as a distinct gender category, while Native American traditions recognize Two-Spirit people. It's like discovering that different languages have always existed—the diversity was always there, even if some cultures tried to deny it. This comprehensive evidence shows that gender diversity represents natural human variation, not modern ideological deviation.

* *Timeless Principle: Gender diversity appears across cultures and ages—its universality reveals its naturalness.*

Ancient wisdom reveals that numerous cultures have recognized third, fourth, or multiple gender categories. Ancient Hindu texts acknowledge hijras as a distinct gender category with specific social roles and spiritual significance. Native American traditions include Two-Spirit people who combine masculine and feminine qualities in recognized social roles. Traditional Thai culture recognizes kathoey as a distinct gender category. Albanian burrnesha, Samoan fa'afafine, and numerous other cultural examples demonstrate that gender diversity appears independently across unrelated societies, proving its natural rather than constructed character.

Modern anthropological research confirms gender diversity appears in most human cultures when examined carefully. Historical records from ancient Egypt, Mesopotamia, Greece, and Rome include references to people who lived outside simple male-female categories. Medieval European records, despite cultural restrictions, still contain evidence of gender-variant individuals. Even within restrictive religious traditions, mystical literature often acknowledges transcendence of gender categories as spiritual attainment.

The philosophy recognizes that universal phenomena indicate natural rather than artificial characteristics. Since gender diversity appears consistently across cultures, time periods, and geographical regions without cross-cultural contact, it must represent inherent human variation rather than learned behavior. The universality of gender diversity reveals its naturalness. It's like how all cultures have music—the universality shows it's human nature.

Practically, this means educational curricula teaching historical gender diversity, legal frameworks acknowledging multiple gender categories as traditional rather than innovative, and social policies recognizing non-binary identities as culturally established rather than recently invented. Some claim only two genders exist naturally. But they must address why gender diversity would appear universally if it weren't natural. The cross-cultural evidence for gender diversity can't be explained by modern influence since it predates contemporary gender theory by millennia. You can't retroactively invent ancient history.

This connects to principles like "gender diversity is natural, not disordered" and "multiple gender identities disprove the binary." Together, they establish historical precedent for gender diversity.

For today's leaders, this demands recognizing current gender diversity as continuation of traditional human variation rather than modern deviation. When we acknowledge non-binary and transgender identities, we're not inventing something new—we're recognizing something that's always existed.

FOR FURTHER READING

Hindu texts acknowledging hijras as distinct gender category

Wilhelm, Amara Das (2008). Tritiya-Prakriti: People of the Third Sex. Philadelphia, PA: Xlibris Corporation.

Native American Two-Spirit traditions

Roscoe, Will (1998). Changing Ones: Third and Fourth Genders in Native North America. New York: St. Martin's Press.

Inner knowledge supersedes external observation.*

Internal knowledge of one's gender identity holds greater validity than external physical evidence. The hierarchy of knowledge sources places self-knowledge above inference from physical signs.

This epistemological teaching establishes the fundamental hierarchy between internal direct knowledge and external observation. It asserts that self-knowledge of gender identity necessarily supersedes external physical indicators because internal experience provides more direct and reliable access to identity truth. Gender identity exists as subjective experience unavailable to external validation. It's like pain or hunger—you have direct access to your experience while others can only guess based on external signs. This makes first-person knowledge superior to third-person inference from physical characteristics.

* *Timeless Principle: This is explicitly an epistemological principle about the hierarchy of knowledge sources that applies universally.*

In human understanding, philosophical traditions have recognized the primacy of internal experience over external observation in matters of consciousness and identity. Cartesian philosophy established the certainty of self-knowledge over external perception—"I think, therefore I am" puts internal knowledge first.[1] Phenomenological traditions emphasize the authority of lived experience over objective measurement in understanding human reality. Buddhist epistemology recognizes that internal states can only be known directly by the experiencing subject, making external inference necessarily secondary and potentially misleading.

Modern cognitive science confirms that internal states like gender identity can't be definitively assessed through external observation. Neuroscience shows that subjective experiences emerge from complex neural networks that can't be fully understood through external physical examination. Research on gender identity proves that chromosomes, hormones, and genital configuration don't reliably predict gender identity, confirming that internal experience provides more accurate information than external physical indicators.

The philosophy recognizes direct perception as the most reliable source of knowledge. Since individuals have direct internal access to their gender experience while others can only make inferences from external signs, self-knowledge necessarily carries greater weight. External observers lack the direct experiential access required for authoritative gender assessment. They're looking through a window while you're inside the room.

Practically, this means medical protocols prioritizing patient self-identification over external testing in gender assessment, legal frameworks accepting self-identification rather than requiring physical examination for gender determination, and social policies respecting individual gender knowledge rather than external verification. Some claim objective external evidence should override subjective internal experience. But they must address why less direct forms of knowledge would be more reliable than more direct ones. If external inference supersedes internal experience, then all self-knowledge becomes questionable. Can a doctor know your thoughts better than you do?

This connects to principles like "self-knowledge of gender identity is supreme authority" and "external body differs from internal identity." Together, they establish the epistemological hierarchy of knowledge sources.

For today's leaders, this demands treating transgender self-identification as more reliable than external assessment. Authentic knowledge emerges from internal experience, not despite it. When someone tells you who they are, they're using the most direct form of knowledge available.

FOR FURTHER READING

Cartesian philosophy establishing certainty of self-knowledge

Descartes, René (1637). Discourse on Method. Translated by Donald A. Cress. Indianapolis: Hackett Publishing, 1998.

Gender diversity is **natural, not disordered**.

Calling trans identity a "disorder" must be rejected because gender diversity is natural. Pathologizing natural variation violates both logic and compassion.

This statement definitively rejects the pathologization of transgender identity. It establishes that gender diversity represents natural human variation rather than mental disorder or dysfunction. Attempts to medicalize or pathologize transgender identity violate both rational analysis and compassionate understanding. It's like how left-handedness was once considered a disorder needing correction—we now recognize it as natural variation. Labeling natural diversity as pathological serves social control, not scientific accuracy, making such pathologization both false and harmful.

Throughout history, pathologizing human diversity has consistently served oppressive rather than healing purposes. Homosexuality was classified as mental illness until 1973, and its depathologization led to improved outcomes without increased social problems. Left-handedness was once considered pathological and subjected to forced correction attempts that caused psychological harm rather than prevented it. This pattern reveals that pathologizing natural variations typically reflects social prejudice rather than medical necessity.

Modern medical understanding increasingly recognizes transgender identity as natural variation rather than pathology. The World Health Organization removed transgender identity from its list of mental disorders in 2019, classifying gender dysphoria—distress caused by societal rejection—rather than transgender identity itself as the clinical concern.[1] Research shows transgender identity appears consistently across cultures and historical periods, suggesting biological rather than pathological origins. Studies prove that family acceptance and social support, not identity change, predict positive mental health outcomes.

The philosophy recognizes that natural phenomena can't simultaneously be pathological. Since transgender identity appears consistently across human populations without external causation, it must represent natural variation rather than dysfunction. Pathologizing natural diversity violates the logical principle that widespread phenomena indicate normalcy rather than disorder. If it's everywhere, it's not a disorder—it's human nature.

Practically, this means medical training treating transgender identity as natural variation, mental health approaches focusing on supporting rather than changing identity, and social policies addressing discrimination rather than transgender people themselves as the problem requiring intervention. Some claim transgender identity requires medical intervention. But they must distinguish between affirming natural identity and pathologizing it. Medical support for transition serves authentic self-expression, not treating pathology. It's like orthodontics—helping achieve desired alignment, not curing disease.

This connects to principles like "multiple genders exist across cultures and history" and "what exists naturally from birth is not disease." Together, they establish non-pathological understanding of gender diversity.

For today's leaders, this demands treating transgender identity as natural human diversity rather than medical problem. When we stop pathologizing difference, we start enabling flourishing.

FOR FURTHER READING

World Health Organization removing transgender identity from mental disorders list

World Health Organization (2019). International Statistical Classification of Diseases and Related Health Problems (11th ed.). Geneva: WHO.

Identity, not anatomy, determines appropriate spaces.

For ritual purity and social spaces (like bathrooms), internal identity takes precedence over physical form. The principle that intention determines ritual validity applies.

|| ॐ ||

This statement establishes that internal gender identity rather than external anatomy should determine access to gendered social spaces. It recognizes that spaces organized around gender serve social rather than biological functions and should therefore align with social identity, not physical characteristics. However, implementing this principle confronts the reality that parents cannot verify the authenticity of strangers' identity claims, creating an irreducible tension between protecting transgender dignity and addressing parental safety concerns, especially for daughters.

For generations, gender-segregated spaces have been organized around social gender roles rather than anatomical inspection. Traditional societies created separate spaces based on social gender presentation and community recognition, not physical examination. Critically, however, these traditional systems operated in smaller communities where people knew each other—vastly different from today's anonymous public spaces where strangers interact without accountability or verification.

Parents of daughters experience a visceral, evolution-honed protective response that no amount of philosophical argument can fully address. This isn't prejudice but biological imperative—mothers and fathers carry deep, embodied knowledge about female vulnerability to male violence. When they imagine their daughter alone in a bathroom with someone who is anatomically male, their nervous systems activate threat responses that bypass rational thought. The statistical reality that sexual violence against women and girls is overwhelmingly perpetrated by people with male anatomy reinforces these protective instincts.

The core epistemological problem is unsolvable: in anonymous public spaces, there is no way to distinguish between genuine transgender individuals deserving of dignity and potential predators exploiting inclusive policies. While research shows that transgender people themselves face extreme violence and that inclusive policies in controlled institutional settings don't increase incidents, parents correctly note that schools and workplaces differ fundamentally from public spaces. In institutions, there's accountability, documentation, and community knowledge. In a highway rest stop or shopping mall bathroom, there's none.

The philosophy recognizes that intention and identity should determine appropriate social participation. Yet this principle assumes we can know intention and verify identity—assumptions that break down in anonymous settings. Bad faith actors exist in every system, and any policy that relies entirely on self-declaration without verification creates exploitable vulnerabilities. This isn't about questioning transgender identity but acknowledging that predators are sophisticated and will exploit any available camouflage.

More nuanced approaches might include: investing in single-occupancy facilities that provide privacy for everyone; creating family/all-gender bathrooms as additional options while maintaining sex-segregated spaces; in institutional settings like schools, implementing policies based on documented, consistent lived identity rather than momentary claims; distinguishing between different contexts—what works in a small school may not work in a large public venue; and focusing enforcement on behavior regardless of gender identity.

Some schools have found middle ground through policies where transgender students use facilities consistent with their identity after engaging with administrators and parents—creating accountability and community knowledge that addresses safety concerns while respecting identity. This works because it transforms anonymous strangers into known community members.

The deeper reality is that both sides have non-negotiable needs that appear mutually exclusive. Transgender people, especially transgender women, face severe violence in male spaces and need access to facilities matching their identity for basic safety and dignity. Parents need assurance that their children won't encounter males in vulnerable spaces, regardless of those males' stated identity. Neither side is wrong—both are responding to real dangers.

Perhaps the binary bathroom system itself is the problem—designed for a world that assumed clear, verifiable gender distinctions. Rather than forcing a binary choice between anatomy and identity, we might need architectural and policy innovations that provide safety and dignity for everyone: true privacy in all facilities, better sight-line management, attendant monitoring in high-risk locations, and community-specific solutions rather than one-size-fits-all mandates.

This connects to principles like "self-knowledge of gender identity is supreme authority" while also acknowledging principles about protecting the vulnerable from those who would exploit systemic trust. The challenge isn't philosophical but practical: implementing identity-based access in a world where identity claims can't be verified and where bad actors exist.

For today's leaders, this demands honesty about irreducible tensions rather than pretending perfect solutions exist. It means investing in infrastructure that provides real privacy, acknowledging that different contexts require different approaches, and respecting that parents' protective instincts and transgender people's dignity needs are both legitimate. Most importantly, it means recognizing that in anonymous public spaces, the impossibility of verifying identity creates vulnerabilities that no amount of good intention can fully resolve—requiring us to seek creative solutions that don't force a choice between competing safety needs.

Children **know their own gender identity**.

Children's knowledge of their gender identity constitutes valid evidence. Age doesn't invalidate self-knowledge; even children possess authoritative knowledge of their internal nature.

|| ॐ ||

This statement establishes that children possess authentic knowledge of their own gender identity. It asserts that age doesn't invalidate self-awareness of internal identity. However, implementing this principle confronts complex realities: distinguishing between gender exploration and fixed identity, developmental fluidity, social influences, and the challenge of supporting children's authentic expression while acknowledging that childhood identity can evolve. Parents face agonizing decisions with imperfect information and high stakes.

Evidence across cultures shows that children's self-knowledge has been recognized in various contexts. Traditional coming-of-age ceremonies acknowledge children's developing self-awareness. Educational psychology recognizes that children possess reliable knowledge about their internal states. We routinely trust children's self-reports about being left-handed, introverted, or athletic. The principle that children can know their own internal experiences has broad acceptance.

Modern research shows that many children expressing transgender identity demonstrate persistence over time, with those who socially transition early often showing positive mental health outcomes.[1] However, the picture is complex. Some children who express gender nonconformity in early childhood don't persist in transgender identity through adolescence. Developmental psychologists note that identity formation is an ongoing process throughout childhood and adolescence, not a single moment of revelation.

Parents face excruciating uncertainties. They see their four-year-old insisting they're a different gender and must decide: Is this exploration or identity? Will supporting transition help or harm? What about the autism correlation—studies show higher rates of gender dysphoria among autistic children, raising questions about whether sensory, social, or identity factors are primary. Parents read about detransitioners and wonder if they're enabling a mistake. They read about transgender suicide rates and fear the consequences of rejection. There's no perfect playbook.

The phenomenon of rapid-onset gender dysphoria in adolescent social groups, particularly among teenage girls, adds another layer of complexity. While many dispute this characterization, parents observe friend groups where multiple children simultaneously identify as transgender and worry about social contagion versus authentic self-discovery. The massive increase in adolescents seeking gender services—increases that can't be explained solely by greater acceptance—raises questions about multiple pathways to gender dysphoria.

The philosophy recognizes that direct experience provides valuable knowledge regardless of age. Children do have authentic internal experiences of gender. Yet childhood development also involves trying on different identities, and not all childhood expressions of gender nonconformity indicate transgender identity. The challenge is that while children know their current feelings, they may not yet know if these feelings are permanent.

Practically, this suggests a middle path: taking children's gender expressions seriously without rushing toward medical interventions; creating space for exploration without either suppressing or cementing identity; distinguishing between social transition (reversible) and medical interventions (some irreversible); providing mental health support that neither dismisses nor automatically affirms; helping families navigate uncertainty with compassion for both children and parents.

Some professionals advocate "watchful waiting" while others recommend immediate affirmation. The reality is that different approaches may be appropriate for different children. A young child with consistent, persistent, insistent gender identity from age three presents differently than a teenager experiencing sudden gender dysphoria during puberty alongside other mental health challenges.

This connects to principles like "self-knowledge of gender identity is supreme authority" while also acknowledging developmental complexity and parental responsibility for children's long-term wellbeing. The challenge is honoring children's self-knowledge while recognizing that childhood identity can be fluid.

For today's leaders, this demands nuanced approaches that neither dismiss children's gender expressions nor rush toward irreversible decisions. It means supporting families through uncertainty rather than providing false certainty. It means acknowledging that both over-medicalization and under-support can cause harm. Most importantly, it means recognizing that parents struggling with these decisions aren't necessarily transphobic—they're often terrified of making mistakes with their children's lives. When a child tells you who they are, listening is essential—but so is recognizing that childhood is a developmental process, not a fixed state.

FOR FURTHER READING

Research on early gender identity development

American Psychological Association (2015). Guidelines for Psychological Practice with Transgender and Gender Nonconforming People. American Psychologist, 70(9), 832-864.

Denying transition **causes harm** through forced delay.

Forcing trans people to delay transition causes psychological and physical harm. Withholding medical care violates the principle of non-violence.

This statement establishes that denying or delaying gender transition constitutes active harm rather than neutral policy. It asserts that withholding medically necessary transition care violates the fundamental principle of non-violence by forcing transgender individuals to endure preventable psychological distress. However, this principle intersects with complex realities: distinguishing between adults and minors, reversible versus irreversible interventions, and the anguishing balance parents face between preventing immediate psychological harm and ensuring long-term wellbeing.

Throughout medical history, gatekeeping has often caused more harm than the conditions it sought to address. Delayed medical interventions in other contexts consistently produce worse outcomes than timely treatment. Modern research shows that delays in transition care correlate with increased suicide risk, depression, and anxiety among transgender individuals.[1] Studies demonstrate that timely access to appropriate transition care improves mental health outcomes and reduces suicidality. The evidence for harm from delays is robust and concerning.

Yet the lived experience of families navigating transition care, particularly for minors, involves excruciating complexity. Parents face seemingly impossible choices: their child is suffering now, but some interventions have permanent effects. They read statistics about suicide risk among transgender youth and feel urgency. They also read accounts from detransitioners—though representing less than 1% of cases—describing regret over irreversible changes made during adolescent turmoil. No parent can easily dismiss even a 1% chance of their child experiencing profound regret.

The medical landscape itself is evolving and contested. Different interventions carry different risk profiles. Social transition is fully reversible. Puberty blockers are largely reversible, though questions remain about bone density and neurological development. Cross-sex hormones cause some irreversible changes. Surgical interventions are permanent. Some European countries that were early adopters of youth transition care have recently pulled back, citing insufficient evidence for long-term outcomes—creating additional uncertainty for parents seeking authoritative guidance.

For adults, the calculus is clearer—autonomous individuals can assess their own risk tolerance and make informed decisions about their bodies. The harm from forced delays for adults seems unambiguous. But for minors, parents must weigh their child's current distress against unknowable future outcomes. A 14-year-old in acute distress may have different needs than a 17-year-old with persistent gender dysphoria since early childhood. Yet systematic protocols often treat these situations similarly.

The philosophy operates through the principle of non-violence (ahimsa), which requires preventing harm when possible. But here we face competing potential harms: the documented harm of delay versus the potential harm of premature intervention. Parents trying to practice non-violence toward their children face choices where every path risks some form of harm. The certainty implied by "denial causes harm" meets the lived uncertainty of families in crisis.

Practically, this suggests differentiated approaches: streamlined access for adults who can make autonomous decisions; graduated protocols for minors that distinguish between reversible and irreversible interventions; comprehensive mental health support that addresses co-occurring conditions without using them to gatekeep; recognition that different developmental stages may warrant different approaches; and honest acknowledgment of what we know and don't know about long-term outcomes.

Some advocate for immediate affirmation and access to all requested interventions. Others support watchful waiting or extended assessment periods. The reality is that both approaches may be appropriate for different individuals. A 25-year-old with persistent gender dysphoria faces different considerations than a 13-year-old experiencing rapid-onset gender dysphoria alongside depression and anxiety. One-size-fits-all protocols serve neither population well.

This connects to principles like "medical transition aligns body with inner truth" while also acknowledging principles about protecting vulnerable populations and the challenges of medical decision-making for minors. The core truth—that unnecessary delays cause harm—remains valid while recognizing that determining what constitutes "necessary" versus "prudent" assessment is complex.

For today's leaders, this demands nuanced protocols that minimize harmful delays while ensuring appropriate assessment, particularly for minors. It means acknowledging that parents agonizing over these decisions aren't necessarily transphobic but are often navigating impossible choices with imperfect information. It means being honest about both the harms of delay AND the reality that some interventions carry irreversible consequences. Most importantly, it means recognizing that behind every statistic is a family trying to prevent their child's suffering while protecting their future—a task that would challenge Solomon himself.

FOR FURTHER READING

Research on mental health impacts of transition care delays

Bauer, G. R., et al. (2015). Intervenable factors associated with suicide risk in transgender persons. BMC Public Health, 15, 525.

Trans people deserve **equal access everywhere**.

Trans people deserve equal access to all spheres of life—employment, housing, public accommodations. Gender identity cannot justify discrimination in any field.

This statement establishes universal equal access for transgender individuals across all spheres of social participation. It asserts that gender identity can't constitute legitimate grounds for exclusion from employment, housing, education, healthcare, public accommodations, or any other domain of civic life. Discrimination based on transgender status violates fundamental equality while serving no legitimate purpose. It's like excluding left-handed people from jobs—arbitrary, harmful, and pointless. The principle demands active inclusion, not just tolerance.

Throughout history, exclusion from social participation has proven harmful to both excluded groups and society overall. Racial segregation in employment, education, and public accommodations harmed not only African Americans but diminished overall social and economic development. Gender exclusions from professions limited both women's opportunities and society's access to their talents. Similar patterns appear with all discrimination—exclusion impoverishes both individuals and communities.

Current evidence shows inclusive policies benefit everyone. Companies with transgender-inclusive employment policies report no operational difficulties while gaining broader talent pools. Schools with inclusive policies show improved climates for all students, not just transgender ones. Healthcare systems providing competent care to transgender patients develop expertise improving care quality generally. Military services including transgender personnel report no degradation in effectiveness while enhancing unit cohesion through inclusive values.

The philosophy recognizes that equal capacity for righteous action demands equal opportunity for social participation. Since transgender people demonstrate equivalent capability across all fields of human endeavor, exclusion violates the logical connection between capacity and access. Denying equal participation wastes human potential while violating justice. It's both wrong and wasteful.

Practically, this means comprehensive non-discrimination laws covering employment, housing, and public accommodations, educational policies ensuring equal access to all programs and facilities, and healthcare systems providing competent care regardless of gender identity or expression. Some claim certain spheres require gender restrictions. But they must address why transgender inclusion would be more disruptive than exclusion itself. Evidence consistently shows inclusion causes fewer problems than discrimination. The feared disruptions simply don't materialize.

This connects to principles like "all humans have equal capacity for righteous action" and "just institutions require representative participation." Together, they establish universal access as necessity.

For today's leaders, this demands proactive inclusion of transgender people in all institutional settings. Equal access constitutes basic justice rather than special accommodation. When we exclude people based on gender identity, we diminish our institutions and ourselves.

Insisting on birth assignment **denies lived experience**.

Insisting on birth-assigned gender despite contrary self-knowledge contradicts valid direct experience. Such insistence values arbitrary assignment over lived truth.

|| ॐ ||

This statement establishes that insisting on birth-assigned gender classification contradicts the primacy of lived experience. It asserts that privileging medical or administrative assignment over transgender individuals' direct knowledge of their identity is a fundamental error. Birth assignment represents a prediction based on external observation, not definitive determination of identity. Meanwhile, lived experience provides direct access to internal reality that external assignment can't override. It's like insisting someone's birth certificate weight is their "real" weight decades later—administrative records don't override current reality.

From time immemorial, administrative classifications have often failed to capture complex human realities, requiring revision when more accurate information becomes available. Medical diagnoses are regularly updated based on patient experience. Legal systems allow name changes, status corrections, and identity modifications when initial records prove inaccurate. Scientific classifications evolve as knowledge improves—biological taxonomy, psychological categories, and social classifications all undergo revision when evidence demands. The principle that initial assignments can be corrected has broad precedent.

Modern understanding recognizes that gender assignment at birth is educated guessing based on external genital configuration, not comprehensive assessment of gender identity. Research shows gender identity develops through complex neurological and psychological processes not visible at birth. Medical organizations increasingly acknowledge that birth assignment, while useful for initial medical care, can't definitively determine lifelong gender identity. Progressive legal systems allow correction of gender markers based on self-identification rather than maintaining outdated records.

The philosophy operates through the hierarchy of knowledge sources, where direct experience supersedes inference from external signs. Since transgender individuals have direct access to their gender experience while birth assignment represents inference from limited external indicators, lived experience necessarily carries greater authority. Privileging assignment over experience reverses this logical hierarchy. It's saying the map is more real than the territory.

Practically, this means legal systems allowing gender marker corrections based on self-identification, institutional policies prioritizing current identity over historical records, and social practices respecting individuals' expressed identity rather than investigating their birth assignment. Some claim birth assignment represents biological reality. But they must address why administrative classification would be more reliable than personal experience. If external assignment supersedes internal knowledge, then no form of self-knowledge would be valid. Can a birth certificate know you better than you know yourself?

This connects to principles like "inner knowledge supersedes external observation" and "self-knowledge of gender identity is supreme authority." Together, they establish experience primacy over administrative records.

For today's leaders, this demands respecting transgender individuals' current identity rather than investigating or privileging their birth assignment. When someone tells you who they are now, that matters more than what someone guessed they were at birth.

Name changes follow **established traditional precedent**.

Traditional literature contains numerous examples of name and identity changes for spiritual or social reasons. Trans name changes follow established precedent.

This statement establishes that transgender name changes align with established traditional precedents for identity transformation. It asserts that changing names to reflect evolved identity has deep historical and spiritual roots rather than being modern innovation. Name changes have served various legitimate purposes across cultures—spiritual initiation, life transitions, social advancement, and personal transformation. It's like how immigrants often changed names for new lives in new countries. Transgender name changes are part of this established tradition, not a departure from it.

The human record demonstrates that name changes have been central to spiritual and social transformation. Hindu traditions include taking new names during sannyasa (renunciation) to reflect spiritual rebirth. Buddhist monks and nuns adopt dharma names upon ordination, signifying identity transformation. Christian confirmation ceremonies often involve choosing new names to mark spiritual maturity. Jewish traditions include Hebrew names adopted at bar/bat mitzvah or conversion. Even secular contexts recognize name changes for marriage, adoption, professional purposes, or personal preference as legitimate exercises of autonomy.

Modern legal systems already accommodate various forms of name change, establishing clear precedents for transgender name modifications. Courts routinely approve name changes for artistic, professional, or personal reasons without requiring extensive justification. Marriage traditionally involves name changes that legal systems readily accommodate. Adoption creates new family names and identities that society accepts without question. The infrastructure for name changes exists precisely because identity evolution has been recognized as legitimate human experience.

The philosophy recognizes that practices aligned with established virtuous precedents carry legitimate authority. Since traditional cultures have consistently recognized name changes as appropriate responses to identity transformation, transgender name changes fall within established parameters of acceptable practice. The precedent validates the principle rather than creating new categories.

Practically, this means legal processes treating transgender name changes as routine administrative matters, social institutions readily adopting new names without lengthy explanations, and cultural recognition that name changes reflect rather than create identity transformation. Some claim transgender name changes differ fundamentally from traditional precedents. But they must address why gender identity transformation would be less legitimate than spiritual, social, or family identity changes. If name changes serve authentic identity expression in other contexts, gender transition can't be arbitrarily excluded.

This connects to principles like "everyone has the right to change name and form" and "self-knowledge of gender identity is supreme authority." Together, they establish traditional legitimacy for transgender name changes.

For today's leaders, this demands treating transgender name changes as continuation of established tradition rather than modern innovation requiring special justification. When we honor someone's new name, we're following ancient precedent.

Transition healthcare serves **righteous purposes**.

Medical transition is a legitimate means of achieving a life fully lived in alignment with one's deepest values. Healthcare that aligns the body with identity is an affirmation of personal truth, not a violation of it.

This statement establishes medical transition as serving fundamentally righteous purposes by enabling authentic self-expression and alleviating suffering. It asserts that transition healthcare is legitimate medical practice that promotes rather than violates ethical principles. Medical interventions designed to align physical reality with internal identity serve the same virtuous goals as other corrective treatments. It's like correcting a cleft palate or treating depression—healthcare that reduces suffering and enables authentic life serves righteousness.

Throughout history, medical interventions correcting misalignments between internal reality and external manifestation have been recognized as legitimate healing. Surgical corrections for cleft palates, limb differences, or sensory impairments align physical reality with normal function and social integration. Mental health treatments address disconnections between internal experience and external functioning. Even cosmetic surgeries for birth defects or traumatic injuries serve psychological and social wellbeing rather than mere vanity. The principle that medical care should address distress and promote functioning has broad acceptance.

Modern medical understanding recognizes gender dysphoria as a legitimate medical condition requiring appropriate treatment, with transition care representing evidence-based intervention rather than experimental procedure. Major medical organizations—the World Medical Association, American Medical Association, and World Health Organization—recognize transition healthcare as medically necessary. Research consistently shows transition care improves mental health outcomes, reduces suicide risk, and enables social functioning. Long-term studies show high satisfaction rates and improved quality of life following transition care.

The philosophy recognizes that actions serving authentic virtue constitute righteous behavior regardless of external appearances. Since transition healthcare serves fundamental virtues of reducing suffering, enabling authentic self-expression, and promoting psychological wellbeing, it fulfills rather than violates moral principles. Aligning internal truth with external reality represents a highest spiritual goal.

Practically, this means healthcare systems providing comprehensive transition care as standard medical treatment, insurance coverage for medically necessary transition procedures, and medical education training providers in competent transition care. Some claim transition healthcare violates natural order. But they must address why alleviating gender dysphoria would be less legitimate than treating other forms of psychological distress. If medical care serves wellbeing in other contexts, transition care can't be arbitrarily excluded.

This connects to principles like "medical transition aligns body with inner truth" and "denying transition causes harm through forced delay." Together, they establish medical legitimacy of transition care.

For today's leaders, this demands treating transition healthcare as legitimate medical practice rather than cosmetic preference. When healthcare enables people to live authentically and reduces suffering, it serves righteousness.

Parents must **accept their children's true identity.***

Parents' virtue requires accepting children's authentic identity. Rejection of trans children violates fundamental parental duty to support and protect offspring.

This statement establishes that parental virtue fundamentally requires accepting and supporting children's authentic gender identity. It asserts that rejection of transgender children violates the essential parental duty to nurture and protect offspring. However, "must accept" implies an instantaneous process when lived experience reveals a complex emotional journey. Parents often navigate grief, fear, religious conflicts, family pressure, and practical concerns while trying to support their child. The path to acceptance is rarely straightforward.

* *Timeless Principle: Parental love means nurturing the child who is, not the child you imagined.*

Across civilizations, successful parenting has emphasized accepting children's inherent nature while providing guidance and support. Religious traditions emphasize parental duties to love and support children unconditionally. Modern research overwhelmingly shows that family acceptance dramatically improves outcomes for transgender children while rejection increases risk of depression, anxiety, self-harm, and suicide.[1] The single strongest predictor of positive outcomes for transgender youth is family support—parental acceptance can be literally life-saving.[2]

Yet the lived experience of parents whose children come out as transgender involves profound complexity rarely captured in prescriptive statements. Many parents describe an intense grieving process—not because they don't love their child, but because they're mourning the future they had imagined. The daughter they pictured walking down the aisle in a wedding dress, the son they imagined teaching to shave—these anticipated moments represent deep emotional investments that don't simply evaporate.

Parents face cascading fears: Will my child be bullied, assaulted, or murdered? Will they find love and acceptance? Can they have children? Will they regret this? Will they face employment discrimination? These aren't abstract concerns—transgender people do face higher rates of violence, discrimination, and other challenges. Parents' protective instincts activate intensely, sometimes manifesting as resistance to transition that stems from fear rather than rejection.

Religious parents face particular anguish. Many deeply believe their faith teaches that God doesn't make mistakes, that biological sex is divinely ordained. They fear not just for their child's earthly wellbeing but for their eternal soul. They face potential ostracization from faith communities that provide essential support. Choosing between their child and their faith community can feel like an impossible choice that tears families apart.

Extended family pressure compounds the challenge. Grandparents may refuse to use new names or pronouns. Siblings may feel confused or resentful about attention shifts. Families divide over holiday gatherings. Parents find themselves defending their child to their own parents, siblings, and communities while still processing their own complex emotions.

Practical concerns are real. Healthcare is expensive and often not covered by insurance. Legal name changes require time and money. School policies vary widely. Some parents worry about younger siblings being influenced. Others fear making irreversible decisions or wonder if they're affirming too quickly or not quickly enough. There's no clear roadmap.

The journey toward acceptance often involves stages. Initial shock and denial: "This is just a phase." Bargaining: "Can't you just be a masculine girl/feminine boy?" Anger: "Why is this happening to our family?" Depression: "I'm losing my child." And eventually, for many, acceptance: "This is who my child is, and I need to support them."

Successful navigation often requires support. Parents benefit from counseling to process their emotions without burdening their child. Support groups like PFLAG connect parents with others who've walked this path.[3] Education helps—understanding that gender identity isn't a choice, learning about treatment options, hearing from thriving transgender adults. Time helps too—many parents who initially struggled become their children's fiercest advocates.

The philosophy recognizes that parental duty requires promoting children's wellbeing. The evidence is clear that acceptance improves outcomes while rejection causes harm. But acceptance is often a destination reached through a difficult journey, not a simple decision. Parents need support and grace during this process, not just mandates to accept.

Practically, this means providing resources for families in transition: counseling that helps parents process emotions while maintaining supportive relationships with their children; support groups connecting families navigating similar challenges; educational resources addressing common concerns and misconceptions; spiritual counseling for religious families struggling to reconcile faith and acceptance; and patience recognizing that acceptance is often a process, not an event.

This connects to principles about children knowing their identity while acknowledging that parents also have their own emotional and spiritual journeys. The challenge is supporting children's immediate needs while giving parents space to process and grow.

For today's leaders, this demands comprehensive family support that recognizes acceptance as a process requiring time, resources, and support. It means acknowledging that parents struggling with acceptance aren't necessarily bad parents—they're often loving parents facing challenges beyond their preparation. Most importantly, it means creating conditions that help families journey toward acceptance together rather than apart.

FOR FURTHER READING

Research on family acceptance and transgender youth outcomes

Ryan, Caitlin, et al. (2010). Family Acceptance in Adolescence and the Health of LGBT Young Adults. Journal of Child and Adolescent Psychiatric Nursing, 23(4), 205-213.

Study on parental support as protective factor for transgender youth

Simons, L., et al. (2013). Parental Support and Mental Health Among Transgender Adolescents. Journal of Adolescent Health, 53(6), 791-793.

PFLAG national organization for family support

PFLAG National. (2024). PFLAG: The First and Largest Organization for LGBTQ+ People, Their Parents and Families, and Allies. https://pflag.org

What exists naturally from birth **is not disease**.

What exists naturally from birth cannot be disease. Trans identity, being innate, requires support not cure. The medical model of pathology fails.

|| ॐ ||

This statement definitively establishes that characteristics present from birth represent natural human variation rather than pathological conditions requiring correction. It asserts that transgender identity, being an innate aspect of human development, should be supported and affirmed rather than treated as disease requiring cure. It's like eye color or handedness—natural variations aren't diseases. The principle recognizes that natural variation can't simultaneously be pathology, making attempts to "cure" transgender identity both illogical and harmful.

Historical evidence confirms that the distinction between natural variation and pathology has been central to ethical medical practice. Left-handedness, once considered pathological and subjected to forced correction, is now recognized as natural variation requiring accommodation. Homosexuality's removal from psychiatric diagnostic manuals reflected understanding that sexual orientation represents natural diversity rather than mental illness. Height, eye color, and numerous human characteristics show natural variation without being considered pathological. The principle that natural variation differs from disease has broad medical and ethical precedent.

Modern scientific understanding increasingly supports transgender identity as natural neurological variation rather than psychological disorder. Brain imaging studies show neurological patterns in transgender individuals aligning with their identified gender rather than assigned sex, suggesting biological rather than pathological origins. Twin studies indicate genetic components to transgender identity, further supporting natural rather than environmental causation. Developmental research shows early emergence of gender identity, typically by age 3-4, consistent with innate rather than acquired characteristics.

The philosophy recognizes that natural phenomena can't simultaneously be pathological. Since transgender identity appears consistently across cultures, historical periods, and family structures without external causation, it must represent natural human variation rather than dysfunction. Natural diversity serves creative purposes rather than requiring correction.

Practically, this means medical approaches supporting rather than attempting to change transgender identity, educational policies treating gender diversity as natural rather than problematic, and social frameworks accommodating rather than pathologizing gender variation. Some claim transgender identity causes distress and therefore constitutes pathology. But they must distinguish between internal identity and external social rejection as sources of distress. Research consistently shows supportive environments eliminate most distress associated with transgender identity. The distress comes from rejection, not the identity itself.[1]

This connects to principles like "gender diversity is natural, not disordered" and "multiple genders exist across cultures and history." Together, they establish transgender identity as natural variation.

For today's leaders, this demands treating transgender identity as natural human diversity requiring support rather than medical condition requiring cure. When we stop trying to fix what isn't broken, we enable flourishing.

FOR FURTHER READING

World Health Organization removing transgender identity from mental disorders

World Health Organization (2019). International Statistical Classification of Diseases and Related Health Problems (11th ed.). Geneva: WHO.

Multiple gender identities **disprove the binary**.

The existence of multiple gender identities disproves rigid binary classification. Reality's complexity exceeds simplistic dual categories.

This statement establishes that the documented existence of multiple gender identities across cultures definitively refutes rigid binary gender classification. It asserts that empirical evidence of gender diversity demonstrates the inadequacy of simplistic dual-category systems. When reality consistently exceeds theoretical frameworks, the frameworks must expand rather than deny reality. It's like insisting there are only two colors when we can see a rainbow. Binary gender models are scientifically and philosophically obsolete.

Throughout history, binary classifications have repeatedly proven inadequate for understanding complex natural phenomena. Early biological classifications assumed simple male-female categories until intersex conditions revealed the inadequacy of strict binaries. Psychological categories once assumed simple normal-abnormal divisions until research revealed spectrum conditions. Even physical sciences moved beyond binary thinking—light exhibits both wave and particle properties, challenging either-or classifications. Reality typically exceeds the boundaries of binary thinking.

Modern research consistently demonstrates gender diversity transcending binary categories. Anthropological studies document numerous cultures with third, fourth, or multiple gender categories. Neurological research reveals brain patterns that don't align neatly with binary classifications. Psychological studies show individuals whose gender identity doesn't fit traditional categories but who demonstrate healthy psychological functioning. Even biological sex reveals complexity—chromosomal, hormonal, and anatomical variations create intersex conditions affecting significant populations.

The philosophy recognizes that valid classification systems must accommodate observed phenomena rather than forcing phenomena into predetermined categories. Since multiple gender identities demonstrably exist across cultures and individuals, classification systems must acknowledge this diversity rather than denying it. Empirical evidence necessarily supersedes theoretical preferences. You can't unsee what exists.

Practically, this means legal systems recognizing non-binary gender options, educational curricula teaching gender diversity rather than binary thinking, and social policies accommodating rather than forcing conformity to traditional gender categories. Some claim binary categories represent natural law. But they must address why natural variation would consistently exceed natural boundaries. If nature truly operated through strict binaries, exceptions wouldn't appear universally across cultures and species. The exceptions prove the rule is wrong.

This connects to principles like "multiple genders exist across cultures and history" and "gender diversity is natural, not disordered." Together, they establish empirical refutation of the binary.

For today's leaders, this demands moving beyond binary gender assumptions in policy and practice. Reality's complexity requires sophisticated rather than simplistic thinking. When we acknowledge the full spectrum of human experience, we create space for everyone to thrive.

Trans joy validates authentic existence.

Transgender joy validates the authenticity of gender-affirming existence. Happiness in authentic identity confirms the rightness of self-determination.

|| ॐ ||

When transgender people experience genuine joy and fulfillment living as their authentic selves, this happiness serves as real-world proof that their identities are valid and that supporting them is the right approach. This principle matters because it shows us that joy isn't just a nice outcome—it's evidence that we're on the right track.

Through human experience, transgender joy serves as real-world proof of authentic existence. When individuals live according to their true gender identity and experience genuine happiness and fulfillment, that joy demonstrates that gender-affirming approaches are correct and necessary. It's like a compass pointing true north—authentic joy shows us we're heading in the right direction, while suffering indicates we've gone astray.

Throughout history, philosophers have recognized that true happiness comes from living authentically. Ancient Greek thinkers like Aristotle taught that flourishing happens when people live according to their true nature.[1] Buddhist philosophy sees genuine happiness as a sign that someone is living righteously.[2] Hindu traditions speak of finding your authentic purpose in life—when you're on the right path, fulfillment naturally follows.[3] Modern psychology confirms this pattern: authenticity leads to well-being, while forcing people to suppress who they are creates distress.

Today, we see this principle clearly in transgender experiences. Research consistently shows that transgender individuals who receive support and can live authentically report dramatically higher levels of happiness, life satisfaction, and psychological well-being. When transgender people access affirming healthcare and supportive environments, their mental health improves significantly. On the flip side, when transgender people are forced to hide or suppress their identities, rates of depression, anxiety, and suicidal thoughts skyrocket. The pattern is unmistakable: authenticity enables joy, while suppression creates suffering.

The philosophy here works through a simple logical principle: valid approaches produce positive outcomes, while invalid approaches create negative consequences. Since gender-affirming approaches consistently produce joy and well-being while suppressive approaches create distress, the evidence validates the authenticity of transgender identities. Joy becomes a form of proof we can measure and observe.

Practically, this means we should prioritize policies and practices that enable rather than restrict transgender joy. It suggests that happiness serves as a measure of how well our policies are working. When we support transgender flourishing, it benefits everyone in society by creating more inclusive, compassionate communities. Some might argue that temporary pleasure is different from authentic joy, questioning whether this happiness is genuine or lasting. But research distinguishes between momentary gratification and deep life satisfaction—gender-affirming approaches produce sustained rather than fleeting happiness, which indicates something much deeper than surface-level pleasure.

This connects to related principles about gender identity deserving recognition and respect, and how transition brings alignment and peace. Together, these teachings create a complete framework for understanding gender authenticity.

For today's leaders, this principle demands measuring success through transgender well-being rather than conformity. It means understanding that authentic joy indicates we're moving in the correct policy direction, while increased suffering suggests we need to change course.

FOR FURTHER READING

Aristotle's concept of eudaimonia (flourishing)

Aristotle. Nicomachean Ethics. 4th century BCE.

Buddhist philosophy on dharma and happiness

Buddhist philosophical traditions on dharma and authentic living.

Hindu concept of svadharma (authentic purpose)

Hindu philosophical traditions on svadharma and life purpose.

ACKNOWLEDGEMENTS

Beyond those to whom this book is dedicated, I have been blessed with remarkable friendships and encounters that have profoundly shaped my understanding of the intersection between ancient wisdom and contemporary justice.

My wife Alice and I had the rare honor and privilege of attending the coronation of Chief Nkosi Langa Zwelidumile Mavuso in the Eastern Cape Province that bears his family name (and incidentally, in the town that bears my wife's name). We were struck not only by his strength and commitment to improving the lives of the thousands of people he governs, but also by the depth of his vision for their future. We learned that the new Xhosa name "Zwelidumile" that was chosen for him by his subjects upon his coronation as Chief literally means "the nation has become renowned"—a reference to the fact that we, as Westerners along with many others, had become active partners and participants in the economic transformation and cultural preservation of their country. As deputy chair of the National House of Traditional and Khoi-San Leaders in South Africa, Chief Mavuso embodies the principle that authentic tradition serves human flourishing.

I have also been blessed through the years with the friendship of two legends in the fields of religion, ethics, spirituality, and civil rights activism. Dean Lawrence Edward Carter, Sr., founding dean of the Martin Luther King Jr. International Chapel at Morehouse College since 1979, has transformed generations of students through his synthesis of Eastern and Western ethical traditions. Personally recruited by Dr.

King as a tenth grader, Carter brings unique authenticity to "Global Ethical Options: In The Tradition Of Gandhi, King, And Ikeda" (co-authored with George David Miller and Neelakanta Radhakrishnan). This innovative workbook demonstrates how the Gandhi-King-Ikeda tradition of nonviolence offers a "force more powerful" for addressing contemporary global challenges. Through his interfaith journey—spanning over 1,000 engagements across diverse religious traditions—and his founding of the Gandhi-King-Ikeda Institute for Global Ethics and Reconciliation, Carter exemplifies how authentic dialogue and practical application can transform King's vision of the Beloved Community into a living framework for global ethics that honors both universal human values and cultural diversity.

Reverend Dr. Gerald L. Durley, Pastor Emeritus of Providence Missionary Baptist Church in Atlanta and Chairman of Interfaith Power & Light, embodies the transformative power of faith in action. From picking cotton in Kansas to marching with Dr. King, from Peace Corps volunteer to White House Champion of Change, his remarkable journey documented in "I Am Amazed!" reveals how the struggle for human dignity naturally extends to defending God's creation. His pioneering vision—that environmental justice is the continuation of the civil rights movement—demonstrates that the same communities bearing the burden of racial injustice suffer most from environmental degradation, making climate activism a moral imperative for people of faith.

The sheer power of their combined vision for humanity was on full display at the International World Culture Festival in New Delhi, India in 2016, and Washington, DC in 2023 where leaders from diverse spiritual and cultural traditions gathered to celebrate our common humanity. Witnessing Dean Carter and Reverend Durley share the stage with my teacher Gurudev Sri Sri Ravi Shankar and other global luminaries reinforced my conviction that ancient wisdom and modern justice are not opposing forces but complementary aspects of humanity's evolution toward greater compassion and understanding.

I am also deeply grateful to Dr. Robert Carter III, whose works "The Morning Mind" and "The Bipartisan Jesus" illuminate both the neuroscience of contemplative practice and the transcendent nature of spiritual truth beyond political divisions -- demonstrating that the transformation of consciousness serves all humanity regardless of ideological boundaries.

I owe a special debt of gratitude to Carol Kline, whose friendship has been one of life's true constants for more than thirty years. When I needed someone to help shape this manuscript into its final form, Carol dove in with the same generous spirit she's brought to our friendship since day one—offering her sharp editorial instincts, her gift for finding the right word, and her brutal honesty when a passage just wasn't working. She never asked for anything except that I trust her judgment (which, after three decades, I've learned to do without question). Carol has this rare ability to see both the forest and the trees, catching typos while never losing sight of the bigger picture. That she would devote her precious time to refining this work, purely out of friendship and a belief in its message, speaks to the kind of person she is. Some people make your work better; Carol makes you want to be better at your work.

No acknowledgment would be complete without recognizing Ben Dinkins, who has been my brother in every way that matters for over fifty years. We met as freshmen at Harvard in the Gung-Fu Club—two kids trying to look tough while learning to throw kicks—and by sophomore year we were roommates, a partnership that somehow survived my late-night coding sessions and his meticulous study habits. Ben's mind for detail, honed through his studies in American History and perfected over decades as a corporate attorney, has always amazed me. When I asked him to review this manuscript, he brought that same laser focus to every page—questioning word choices, probing themes for unintended implications, and pushing me to clarify arguments I thought were already clear. He caught nuances I'd missed and potential interpretations I hadn't considered, all while somehow maintaining enthusiasm for a project that required him to wade through dense philosophical arguments about ancient Sanskrit texts. That's Ben—still looking out for me after half a century, still making sure I don't embarrass myself, still the friend who tells you what you need to hear, not what you want to hear. Some friendships are measured in years; ours is measured in lifetimes.

To all who have contributed to this work through their example, their scholarship, and their friendship—my heartfelt thanks. May these ancient tools continue to serve the cause of justice and human dignity for generations to come.

NOTES

1.1 : Birth and race do not determine virtue or worth.

[1] Marcus Aurelius (167-180 CE). Meditations, Book II. Various modern translations available. *Marcus Aurelius - Stoic assertion that 'we were born to work together' regardless of origin*

[2] Husserl, Edmund (1913). Ideas: General Introduction to Pure Phenomenology. Translated by W.R. Boyce Gibson. New York: Macmillan, 1931. *Edmund Husserl - phenomenological tradition supporting direct perception of moral agency*

[3] Merleau-Ponty, Maurice (1945). Phenomenology of Perception. Translated by Colin Smith. London: Routledge, 1962. *Maurice Merleau-Ponty - phenomenological insights on perception preceding categorization*

[4] Executive Order 9981 (1948). Desegregation of the Armed Forces. Harry S. Truman Presidential Library. *U.S. military racial integration - historical example of successful institutional change*

1.2 : Systemic racism exists even when not visible.

[1] DuBois, W.E.B. (1903). The Souls of Black Folk. Chicago: A.C. McClurg & Co. *W.E.B. DuBois - concept of 'double consciousness' affecting African Americans*

[2] Gramsci, Antonio (1971). Selections from the Prison Notebooks. Edited and translated by Quintin Hoare and Geoffrey Nowell Smith. New York: International Publishers. *Antonio Gramsci - theory of hegemonic power structures maintaining dominance through cultural means*

[3] Horkheimer, Max and Theodor W. Adorno (1947). Dialectic of Enlightenment. Stanford: Stanford University Press, 2002. *The Frankfurt School - analysis of the 'culture industry' and embedded institutional bias*

[4] Bonilla-Silva, Eduardo (2003). Racism Without Racists: Color-Blind Racism and the Persistence of Racial Inequality in the United States. Lanham, MD: Rowman & Littlefield. *Eduardo Bonilla-Silva - concept of 'racism without racists' describing systemic inequalities through race-neutral processes*

1.3 : All humans have equal capacity for righteous action.

[1] Marcus Aurelius (167-180 CE). Meditations. Various modern translations available. *Marcus Aurelius - The Roman emperor who believed all humans were part of one global community*

[2] Nagarjuna (c. 150-250 CE). Mūlamadhyamakakārikā (Fundamental Verses on the Middle Way). Various translations available. *Nagarjuna - Buddhist teacher who taught that everyone has the potential for enlightenment*

[3] Mencius (c. 372-289 BCE). The Mencius. Translated by D.C. Lau. London: Penguin Classics, 1970. *Mencius - Chinese philosopher who said all people are born with the same basic goodness*

[4] Al-Ghazali (1058-1111). The Revival of the Religious Sciences (Ihya Ulum al-Din). Various translations available. *Al-Ghazali - Islamic scholar who taught everyone has equal spiritual and moral potential*

[5] Aquinas, Thomas (1265-1274). Summa Theologica. Various modern editions available. *Thomas Aquinas - Christian thinker who taught equal moral potential regardless of social status*

[6] Hauser, Marc (2006). Moral Minds: How Nature Designed Our Universal Sense of Right and Wrong. New York: Ecco/HarperCollins. *Marc Hauser - studies showing we're all born with similar ethical instincts*

[7] de Waal, Frans (1996). Good Natured: The Origins of Right and Wrong in Humans and Other Animals. Cambridge, MA: Harvard University Press. *Frans de Waal - research on primates showing moral behavior comes from shared evolution*

[8] Kant, Immanuel (1785). Groundwork of the Metaphysics of Morals. Various modern translations available. *Immanuel Kant - philosopher who argued all people have dignity through their capacity for reason*

1.4 : Racial categories are social constructs, not natural facts.

[1] Whorf, Benjamin Lee (1956). Language, Thought, and Reality: Selected Writings. Cambridge, MA: MIT Press. *Sapir-Whorf hypothesis - theory about language shaping perception*

[2] International Human Genome Sequencing Consortium (2001). "Initial

sequencing and analysis of the human genome." Nature 409(6822): 860-921. *The Human Genome Project - revealed greater genetic variation within racial groups than between them*

[3] Goodman, Alan H. (2000). "Why Genes Don't Count (for Racial Differences in Health)." American Journal of Public Health 90(11): 1699-1702. *Alan Goodman - research showing racial categories explain less than 0.1% of human genetic variation*

[4] Omi, Michael and Howard Winant (1994). Racial Formation in the United States: From the 1960s to the 1990s. New York: Routledge. *Critical race theory documentation of how racial categories emerged to justify slavery and colonization*

1.5 : Equal or comparable achievement demonstrates equal rights to opportunity.

[1] Lewis, David Levering (1981). When Harlem Was in Vogue. New York: Knopf. *The Harlem Renaissance - period demonstrating African American achievement when barriers lowered*

[2] Robinson, Jackie (1972). I Never Had It Made: An Autobiography. New York: G.P. Putnam's Sons. *Jackie Robinson's integration of baseball - proving athletic equality when opportunity opened*

[3] Sahlberg, Pasi (2011). Finnish Lessons: What Can the World Learn from Educational Change in Finland? New York: Teachers College Press. *Finland's comprehensive school reforms - showing achievement gaps vanish with educational equality*

1.6 : Discriminatory traditions have no moral authority.

[1] Aristotle (350 BCE). Politics. Translated by Ernest Barker. Oxford: Oxford University Press, 1995. *Aristotle's distinction between good and bad customs*

[2] Mill, John Stuart (1859). On Liberty. London: John W. Parker and Son. *John Stuart Mill's harm principle that invalidates traditions causing unjustified suffering*

[3] Chinese Exclusion Act (1882). 22 Stat. 58, enacted May 6, 1882. *Chinese Exclusion Act - example of discriminatory law lacking moral authority*

1.7 : Excellence from any group disproves natural inferiority.

[1] Popper, Karl (1959). The Logic of Scientific Discovery. London: Hutchinson. *Karl Popper's philosophy of science - falsification through counterexamples*

[2] Douglass, Frederick (1845). Narrative of the Life of Frederick Douglass, an American Slave. Boston: Anti-Slavery Office. *Frederick Douglass's eloquence disproving claims about African intellectual inferiority*

[3] Nobel Prize Awards: Marie Curie - Physics (1903) and Chemistry (1911). Nobel Foundation Archives. *Marie Curie's Nobel Prizes falsifying theories about women's scientific incapacity*

[4] Robinson, Jackie (1972). I Never Had It Made: An Autobiography. New York: G.P. Putnam's Sons. *Jackie Robinson's athletic excellence demolishing theories about Black athletic inferiority*

1.8 : Judge individuals by their actions, not their group.

[1] Aristotle (350 BCE). Nicomachean Ethics. Translated by Terence Irwin. Indianapolis: Hackett Publishing, 1999. *Aristotle's Nicomachean Ethics - virtue depends on voluntary action by rational agents*

[2] Executive Order 9066 (1942). Authorizing the Secretary of War to Prescribe Military Areas. Franklin D. Roosevelt Presidential Library. *Japanese American internment - historical violation of individual judgment principle*

[3] Kant, Immanuel (1785). Groundwork of the Metaphysics of Morals. Translated by Mary Gregor. Cambridge: Cambridge University Press, 1997. *Kant's categorical imperative - treating people as ends in themselves*

1.9 : Claims of racial superiority are propaganda, not truth.

[1] Aristotle (350 BCE). Rhetoric. Translated by W. Rhys Roberts. New York: Modern Library, 1954. *Aristotle's distinction between epistemic discourse (truth-seeking) and deliberative rhetoric (persuasion)*

[2] Rosenberg, Alfred (1930). Der Mythus des 20. Jahrhunderts. Munich: Hoheneichen-Verlag. *Alfred Rosenberg's 'Myth of the Twentieth Century' - example of propaganda disguised as scholarship*

[3] Gould, Stephen Jay (1981). The Mismeasure of Man. New York: W.W. Norton & Company. *American 'scientific racism' period using statistical manipulation*

1.10 : Prejudice requires ignoring evidence of human equality.

[1] Festinger, Leon (1957). A Theory of Cognitive Dissonance. Stanford: Stanford University Press. *Leon Festinger's cognitive dissonance theory - explaining how people reject evidence contradicting beliefs*

[2] Eberhardt, Jennifer L. (2019). Biased: Uncovering the Hidden Prejudice That Shapes What We See, Think, and Do. New York: Viking. *Jennifer Eberhardt's research on how racial assumptions override direct observation*

[3] Goldin, Claudia and Cecilia Rouse (2000). "Orchestrating Impartiality: The Impact of 'Blind' Auditions on Female Musicians." American Economic Review 90(4): 715-741. *Blind auditions in orchestras eliminating gender bias*

1.11 : Failed segregation shows racial divisions are artificial.

[1] Woodward, C. Vann (1955). The Strange Career of Jim Crow. New York: Oxford University Press. *American segregation period promising but failing to deliver social harmony*

[2] Thompson, Leonard (2001). A History of South Africa. New Haven: Yale University Press. *South African apartheid system and its internal contradictions*

[3] Massey, Douglas S. and Nancy A. Denton (1993). American Apartheid: Segregation and the Making of the Underclass. Cambridge, MA: Harvard University Press. *Contemporary residential segregation patterns and their negative outcomes*

1.12 : Excluding any group diminishes society's virtue.

[1] King, Martin Luther Jr. (1963). "Letter from Birmingham Jail." American Friends Service Committee. *Martin Luther King Jr.'s assertion about injustice affecting justice everywhere*

[2] Page, Scott E. (2007). The Difference: How the Power of Diversity Creates Better Groups, Firms, Schools, and Societies. Princeton: Princeton University Press. *Scott Page's work demonstrating diverse groups outperform*

homogeneous ones

[3] Florida, Richard (2002). The Rise of the Creative Class. New York: Basic Books. *Richard Florida's research on diversity driving economic growth and innovation*

[4] Mill, John Stuart (1859). On Liberty. London: John W. Parker and Son. *John Stuart Mill's concept of the 'marketplace of ideas'*

1.13 : Racial prejudice stems from misperception becoming delusion.

[1] Morton, Samuel George (1839). Crania Americana. Philadelphia: J. Dobson. *Samuel Morton's cranial studies exemplifying measurement errors from racial bias*

[2] Eberhardt, Jennifer L. (2019). Biased: Uncovering the Hidden Prejudice That Shapes What We See, Think, and Do. New York: Viking. *Jennifer Eberhardt's studies on how racial categories prime perception*

[3] Steele, Claude M. (2010). Whistling Vivaldi: How Stereotypes Affect Us and What We Can Do. New York: W.W. Norton & Company. *Claude Steele's stereotype threat research on self-fulfilling prophecies*

[4] Simmel, Georg (1908). Sociology: Investigations on the Forms of Sociation. Berlin: Duncker & Humblot. *Georg Simmel's sociology on how social categories become reified*

[5] Greenwald, Anthony G., Debbie E. McGhee, and Jordan L.K. Schwartz (1998). "Measuring Individual Differences in Implicit Cognition: The Implicit Association Test." Journal of Personality and Social Psychology 74(6): 1464-1480. *Harvard's Project Implicit revealing unconscious associations*

1.14 : Human worth cannot be ranked or compared.

[1] Kant, Immanuel (1785). Groundwork of the Metaphysics of Morals. Translated by Mary Gregor. Cambridge: Cambridge University Press, 1997. *Kant's categorical imperative establishing rational beings as 'ends in themselves'*

[2] Comte, Auguste (1830-1842). The Course of Positive Philosophy. Paris: Bachelier. *Auguste Comte's positivist hierarchy attempting to rank cultures*

[3] Hofstadter, Richard (1944). Social Darwinism in American Thought.

Philadelphia: University of Pennsylvania Press. *Social Darwinist theories misapplying evolution to human societies*

1.15 : Universal ethics override discriminatory rules.

[1] Thoreau, Henry David (1849). "Civil Disobedience." Aesthetic Papers. Boston: Elizabeth P. Peabody. *Henry David Thoreau's argument that unjust laws lack moral authority*

[2] King, Martin Luther Jr. (1963). "Letter from Birmingham Jail." American Friends Service Committee. *Martin Luther King Jr.'s distinction between just and unjust laws*

[3] Dworkin, Ronald (1977). Taking Rights Seriously. Cambridge, MA: Harvard University Press. *Ronald Dworkin's jurisprudence distinguishing between rules and principles*

[4] Still, William (1872). The Underground Railroad: A Record of Facts, Authentic Narratives, Letters, &c. Philadelphia: Porter & Coates. *The Underground Railroad as practical application of universal principles over law*

1.16 : Equal treatment serves the common good.

[1] Aristotle (350 BCE). Politics. Translated by Ernest Barker. Oxford: Oxford University Press, 1995. *Aristotle's concept of the common good (koinon agathon)*

[2] Cicero, Marcus Tullius (54-51 BCE). De Re Publica. Translated by Clinton W. Keyes. Cambridge, MA: Harvard University Press, 1928. *Cicero's concept of res publica (public good)*

[3] Rawls, John (1971). A Theory of Justice. Cambridge, MA: Harvard University Press. *John Rawls's theory that just institutions benefit society as a whole*

[4] DuBois, W.E.B. (1935). Black Reconstruction in America, 1860-1880. New York: Harcourt, Brace and Company. *W.E.B. DuBois's economic analyses of how discrimination harmed Southern workers*

1.17 : Eternal principles of justice supersede unjust laws.

[1] Aristotle (350 BCE). Nicomachean Ethics, Book V. Translated by Terence Irwin. Indianapolis: Hackett Publishing, 1999. *Aristotle's distinction between conventional and natural justice*

[2] Cicero, Marcus Tullius (52 BCE). De Legibus (On the Laws). Translated by Clinton W. Keyes. Cambridge, MA: Harvard University Press, 1928. *Cicero's assertion that unjust laws aren't truly laws*

[3] Aquinas, Thomas (1265-1274). Summa Theologica, I-II, Question 91. Various modern editions available. *Thomas Aquinas's hierarchy placing eternal law above human law*

[4] Sophocles (441 BCE). Antigone. Translated by Robert Fagles. New York: Penguin Classics, 1984. *Sophocles's Antigone dramatizing conflict between divine and human law*

[5] Dworkin, Ronald (1977). Taking Rights Seriously. Cambridge, MA: Harvard University Press. *Ronald Dworkin's legal theory distinguishing rules and principles*

1.18 : Achievement from the oppressed demonstrates universal potential.

[1] Douglass, Frederick (1845). Narrative of the Life of Frederick Douglass, an American Slave. Boston: Anti-Slavery Office. *Frederick Douglass's oratory and writing demonstrating intellectual brilliance*

[2] Wheatley, Phillis (1773). Poems on Various Subjects, Religious and Moral. London: A. Bell. *Phillis Wheatley's poetry creating cognitive dissonance about slavery*

[3] Obama, Barack (2009-2017). 44th President of the United States. Presidential Archives. *Barack Obama's presidency as contemporary example of excellence from oppressed group*

2.1: Physical differences don't extend to consciousness or capability.

[1] Plato (380 BCE). Phaedo. Translated by G.M.A. Grube. Indianapolis: Hackett Publishing, 1977. *Platonic philosophy separating soul from body*

[2] Shankara (8th century CE). Vivekachudamani (Crest Jewel of

Discrimination). Translated by Swami Madhavananda. Kolkata: Advaita Ashrama, 1921. *Vedantic thought distinguishing eternal self (atman) from physical form*

[3] Descartes, René (1637). Discourse on Method. Translated by Donald A. Cress. Indianapolis: Hackett Publishing, 1998. *Cartesian dualism recognizing mind as separate from material extension*

[4] Chalmers, David J. (1996). The Conscious Mind: In Search of a Fundamental Theory. Oxford: Oxford University Press. *Contemporary philosophy of mind on consciousness transcending physical properties*

2.4 : Women's virtue encompasses all spheres, not just domestic.

[1] Nightingale, Florence (1859). Notes on Nursing: What It Is, and What It Is Not. London: Harrison. *Florence Nightingale revolutionizing medical care and hospital sanitation*

[2] Roosevelt, Eleanor (1958). On My Own. New York: Harper & Brothers. *Eleanor Roosevelt advancing human rights globally*

[3] Curie, Marie (1923). Pierre Curie. New York: The Macmillan Company. *Marie Curie transforming scientific understanding*

2.5 : Gender roles are social constructions, not natural law.

[1] Butler, Judith (1990). Gender Trouble: Feminism and the Subversion of Identity. New York: Routledge. *Anthropological research on cultural construction of gender roles*

2.6 : Women achieve all life goals without needing men.

[1] Tyldesley, Joyce (1996). Hatchepsut: The Female Pharaoh. London: Viking. *Queen Hatshepsut ruling Egypt successfully for decades*

[2] Curie, Eve (1937). Madame Curie: A Biography. Garden City, NY: Doubleday. *Marie Curie achieving scientific breakthroughs*

[3] Spink, Kathryn (1997). Mother Teresa: A Complete Authorized Biography. San Francisco: HarperSanFrancisco. *Mother Teresa embodying spiritual realization*

2.7 : Intelligence, not gender, determines educational access.

[1] Newman, Barbara (1987). Sister of Wisdom: St. Hildegard's Theology of the Feminine. Berkeley: University of California Press. *Hildegard of Bingen producing sophisticated theological and scientific works*

2.8 : Self-determination is a universal human right.

[1] Kant, Immanuel (1785). Groundwork of the Metaphysics of Morals. Translated by Mary Gregor. Cambridge: Cambridge University Press, 1998. *Kantian philosophy on autonomy as fundamental to human dignity*

2.9 : Work results demonstrate gender is irrelevant to achievement.

[1] Shetterly, Margot Lee (2016). Hidden Figures: The American Dream and the Untold Story of the Black Women Mathematicians Who Helped Win the Space Race. New York: William Morrow. *Katherine Johnson's NASA calculations*

2.11: Equal work demands equal pay, regardless of gender.

[1] Act on Equal Status and Equal Rights of Women and Men No. 10/2008, as amended by Act No. 56/2017 (Iceland). *Iceland's pay equity requirements demonstrating improved economic efficiency*

2.13 : Restrictive gender roles obstruct self-realization.

[1] DeVries, Kelly (1999). Joan of Arc: A Military Leader. Stroud: Sutton Publishing. *Joan of Arc transcending gender roles through military leadership*

[2] Somerset, Anne (1991). Elizabeth I. London: Weidenfeld & Nicolson. *Elizabeth I succeeding by rejecting gender limitations*

[3] Harlan, Elizabeth (2004). George Sand. New Haven: Yale University Press. *George Sand achieving literary success by transcending gender restrictions*

2.14 : Universal duties override gender-based prohibitions.

[1] Bostridge, Mark (2008). Florence Nightingale: The Making of an Icon.

London: Viking. *Florence Nightingale violating Victorian gender norms to serve wounded soldiers*

[2] Parks, Rosa with Jim Haskins (1992). Rosa Parks: My Story. New York: Dial Books. *Rosa Parks defying social expectations to advance civil rights*

2.15 : In highest consciousness, gender becomes irrelevant.

[1] Newman, Barbara (1987). Sister of Wisdom: St. Hildegard's Theology of the Feminine. Berkeley: University of California Press. *Hildegard of Bingen achieving recognition through mystical insights*

[2] Barks, Coleman (1995). The Essential Rumi. San Francisco: HarperSanFrancisco. *Rumi's spiritual poetry transcending gender categories*

3.1 : Diversity is nature's fundamental principle.

[1] Heraclitus (535-475 BCE). Fragments. In Kirk, G.S., Raven, J.E., and Schofield, M. (1983). The Presocratic Philosophers. Cambridge: Cambridge University Press. *Heraclitus's identification of unity of opposites as reality's fundamental structure*

[2] Darwin, Charles (1859). On the Origin of Species by Means of Natural Selection. London: John Murray. *Charles Darwin's evolutionary theory demonstrating how diversity drives adaptation*

[3] Frankham, Richard (2005). "Genetics and extinction." Biological Conservation 126(2): 131-140. *Population genetics showing genetic diversity essential for species survival*

[4] McCann, Kevin Shear (2000). "The diversity-stability debate." Nature 405(6783): 228-233. *Ecosystem complexity and stability relationship*

3.2 : Uniformity leads to systemic collapse.

[1] Irish Potato Famine. (1845-1852). [Historical Event] *The Irish Potato Famine historical event*

[2] Global Financial Crisis. (2008). [Economic Event] *The 2008 global financial crisis*

[3] Kauffman, Stuart. (1993). The Origins of Order: Self-Organization and Selection in Evolution. Oxford University Press. *Stuart Kauffman's research on complex systems*

[4] Tilman, David (1999). "The ecological consequences of changes in biodiversity: a search for general principles." Ecology 80(5): 1455-1474. *Ecological research on monoculture vulnerability*

3.3 : Present action must address historical injustices.

[1] Reparations Agreement between Israel and West Germany. (1952). [Historical Agreement] *Germany's reparations to Holocaust survivors*

[2] Truth and Reconciliation Commission (South Africa). (1995-1998). [Commission Report] *South Africa's Truth and Reconciliation Commission*

[3] European Recovery Program [Marshall Plan]. (1948-1951). [U.S. Legislation] *The Marshall Plan for European recovery*

[4] Aristotle. (c. 350 BCE). Nicomachean Ethics. Book V. *Aristotle's theory of corrective justice*

3.4 : Pure meritocracy ignores systemic advantages.

[1] Bertrand, Marianne and Sendhil Mullainathan (2003). "Are Emily and Greg More Employable Than Lakisha and Jamal? A Field Experiment on Labor Market Discrimination." National Bureau of Economic Research Working Paper No. 9873. *Marianne Bertrand and Sendhil Mullainathan's study on racial bias in hiring*

[2] Bourdieu, Pierre (1986). "The Forms of Capital." In J. Richardson (Ed.), Handbook of Theory and Research for the Sociology of Education (pp. 241-258). New York: Greenwood. *Pierre Bourdieu's concept of 'cultural capital'*

3.5 : Just institutions require representative participation.

[1] Branch, Taylor (1988-2006). America in the King Years (trilogy). New York: Simon & Schuster. *U.S. Civil Rights Movement demanding meaningful political representation*

[2] Sparks, Allister (1995). Tomorrow is Another Country: The Inside Story

of South Africa's Road to Change. Chicago: University of Chicago Press. *South Africa's transition from apartheid requiring inclusive representation*

[3] Locke, John (1689). Two Treatises of Government. London: Awnsham Churchill. *Democratic theory on consent of the governed*

3.6 : Including everyone maintains social harmony.

[1] Garnsey, Peter and Richard Saller (1987). The Roman Empire: Economy, Society and Culture. Berkeley: University of California Press. *Roman Empire's inclusive policies during peak periods*

[2] Menocal, María Rosa (2002). The Ornament of the World: How Muslims, Jews, and Christians Created a Culture of Tolerance in Medieval Spain. Boston: Little, Brown and Company. *Medieval Spain's convivencia period of peaceful coexistence*

3.7 : Invisible barriers need visible remedies.

[1] Civil Rights Act of 1964, Pub. L. 88-352, 78 Stat. 241 (1964). *The Civil Rights Act of 1964 and its limitations in addressing subtle bias*

[2] Greenwald, Anthony G., Debbie E. McGhee, and Jordan L.K. Schwartz (1998). "Measuring Individual Differences in Implicit Cognition: The Implicit Association Test." Journal of Personality and Social Psychology 74(6): 1464-1480. *Harvard's Project Implicit demonstrating unconscious associations*

3.8 : Biased conditioning requires active correction.

[1] MacGregor, Morris J. (1981). Integration of the Armed Forces, 1940-1965. Washington, D.C.: Center of Military History. *U.S. military integration efforts including deliberate contact programs*

[2] Truth and Reconciliation Commission of South Africa Report (1998). Cape Town: Truth and Reconciliation Commission. *South Africa's Truth and Reconciliation Commission recognizing need for active dialogue*

[3] Devine, Patricia G. (1989). "Stereotypes and Prejudice: Their Automatic and Controlled Components." Journal of Personality and Social Psychology 56(1): 5-18. *Patricia Devine's work on bias interruption and prejudice reduction*

[4] Greenwald, Anthony G. and Mahzarin R. Banaji (1995). "Implicit social cognition: Attitudes, self-esteem, and stereotypes." Psychological Review 102(1): 4-27. *Psychology research on how biased patterns form through repetition*

3.9 : Refusing to see race prevents addressing racism.

[1] Scalia, Antonin (1995). Adarand Constructors, Inc. v. Peña, 515 U.S. 200 (concurring opinion). *Justice Antonin Scalia's assertion about colorblind Constitution*

[2] Bonilla-Silva, Eduardo (2003). Racism Without Racists: Color-Blind Racism and the Persistence of Racial Inequality in the United States. Lanham, MD: Rowman & Littlefield. *Eduardo Bonilla-Silva's work on colorblind racism*

3.10 : True equality means equal opportunity, not just outcomes.

[1] Johnson, Lyndon B. (1964). "The Great Society." Speech at University of Michigan, May 22, 1964. Presidential Archives. *The Great Society programs attempting to provide equal opportunity through compensatory measures*

[2] Roemer, John E. (1998). Equality of Opportunity. Cambridge, MA: Harvard University Press. *Economic and philosophical discussion of equality of initial conditions*

3.11 : Multicultural environments increase collective strength.

[1] Saliba, George (2007). Islamic Science and the Making of the European Renaissance. Cambridge, MA: MIT Press. *The Islamic Golden Age flourishing through cultural synthesis*

[2] Page, Scott E. (2007). The Difference: How the Power of Diversity Creates Better Groups, Firms, Schools, and Societies. Princeton: Princeton University Press. *Scott Page's work on diverse groups outperforming homogeneous groups*

[3] Hunt, Vivian, Dennis Layton, and Sara Prince (2015). "Why Diversity Matters." McKinsey & Company Report. *McKinsey research on diversity and company performance*

[4] Ashby, W. Ross (1956). An Introduction to Cybernetics. London: Chapman & Hall. *Systems theory concept of requisite variety*

3.12 : Like music, society needs multiple voices.

[1] Lewis, David Levering (1981). When Harlem Was in Vogue. New York: Knopf. *The Harlem Renaissance exemplifying cultural cross-pollination*

[2] Lewis, Mark Edward (2009). China's Cosmopolitan Empire: The Tang Dynasty. Cambridge, MA: Harvard University Press. *Tang Dynasty's cultural flowering through cosmopolitan openness*

[3] Florida, Richard (2002). The Rise of the Creative Class. New York: Basic Books. *Richard Florida's work on creative professionals gravitating toward diverse environments*

3.13 : Denying qualified people opportunities is unjust.

[1] Robinson, Jackie (1972). I Never Had It Made: An Autobiography. New York: G.P. Putnam's Sons. *Jackie Robinson's baseball integration revealing previously excluded talent*

3.14 : Diversity programs often lack genuine commitment.

[1] Dobbin, Frank and Alexandra Kalev (2016). Why Diversity Programs Fail. Harvard Business Review, 94(7), 52-60. *Research on ineffective diversity training and potential backlash*

[2] Kalev, Alexandra, Frank Dobbin, and Erin Kelly (2006). Best Practices or Best Guesses? Assessing the Efficacy of Corporate Affirmative Action and Diversity Policies. American Sociological Review, 71(4), 589-617. *Study on how mandatory diversity training can increase bias*

[3] Leon, Raul A. (2014). The Chief Diversity Officer: An Examination of CDO Models and Strategies. Journal of Diversity in Higher Education, 7(2), 77-91. *Research on Chief Diversity Officer challenges and turnover*

[4] Thomas, Kecia M. and Victoria C. Plaut (2008). The Many Faces of Diversity Resistance in the Workplace. In K.M. Thomas (Ed.), Diversity Resistance in Organizations (pp. 1-22). New York: Lawrence Erlbaum. *Analysis of middle management resistance to diversity initiatives*

[5] Ahmed, Sara (2012). On Being Included: Racism and Diversity in Institutional Life. Durham, NC: Duke University Press. *Research on the gap*

between diversity rhetoric and practice

[6] Dover, Tessa L., Brenda Major, and Cheryl R. Kaiser (2016). Members of High-Status Groups Are Threatened by Pro-Diversity Organizational Messages. Journal of Experimental Social Psychology, 62, 58-67. *Study on unintended consequences of diversity initiatives*

3.15 : Justice requires substantive, not just formal, equality.

[1] Aristotle (350 BCE). Nicomachean Ethics, Book V. Translated by Terence Irwin. Indianapolis: Hackett Publishing, 1999. *Aristotle's concept of distributive justice recognizing treating unequals equally as injustice*

[2] Plessy v. Ferguson, 163 U.S. 537 (1896) and Brown v. Board of Education, 347 U.S. 483 (1954). *Supreme Court's evolution from Plessy v. Ferguson to Brown v. Board of Education*

[3] Rawls, John (1971). A Theory of Justice. Cambridge, MA: Harvard University Press. *John Rawls's concept of 'fair equality of opportunity'*

3.17: Universal acceptance protects existence itself.

[1] Popper, Karl. The Open Society and Its Enemies. Vol. 1. London: Routledge, 1945. *Karl Popper's formulation of the paradox of tolerance*

[2] The Bhagavad Gita. Translated by Eknath Easwaran. 2nd ed. Tomales, CA: Nilgiri Press, 2007. Chapter 2, verses 31-38. *The Bhagavad Gita's discussion of protecting dharma through righteous action*

4.2: Unrestricted weapon access endangers society.

[1] Mill, John Stuart (1859). On Liberty. London: John W. Parker and Son. *John Stuart Mill's principle balancing individual liberty with collective harm prevention*

[2] National Research Council (2013). Priorities for Research to Reduce the Threat of Firearm-Related Violence. Washington, DC: The National Academies Press. *National Research Council report discussing the wide range of defensive gun use estimates*

[3] Castle Rock v. Gonzales, 545 U.S. 748 (2005). *Supreme Court case*

establishing that police have no constitutional duty to protect individuals

4.3: Easy access to lethal force increases violence.

[1] Chapple, Christopher Key (1993). Nonviolence to Animals, Earth, and Self in Asian Traditions. Albany: State University of New York Press. *The principle of non-violence (ahimsa) in ancient Eastern philosophy*

4.15: Even constitutional rights include 'well-regulated.'

[1] U.S. Const. amend. II. *The Second Amendment's text including 'well-regulated militia' language*

5.1: Control over one's body is the foundation of autonomy.

[1] Locke, John (1689). Two Treatises of Government. London: Awnsham Churchill. *John Locke's theory of self-ownership*

[2] Kant, Immanuel (1785). Groundwork of the Metaphysics of Morals. Translated by Mary Gregor. Cambridge: Cambridge University Press, 1997. *Immanuel Kant's concept of human dignity as self-determination*

5.3: Without consciousness, personhood is not established.

[1] Aristotle (350 BCE). De Anima (On the Soul). Translated by Hugh Lawson-Tancred. London: Penguin Classics, 1986. *Aristotle's concept of consciousness and rationality as defining human characteristics*

[2] Pew Research Center (2022). America's Abortion Quandary: Majority of Americans say abortion should be legal in some cases, illegal in others. *Survey research on American beliefs about when life begins*

[3] Morgan, Lynn M. (1989). When does life begin? A cross-cultural perspective on the personhood of fetuses and young children. Abortion Rights and Fetal Personhood, 97-114. *Cross-cultural analysis of personhood concepts and religious influences*

[4] Gallup (2023). Abortion Trends and Attitudes in America. Gallup Historical Trends. *Polling data on beliefs about when human life begins*

[5] Layne, Linda L. (2003). Motherhood Lost: A Feminist Account of Pregnancy Loss in America. Routledge. *Qualitative research on experiences of early pregnancy loss*

[6] Congregation for the Doctrine of the Faith (1987). Donum Vitae: Instruction on Respect for Human Life. *Catholic theological perspective on ensoulment and personhood*

[7] Atighetchi, Dariusch (2007). Islamic Bioethics: Problems and Perspectives. Springer. *Islamic jurisprudential views on ensoulment and fetal development*

[8] Lee, Patrick & George, Robert P. (2008). Body-Self Dualism in Contemporary Ethics and Politics. Cambridge University Press. *Philosophical critique of consciousness-based personhood criteria*

[9] Kaczor, Christopher (2014). The Ethics of Abortion: Women's Rights, Human Life, and the Question of Justice. Routledge. *Substance view of human dignity and personhood*

[10] Van der Sijpt, Erica (2018). The Pain and Pride of 'Repeat Pregnancy Loss' in Cameroon. Medical Anthropology Quarterly, 32(2), 241-259. *Anthropological study of miscarriage grief and recognition practices*

[11] Murphy, Fiona & Merrell, Jean (2009). Negotiating the transition: caring for women through the experience of early miscarriage. Journal of Clinical Nursing, 18(11), 1583-1591. *Cross-cultural funeral and memorial practices for pregnancy loss*

[12] Beckwith, Francis J. (2007). Defending Life: A Moral and Legal Case Against Abortion Choice. Cambridge University Press. *Arguments about potentiality and consciousness in bioethics debates*

[13] Foster, Diana Greene, et al. (2012). Attitudes and decision making among women seeking abortions at one U.S. clinic. Perspectives on Sexual and Reproductive Health, 44(2), 117-124. *Women's diverse beliefs about fetal status in abortion decisions*

5.5: Fertilized eggs lack the characteristics of persons.

[1] George, Robert P. & Tollefsen, Christopher (2008). Embryo: A Defense of Human Life. Doubleday. *Philosophical argument for embryonic personhood based on substantial identity*

[2] Kittay, Eva Feder (2005). At the Margins of Moral Personhood. Ethics, 116(1), 100-131. *Analysis of inherent dignity arguments in bioethics*

[3] Condic, Maureen L. (2014). Totipotency: What it is and what it is not. Stem Cells and Development, 23(8), 796-812. *Perspectives on continuous human identity from conception*

[4] Ehrich, K., et al. (2010). Embryo futures and stem cell research: The management of informed uncertainty. Sociology of Health & Illness, 32(1), 1-17. *Healthcare worker experiences with embryo-related procedures*

[5] Oderberg, David S. (2008). Applied Ethics: A Non-Consequentialist Approach. Blackwell. *Thomistic philosophy on continuous human identity*

[6] Condic, Maureen L. (2008). When does human life begin? A scientific perspective. Westchester Institute White Paper, 1(1), 1-18. *Scientific argument for organismal behavior from fertilization*

[7] Gilbert, Scott F. (2017). When 'personhood' begins in the embryo: Avoiding a syllabus of errors. Birth Defects Research, 109(8), 553-562. *Embryological perspectives on early human development*

[8] Hurlbut, William B. (2017). Biology and Being: The Emerging Science of Human Nature. Notre Dame Press. *Varied scientific interpretations of embryonic development*

[9] Marquis, Don (1989). Why abortion is immoral. Journal of Philosophy, 86(4), 183-202. *Critique of potentiality arguments and defense of developmental view*

[10] Provoost, V., et al. (2009). Infertility patients' beliefs about their embryos and their disposition preferences. Human Reproduction, 24(4), 896-905. *IVF patients' complex attitudes toward embryo status*

[11] Austriaco, Nicanor (2002). On Static Eggs and Dynamic Embryos. National Catholic Bioethics Quarterly, 2(4), 659-683. *Organismic view of embryonic life versus tissue view*

[12] Camosy, Charles (2015). Beyond the Abortion Wars: A Way Forward for a New Generation. Eerdmans. *Pro-life perspectives on protecting vulnerable life*

[13] Munson, Ziad (2009). The Making of Pro-life Activists: How Social Movement Mobilization Works. University of Chicago Press. *Women's*

motivations in pro-life advocacy

[14] Evans, John H. & Hudson, Kathy (2007). Religion and reproductive genetics: Beyond views of embryonic life? Journal for the Scientific Study of Religion, 46(4), 565-581. *Public opinion research on graduated views of embryonic status*

5.6 : No one else may control your bodily functions.

[1] Locke, John (1689). Two Treatises of Government. London: Awnsham Churchill. *John Locke's classical liberal theory recognizing the body as first property*

5.7 : Ending one's own suffering is legitimate self-care.

[1] Rocca, Corinne H., et al. (2020). Emotions and decision rightness over five years following an abortion: An examination of decision difficulty and abortion stigma. Social Science & Medicine, 248, 112704. *Research on emotional complexity following abortion*

[2] Hursthouse, Rosalind (1991). Virtue Theory and Abortion. Philosophy & Public Affairs, 20(3), 223-246. *Philosophical frameworks for approaching abortion ethics*

[3] Foster, Diana Greene (2020). The Turnaway Study: Ten Years, a Thousand Women, and the Consequences of Having—or Being Denied—an Abortion. New York: Scribner. *Research on moral perspectives and abortion*

[4] Kimport, Katrina, et al. (2012). Social Sources of Women's Emotional Difficulty After Abortion: Lessons from Women's Abortion Narratives. Perspectives on Sexual and Reproductive Health, 44(2), 103-109. *Study on diverse women's experiences of abortion*

5.9: Personal virtue choices supersede state authority.

[1] Luker, Kristin (1984). Abortion and the Politics of Motherhood. University of California Press. *Analysis of pro-life framing around protecting life versus controlling women*

[2] Jelen, Ted G. & Wilcox, Clyde (2003). Causes and consequences of public attitudes toward abortion. Annual Review of Political Science, 6, 489-518.

Survey research on abortion opponents' primary motivations

[3] Finnis, John (1973). The rights and wrongs of abortion. Philosophy & Public Affairs, 2(2), 117-145. *Legal argument about limits of autonomy when others are affected*

[4] Glendon, Mary Ann (1987). Abortion and Divorce in Western Law. Harvard University Press. *Comparative analysis of state duties regarding fetal versus born life*

[5] Arkes, Hadley (1986). First Things: An Inquiry into the First Principles of Morals and Justice. Princeton University Press. *Democratic theory and protection of vulnerable populations*

[6] Rubenfeld, Jed (1989). The Right of Privacy. Harvard Law Review, 102(4), 737-807. *Arguments for legitimate state interest in potential life*

[7] Mackenzie, Catriona & Stoljar, Natalie (2000). Relational Autonomy: Feminist Perspectives on Autonomy, Agency, and the Social Self. Oxford University Press. *Relational autonomy theory in reproductive ethics*

[8] Zampas, Christina & Gher, Jaime M. (2008). Abortion as a human right. Human Rights Law Review, 8(2), 249-294. *Analysis of competing human rights frameworks on abortion*

[9] Callahan, Daniel & Callahan, Sidney (1984). Abortion: Understanding Differences. Plenum Press. *State intervention to protect vulnerable populations*

[10] Beckwith, Francis J. (1993). Politically Correct Death: Answering Arguments for Abortion Rights. Baker Books. *Comparison of abortion restrictions to other protective laws*

[11] Tollefsen, Christopher (2008). Biomedical Research and Beyond: Expanding the Ethics of Inquiry. Routledge. *Arguments about state interest in protecting human life*

[12] Shields, Jon A. (2009). The Democratic Virtues of the Christian Right. Princeton University Press. *Research on pro-life support for social welfare programs*

[13] Saad, Lydia (2023). Broader Support for Abortion Rights Continues Post-Dobbs. Gallup Poll Social Series. *Public opinion on abortion restrictions and moral complexity*

5.11: Moral duties vary with developmental stages.

[1] Aquinas, Thomas (1273). Summa Theologica. Translated by Fathers of the English Dominican Province. New York: Benziger Brothers, 1947. *Thomas Aquinas's theory of delayed ensoulment distinguishing developmental stages*

5.12: Full personhood rights begin at birth.

[1] Blackstone, William (1765-1769). Commentaries on the Laws of England. Oxford: Clarendon Press. *English common law's 'born alive' rule as legal foundation*

5.15 : True compassion respects autonomous decisions.

[1] Harvey, Peter (2000). An Introduction to Buddhist Ethics. Cambridge: Cambridge University Press. *Buddhist concept of compassion (karuna) emphasizing skillful means respecting individual wisdom*

[2] Altshuler, A. L., et al. (2017). Male partners' involvement in abortion care: A mixed-methods systematic review. Perspectives on Sexual and Reproductive Health, 49(2), 71-84. *Qualitative research on support needs and autonomy during reproductive decision-making*

[3] Foster, D. G. (2020). The Turnaway Study: Ten Years, a Thousand Women, and the Consequences of Having—or Being Denied—an Abortion. Scribner. *Study on autonomy and relational decision-making in reproductive choices*

[4] Rocca, C. H., et al. (2015). Decision rightness and emotional responses to abortion in the United States. PLOS One, 10(7), e0128832. *Research on emotional complexity and ambivalence in abortion decisions*

[5] Mumtaz, Z., et al. (2014). Unintended pregnancy in Pakistan: The role of gender and empowerment. International Journal of Gynecology & Obstetrics, 124(3), 250-253. *Cross-cultural perspectives on family involvement in reproductive decision-making*

[6] Roberts, D. (1997). Killing the Black Body: Race, Reproduction, and the Meaning of Liberty. Pantheon Books. *Analysis of structural barriers to reproductive autonomy*

[7] Lipp, A. (2011). Self-preservation in abortion care: A grounded theory

study. Journal of Clinical Nursing, 20(5-6), 892-900. *Healthcare provider perspectives on balancing autonomy and care*

[8] Biggs, M. A., et al. (2017). Women's mental health and well-being 5 years after receiving or being denied an abortion. JAMA Psychiatry, 74(2), 169-178. *Long-term outcomes and decision satisfaction research*

5.16 : Actual persons take precedence over potential ones.

[1] Pew Research Center (2022). Public Opinion on Abortion: Views on abortion by trimester. Pew Research Center Religion & Public Life. *Public opinion research on gradated views of fetal moral status*

[2] MacIntyre, Alasdair (1999). Dependent Rational Animals: Why Human Beings Need the Virtues. Open Court. *Philosophical argument about vulnerability creating moral obligations*

[3] Warren, Mary Anne (1997). Moral Status: Obligations to Persons and Other Living Things. Oxford University Press. *Analysis of gradated moral status in reproductive ethics*

[4] Kjelsvik, M. & Gjengedal, E. (2011). First-trimester abortion: Women's experiences of the decision and the procedure. Scandinavian Journal of Caring Sciences, 25(3), 449-457. *Women's moral reasoning in abortion decisions*

[5] Kaczor, Christopher (2011). The Ethics of Abortion: Women's Rights, Human Life, and the Question of Justice. Routledge, pp. 165-178. *Catholic doctrine on double effect and maternal life exceptions*

[6] Cavanaugh, T.A. (2006). Double-Effect Reasoning: Doing Good and Avoiding Evil. Oxford University Press. *Analysis of double-effect reasoning in medical ethics*

[7] Steinbock, Bonnie (2011). Life Before Birth: The Moral and Legal Status of Embryos and Fetuses, 2nd ed. Oxford University Press. *Gradated approaches to fetal moral status in bioethics*

[8] Wilkinson, Dominic (2013). Death or Disability?: The 'Carmentis Machine' and Decision-making for Critically Ill Children. Oxford University Press. *Neonatal care and moral status at margins of viability*

[9] McMahan, Jeff (2002). The Ethics of Killing: Problems at the Margins of

Life. Oxford University Press. *Cognitive disability and personhood debates*

[10] Marquis, Don (1989). Why abortion is immoral. Journal of Philosophy, 86(4), 183-202. *Future-like-ours account of abortion ethics*

[11] Stone, Jim (1987). Why potentiality matters. Canadian Journal of Philosophy, 17(4), 815-830. *Distinguishing actual potential from merely possible life*

[12] Center for Reproductive Rights (2021). The World's Abortion Laws. Center for Reproductive Rights Global Maps. *International comparison of gestational limits in abortion law*

[13] Lafarge, C., Mitchell, K., & Fox, P. (2013). Women's experiences of coping with pregnancy termination for fetal abnormality. Qualitative Health Research, 23(7), 924-936. *Parents' experiences with abortion for fetal abnormalities*

5.17 : Individual conscience governs personal moral choices.

[1] Luther, Martin (1520). On the Freedom of a Christian. Wittenberg: Melchior Lotter. *Protestant Reformation theology emphasizing individual's direct relationship with divine authority*

[2] Kant, Immanuel (1785). Groundwork of the Metaphysics of Morals. Translated by Mary Gregor. Cambridge: Cambridge University Press, 1997. *Kant establishing personal moral autonomy as fundamental to human dignity*

6.2: Self-knowledge of gender identity is supreme authority.

[1] Descartes, René (1637). Discourse on Method. Translated by Donald A. Cress. Indianapolis: Hackett Publishing, 1998. *Descartes establishing the primacy of self-knowledge*

6.5 : Multiple genders exist across cultures and history.

[1] Wilhelm, Amara Das (2008). Tritiya-Prakriti: People of the Third Sex. Philadelphia, PA: Xlibris Corporation. *Hindu texts acknowledging hijras as distinct gender category*

[2] Roscoe, Will (1998). Changing Ones: Third and Fourth Genders in Native North America. New York: St. Martin's Press. *Native American Two-Spirit*

traditions

6.6 : Inner knowledge supersedes external observation.

[1] Descartes, René (1637). Discourse on Method. Translated by Donald A. Cress. Indianapolis: Hackett Publishing, 1998. *Cartesian philosophy establishing certainty of self-knowledge*

6.7 : Gender diversity is natural, not disordered.

[1] World Health Organization (2019). International Statistical Classification of Diseases and Related Health Problems (11th ed.). Geneva: WHO. *World Health Organization removing transgender identity from mental disorders list*

6.9 : Children know their own gender identity.

[1] American Psychological Association (2015). Guidelines for Psychological Practice with Transgender and Gender Nonconforming People. American Psychologist, 70(9), 832-864. *Research on early gender identity development*

6.10 : Denying transition causes harm through forced delay.

[1] Bauer, G. R., et al. (2015). Intervenable factors associated with suicide risk in transgender persons. BMC Public Health, 15, 525. *Research on mental health impacts of transition care delays*

6.15: Parents must accept their children's true identity.

[1] Ryan, Caitlin, et al. (2010). Family Acceptance in Adolescence and the Health of LGBT Young Adults. Journal of Child and Adolescent Psychiatric Nursing, 23(4), 205-213. *Research on family acceptance and transgender youth outcomes*

[2] Simons, L., et al. (2013). Parental Support and Mental Health Among Transgender Adolescents. Journal of Adolescent Health, 53(6), 791-793. *Study on parental support as protective factor for transgender youth*

[3] PFLAG National. (2024). PFLAG: The First and Largest Organization for LGBTQ+ People, Their Parents and Families, and Allies. https://pflag.org

PFLAG national organization for family support

6.16: What exists naturally from birth is not disease.

[1] World Health Organization (2019). International Statistical Classification of Diseases and Related Health Problems (11th ed.). Geneva: WHO. *World Health Organization removing transgender identity from mental disorders*

6.18: Trans joy validates authentic existence.

[1] Aristotle. Nicomachean Ethics. 4th century BCE. *Aristotle's concept of eudaimonia (flourishing)*

[2] Buddhist philosophical traditions on dharma and authentic living. *Buddhist philosophy on dharma and happiness*

[3] Hindu philosophical traditions on svadharma and life purpose. *Hindu concept of svadharma (authentic purpose)*

INDEX

Made in the USA
Coppell, TX
13 February 2026

72013098R00292